Japan's New World Role

Other Titles of Interest

The Modernizers: Overseas Students, Foreign Employees, and Meiji Japan, edited by Ardath W. Burks

The Armed Forces in Contemporary Asian Societies, edited by Edward A. Olsen and Stephen Jurika, Jr.

Food and Development in the Pacific Basin, G. Edward Schuh and Jennifer McCoy

A Japanese Journalist Looks at U.S.-Japan Relations, Yukio Matsuyama

Japan's Foreign Relations: A Global Search for Economic Security, edited by Robert S. Ozaki and Walter Arnold

The Emerging Pacific Community: A Regional Perspective, edited by Robert L. Downen and Bruce J. Dickson

Japan: Profile of a Post Industrial Power (second edition), Ardath W. Burks

About the Book and Editors

Despite Japan's status as a global economic power and its position as the world's second-largest market economy, institutional, historical, and cultural factors have combined to limit Japan's political and military roles. In this volume, a reprint of a 1983 issue of the *Journal of International Affairs* (*JIA*), a group of prominent Japanese and American scholars address Japan's potential for an expanded world role and the responsibilities and policy choices entailed in becoming a truly global power. Some of the specific issues covered include East Asian regional security, international trade, and Japan's relations with the United States, China, and the European Community.

Joshua D. Katz is managing editor of *Financing Foreign Operations* at Business International. He was formerly editor in chief of the *Journal of International Affairs*. **Tilly C. Friedman-Lichtschein** is managing editor of *Political Science Quarterly*. She was formerly managing editor of *JIA*.

Japan's New World Role

edited by
Joshua D. Katz and
Tilly C. Friedman-Lichtschein

LONDON AND NEW YORK

First published 1983 by Westview Press

Published 2018 by Routledge
52 Vanderbilt Avenue, New York, NY 10017
2 Park Square, Milton Park, Abingdon, Oxon OX14 4RN

Routledge is an imprint of the Taylor & Francis Group, an informa business

Copyright © 1983,1985 by the Trustees of Columbia University in the City of New York

All rights reserved. No part of this book may be reprinted or reproduced or utilised in any form or by any electronic, mechanical, or other means, now known or hereafter invented, including photocopying and recording, or in any information storage or retrieval system, without permission in writing from the publishers.

Notice:
Product or corporate names may be trademarks or registered trademarks, and are used only for identification and explanation without intent to infringe.

Library of Congress Catalog Number 85-50889

ISBN 13: 978-0-367-00607-5(hbk)
ISBN 13: 978-0-367-15594-0(pbk)

CONTENTS

Editor's Foreword ix
Preface xiii
About the Authors 1

East Asia and Global Security: Implications for Japan 5
Zbigniew Brzezinski

Japan and the Pacific Basin 13
Saburo Okita

Toward a Bilateral Partnership: Improving Economic Relations 21
Robert S. Ingersoll

The Changing Role of Japan in the United Nations 29
Sadako Ogata

The U.S.-Japan Connection in the Changing World Marketplace: A Trader's Perspective 43
Toshihiro Tomabechi

Evolving Sino-Japanese Relations 49
Shinkichi Eto

Industrial Structure and Japanese Trade Friction: U.S. Policy Responses 67
William V. Rapp

The Soviet Proposal on Confidence-Building Measures and the Japanese Response   81
Hiroshi Kimura

The Politics of Trade Liberalization in Japan   105
Timothy J. Curran

Japan and the U.S. Congress: Problems and Prospects   123
Susan C. Schwab

Business and Japan's New World Role: As Seen Through Personal Experience   141
Akio Morita

The European Community and Japan: Beyond the Economic Dimension   147
Reinhard Drifte

Sharing the Burden on the Far Side of the Alliance: Japanese Security in the 1980s   163
R. B. Byers and Stanley C. M. Ing

The Andrew Wellington Cordier Essay: Carrots, Sticks, and Rice: Japan's Search for Food Security   177
Tim Sears

EDITOR'S FOREWORD

Few would dispute the assertion that Japan's postwar recovery and rapid emergence as an economic superpower constitute one of the major transformations in the international system since 1945. Yet, despite the revolutionary changes that phenomenal growth and prosperity have brought about in the Japanese standard of living, Japan's role in international relations has not kept pace. An active world role demands not only a powerful economic base, but also a decision to allocate resources on a national scale toward particular international goals, as well as a choice of the specific means—political, diplomatic, or military—for pursuing the desired ends. At the same time, the exercise of national power on the international scene requires a consciousness—at least among the policymaking elite—of the state as a global actor.

Observers of international relations have foreseen a gradual restructuring of the world system, away from the strictly bipolar confrontation between the Soviet Union and the United States of the 1940s and 1950s, toward a multipolar system in which Japan, China, and Western Europe would each make inroads into the relative strength of the superpowers. Until the recent resurgence of Soviet-American confrontation, it was widely hoped that détente between the superpowers, along with a general diffusion of world power, could engender a more stable world. While this vision may still prove viable in the long run, it has so far failed to supplant bipolarity, leading some to question its original premises.

One source of disappointment for advocates of multipolarity has been the slow pace with which Japan has assumed a responsible international political role commensurate with its status as the world's second largest market economy. Japan's current posture may appear paradoxical: *Global* in its economic outreach, as a major exporter to both industrialized and developing countries and as a resource-poor importer of primary products essential to its national survival, Japan remains *insular* in its belief that it cannot or should not project its power politically or militarily to pursue its economic interests in an independent way. Of course, there has indeed been a movement away from the postwar role of junior partner to the United States, as evidenced in diverging positions on the Middle East and certain East-West issues. There is also a growing awareness among Japanese leaders that Japan *should* in one way or another develop an active global policy, rather than merely reacting to foreign pressures and changing external circumstances. At present, however, there is no clear consensus on the road to be taken.

This paradox has been internalized, both by Japanese and foreigners. Perceptions tend to lag behind economic growth. Despite a renewal of national pride in Japanese economic accomplishments and demands that Japan be treated as a full member of the Western alliance, many Japanese still view their country as small and vulnerable, incapable of having a major impact on world politics. In an age which has witnessed the limitations of American power, the United States is still widely regarded in the framework of its postwar role—as a dominant senior partner on whom Japan should depend for its security and place in international relations. At the same time, there is a large body of Japanese public opinion which resents Japan's postwar dependence on the United States and would advocate a more independent course for the post-*Pax Americana* period.

Americans and Europeans, on the other hand, while in awe of Japanese economic success—as clearly evidenced by the recent popularity of books on the "Japanese challenge" and business practices—have only recently and reluctantly begun to open the door to full Japanese membership in the club of advanced industrial democracies. Japanese participation in "trilateral" economic and security cooperation is barely a decade old and still far from adequate, in view of the extensive shared interests and problems.

Developing nations, especially those which were victims of Japanese expansion and colonialism prior to 1945, have understandably ambivalent feelings toward Japan. As proof that a non-Western nation can modernize and achieve prosperity, Japan is to be respected and even emulated. But such laudatory attitudes are in delicate balance with apprehensions over the potential for Japanese "economic imperialism" or even rearmament and renewed militarism.

Our authors have referred to these and other paradoxes in their discussions of the many aspects of Japan's global role. They have also seen distinguishing characteristics of the Japanese experience, which form the basis for Japan's relations with other countries now and will continue to do so in the future. Many of these are well known in their broadest outlines: Japan's frenzied efforts to resist Western colonialism by rapid modernization, its overriding concern with its perceived vulnerability, the legacy of postwar reforms under American occupation, and the "special relationship" that developed between Japan and the United States. Each article includes at least passing mention of the fundamental linguistic, cultural, and institutional differences separating Japan from the Western-oriented mainstream of international relations discourse. Such differences necessarily lead to a divergence of expectations in all spheres of international relations and can easily lead to conflict if not recognized and addressed.

Japan appears unique, not only in its culture and history, but also in its postwar development into a global *economic* force, without becoming a correspondingly important *military* power. Historically, the great economic powers, almost without exception, have required great military forces to realize their aims as colonialists or prosperous global traders. A variety of circumstances particular to the postwar world—including the inclusion of an anti-military clause (Article IX) into Japan's revised constitution, the presence of the United States, a *status quo* power with global interests, as a guarantor of Japanese security, and an increasing open international economy—have enabled Japan to pursue worldwide economic objectives without developing the military potential to enforce its position directly. Yet outside pressures for more "sharing of burdens" by Japan are mounting, as documented in many of the articles. The basic question of Japan's security needs—and the proper means required to meet these needs— remains unresolved.

The results of Japanese economism have included not only steadily rising domestic prosperity but also conflict with the Western democracies. During the recent recession, tensions resulting from Japanese inroads into important Western domestic markets and perceived trade barriers have reached a critical level. Indeed, the liberal postwar trading system from which Japan and other nations have derived great economic benefit may be in danger of collapse. Protectionist measures have entered the policy arena of the Western nations in a serious way—with the "Japanese threat" raised increasingly often as a theme in political advocacy. Japan is being called upon with increasing urgency to share responsibility for the health of the world economy. The success of Japanese policymakers, private sector leaders, and scholars in responding to these challenges will have far-reaching consequences.

Finally, if Japan is to pursue an independent global policy, it must balance off its policies toward those areas vital to its international position: the United States, the Soviet Union, China, the Pacific Basin, Europe, and the Middle East. The articles in this volume attest to the complexities of adjusting relations with each of these areas to changing world circumstances. Synthesizing a coherent overall foreign policy will present an even more difficult task.

Clearly, Japan's current position is one of vast *potentiality*. Once a national consensus has developed that a "new world role" for Japan is desirable—or at least unavoidable—the content of this role will remain to be determined by the Japanese policymaking process. Our aim in publishing this issue is to provide a glimpse into the vital debate currently underway among Japanese and Western scholars, policymakers, and private sector leaders concerning Japan's future course—a process with implications extending far beyond Japan to the entire world political system.

J.D.K.
1983

PREFACE

Since the original publication of *Japan's New World Role* in June 1983, few if any of the issues discussed have been definitively resolved. Prime Minister Nakasone's ambitious leadership has given Japan a far more assertive posture in global *economic* relations; Japan has come to see a clear international role for itself while the West seemingly stands ready to accept Japan as a full partner. Yet in the diplomatic and military spheres, history and domestic political forces still pose obstacles to Japan's full-fledged entry onto the world stage.

Despite continued U.S. pressures and Japanese acceptance of certain expanded regional defense responsibilities, any hint of military growth is anathema to popular sentiment and harks back to the dark years of the 1930s. The conventional 1 percent GNP limit on defense spending has been stretched but not discarded. In fact, defense was one of the few areas to escape cutbacks in the most recent national budget, actually increasing in real terms.

As evidenced by recent events, trade issues remain at the forefront of international concern. Record Japanese trade surpluses have engendered record external investments—largely in foreign government securities, as well as protectionist demands by affected industries in the United States and elsewhere. Thus the Japanese economic scope continues to expand, though not always with the complete blessing of foreign countries.

One important development covered only tangentially in *Japan's New World Role* is the liberalization of Japanese financial markets currently under way. The internationalization of the yen, the development of the Euroyen bond market, and the opening of internal financial markets to foreigners will multiply international contacts and interdependencies. This also presents new opportunities for Japan to exert its economic weight in an internationally acceptable arena.

We believe this volume will continue to prove useful to students of Japanese international relations, as these same basic issues will continue to pose a challenge to policymakers, economists, political scientists, and the people of Japan. Since its inception in 1947, the *Journal of International Affairs* has approached important international issues by covering the selected theme from various frameworks through writers world-wide. We hope that the success of this volume inspires others to approach the continuing issues of our time through a truly international perspective.

The editors wish to express their thanks to Steven Eisner and Wendie Lubic for organizing this issue for publication by Westview Press.

J.D.K.
T.C.F.-L.

ABOUT THE AUTHORS

ZBIGNIEW BRZEZINSKI is Herbert Lehman Professor of Government at Columbia University. He served as Assistant to the President for National Security Affairs from 1977 to 1981. In the early 1970s, Dr. Brzezinski was instrumental in founding the Trilateral Commission, a private organization dedicated to fostering better relations between Japan, the United States, and Western Europe. His many publications include *Power and Principle* (Farrar Straus & Giroux, 1983), *The Fragile Blossom: Crisis and Change in Japan* (Harper and Row, 1972), and *The Soviet Bloc—Unity and Conflict* (Harvard University Press, 1960).

SABURO OKITA was Foreign Minister of Japan, 1979-80. Initially trained in electrical engineering, Dr. Okita's interest in economics came to light early in his career. In 1946, the author participated in the Foreign Ministry task force which published *The Past, Present and Future of Japan's Economy: Basic Problems of Japan's Reconstruction,* a report credited by many as having established the guidelines for Japan's postwar recovery. In 1952, he was appointed Japan's first member of the international secretariat of the UN Economic Commission for Asia and the Far East. The following year, Dr. Okita directed the Economic Cooperation Section of the Economic Planning Agency and was in charge of setting priorities for Japan's first five-year plan. In 1960, Dr. Okita assisted in elaborating the "income-doubling plan," which Japan fulfilled by doubling its GNP within seven years. The author also served on the Lester B. Pearson Commission on International Development in 1968-69 and participated in writing the commission report, *Partners in Development.* In 1978, he was appointed to organize an Advisory Group on Pacific Basin Cooperation and in 1979, he headed a Japanese delegation of economists who were sent to advise China on state planning and set the stage for the 1979 Sino-Japanese economic agreements.

ROBERT S. INGERSOLL was the United State Ambassador to Japan from 1972 to 1973. He was also Assistant Secretary of State for East Asian and Pacific Affairs in 1974 and served as Deputy Secretary of State from 1974 to 1976. Mr. Ingersoll worked with Borg-Warner Corporation for 33 years and was Chairman of the Board. He co-chaired the Japan-U.S. Economic Relations Group from 1979 to 1981. He is currently Chairman of the Japan Society.

SADAKO OGATA is presently a professor at the Institute of International Relations of Sophia University in Tokyo. She received her Ph.D. in Political Science from the University of California at Berkeley. Following two international relations teaching appointments in Japan, the author was named Minister Plenepotentiary of the Japanese Permanent Mission to the United Nations, where she served from 1976 through 1979. She was an active member of committees relating to disarmament and Cambodian relief. In 1982, she represented Japan on the UN Human Rights Commission. Dr. Ogata has published numerous articles and books, including: *Defiance in Manchuria—The Making of Japanese Foreign Policy: 1931-1932* (University of California Press, 1964) and *Vantage Point from the United Nations* [*Kokuren kara no shiten*] (*Asahi Evening News* Publication, 1980).

TOSHIHIRO TOMABECHI is President of Mitsubishi International Corporation, New York. A graduate of the Tokyo University of Commerce, Mr. Tomabechi has served in various capacities with Mitsubishi Corporation since 1941. Actively promoting improved business relations between the United States and Japan, the author has been a member of the Board of Directors of the Japanese Chamber of Commerce of New York and the Board of Directors of the Japanese-American Association of New York. Mr. Tomabechi has also served as a council member at the Woodrow Wilson International Center for Scholars and as a member of the Business Committee for the Museum of Modern Art in New York.

SHINKICHI ETO is Professor of International Relations at the University of Tokyo. During the 1982-3 academic year, he has been a Visiting Fellow at the Research School of Pacific Studies of the Australian National University in Canberra.

WILLIAM V. RAPP has recently been appointed Commercial Counselor at the American Embassy in Tokyo.

He received his Ph.D. in Economics from Yale University and has served as Vice President of the Bank of America. His individual and joint publications include *A Theory of Changing Trade Patterns: Tested for Japan, Effective Protective Rates for Korean Industries,* and a wide variety of articles on Japanese business and economic policy.

HIROSHI KIMURA is Professor of Political Science at the Slavic Research Center, Hokkaido University. He was director of the center from 1975 to 1977 and has served as a Special Research Associate with the Japanese Embassy in Moscow. He is spending the 1982-83 academic year at Stanford University as a Visiting Fellow with the Arms Control and Disarmament Program, where he is engaged in research and writing on Soviet-Japanese relations, with a special emphasis on security. Professor Kimura holds a Ph.D. in Politicial Science from Columbia University.

TIMOTHY J. CURRAN is Associate Director of the Project on the United States, Japan, and Southeast Asia at the East Asian Institute of Columbia University and a Lecturer in the Department of Political Science. He has been a Guest Scholar at the Japan Economic Research Center in Tokyo and a consultant to the U.S.-Japan Economic Relations Group. The author received his Ph.D. in Political Science from Columbia in 1982 and is currently preparing to publish his dissertation on Japan's trade policy during the Tokyo Round of trade negotiations.

SUSAN C. SCHWAB holds the post of Legislative Assistant to Senator John C. Danforth of Missouri, where she is responsible for trade, agriculture, and foreign policy issues. She served as Trade Policy Officer at the American Embassy in Tokyo (1980-81) and worked at the Office of the Special Representative for Trade Negotiations (1977-79). Ms. Schwab received her M.A. in Economics from the Stanford University Food Research Center, where she specialized in international trade, development economics, and agriculture.

AKIO MORITA has been Chairman of the Board and Chief Executive Officer of SONY Corporation since 1976. Educated at Osaka Imperial University, Mr. Morita was co-founder of SONY in 1946. He was awarded the Edwardo Rihan Award for International Marketing in 1969. In 1979, he was named to serve on the Japan-United States Economic Relations Group (the "Wisemen's Group"), which produced a set of joint recommendations that was presented to President Carter and Prime Minister Ohira.

REINHARD DRIFTE is presently a research fellow at the Graduate Institute of International Studies in Geneva. He worked with the Commission of the European Community on EC-Japan Industrial Relations in 1979-80. The author has published extensively in French, German, and English, with emphasis on Japanese foreign policy and security issues. Upcoming publications include *Security in Japan's Foreign Policy 1945-52*, and *Japan's Quest for Comprehensive Security*, coauthored with John Chapman and Ian Gow. The author graduated from the University of Bochum in East Asian Studies in 1979, and has worked part-time as a broadcaster with Radio Japan for four summers.

R. B. BYERS is Director of the Research Programme in Strategic Studies and Associate Professor of Political Science at York University, Toronto. He is also the Research Director of the Canadian Institute of Strategic Studies and editor of *The Canadian Strategic Review, 1982*. Dr. Byers is editor of *Arms Limitation and the United Nations* and *Superpower Intervention in the Persian Gulf*, published by the Canadian Institute of Strategic Studies. In addition, he is co-author of *Canada and Western Security: The Search for New Options*.

STANLEY ING is a Research Associate in the Research Programme in Strategic Studies at York University, Toronto and is the co-editor of *Arms Limitation and the United Nations*. He is also a contributor to the *Canadian Strategic Review, 1982*.

Zbigniew Brzezinski

EAST ASIA AND GLOBAL SECURITY:
Implications for Japan[*]

The emerging centrality of Asia in American foreign policy is a relatively recent phenomenon. The United States has been deeply involved in postwar Asian problems, most notably in Korea and Vietnam. The U.S. has also stressed relations with Japan and, in recent years, turned its attention to China. But it is still fair to say that, on the whole, Asia was once considered of secondary strategic importance. This perception is now changing.

In the postwar era American foreign policy has been anchored in the preponderant Atlantic connection. This has reflected, among other things, an intellectual and sentimental affinity toward Europeans. Only in recent years has there emerged a strategic realization that U.S. security and well-being depend on the maintenance of stability and security in two other, interrelated zones — the Middle East and Persian Gulf and the Far East.

This strategic reorientation has significant implications for the United States in Asia. Asia policy must now reflect a broader, more equally balanced involvement in maintenance of security in the three central, interrelated strategic zones. Recognition of the increasing importance of these zones challenges American policy-makers to devise new approaches to regional diplomacy and to global strategic planning to meet this new reality.

A number of factors precipitated the change in American strategic perceptions and focus. First, the Far East today is the most economically successful region in the world. The recovery of Japan and Korea and the vitality of other Asian economies stimulated an awareness of the region's importance for overall global security.

In some respects, the Far East is an unquestioned success story of recent American foreign policy. For the first time in many decades, the United States simultaneously enjoys good relations with the two most important Asian countries, Japan and China. For the first time, these relations are not viewed as inherently competitive or contradictory. The American relationship with the Japanese and Chinese is infinitely better than the relations of either with the Soviet Union. In other words, the economic vitality of the region has bred success, and the United States has the additional advantage of good relations with both Peking and Tokyo.

In addition, a balance in the Far East has emerged in the post-Vietnam era that was not fully anticipated by those who speculated on the consequences of the Vietnam war. Many feared that its hasty termination would precipitate regional destabilization. But not only does the United States today have close and friendly relations with Japan and China, it has also been able to develop a reasonably good relationship with most of

---

[*] This article combines remarks delivered by Dr. Brzezinski to the Columbia University East Asian Institute Toyota seminar in May 1982 with excerpts from an exclusive interview with the *Journal* in March 1983.

the ASEAN (Association of Southeast Asian Nations) countries. These countries enjoy a high degree of economic prosperity, though not equaled in all cases by political stability. This prosperity is quiet impressive and contributes to a sense of well-being and greater stability.

We must also acknowledge the growing importance of Australia and New Zealand. Their role as a pillar of support for our increased presence in the Indian Ocean has become vital. The widening American involvement in the protection of the second strategic zone—the Middle East and the Persian Gulf—has enhanced the salience of Austrialia as a logistical and staging base in the event of an outbreak of hostilities. This is all in keeping with the emerging strategic thinking in the United States, at least in war-planning echelons and the political sector of the government, about the importance of the interrelationship of the three zones.

These developments are underscored by the nature of Soviet policy. There are many ways to analyze recent Soviet foreign policy. Much of the debate focuses on whether the Soviet Union has aggressive strategic ambitions or whether it acts defensively. Whatever one's assessment of Soviet motivations may be, there does appear to be a concrete manifestation of Soviet assertiveness that underlines the interrelationship between the three central strategic zones.

For much of the postwar era, the East-West conflict has been dominated by contests that involved first a westward and then an eastward Soviet push. Rightly or wrongly, principal American policymakers felt that preservation of key outposts in the West was central to the maintenance of America's position in the Atlantic world. That is why the United States declared its security to be irrevocably bound to the security of Turkey, Greece, and Berlin.

When President Truman made these commitments,

the United States did not have the capacity to defend those areas. The purpose of the commitment, and one can readily see the analogy in subsequent commitments, was to make clear to the Soviets that an intrusion into any one of these designated vital areas would precipitate a massive engagement with the United States. The line held despite some intensive probes, particularly in Berlin, and an attempt at subversion in Greece.

The next series of confrontations occurred in the Far East. American policymakers perceived, again rightly or wrongly, the defense of Korea as absolutely necessary for the defense of Japan. The underlying motivation, the central stake in the American strategic reaction, was Japan and not just Korea. By standing fast in Korea the United States contributed to the defense of Japan.

Then came the Vietnam war, which U.S. policymakers again viewed in strategic terms not only as involving the territory by South Vietnam but as representing a thrust by a major nation thought to be an extension of Soviet power, Red China. U.S. policymakers felt that standing fast in Vietnam was necessary to prevent a power imbalance in the Far East that would have far-reaching consequences for America's global strategic interest.

The United States lost the war in Vietnam, but fortune smiled on us. A resurgence of ASEAN and economic progress in the region followed the defeat, as did a rift between the Soviet Union and China, which eliminated the strategic danger that some perceived as the inevitable consequence of a communist victory in Vietnam. For better or worse, the strategic assumptions that underlined American involvement in defending lines in the West and East seemed historically validated.

Soviet foreign policy today is viewed as manifesting a southward push, in some ways historically rooted and in some ways novel. The push southward toward the

Persian Gulf has obvious historical precedents. In November 1940, for example, when Hitler and Stalin were engaged in sensitive negotiations on the possibility of Soviet membership in the Rome-Berlin-Tokyo tripartite pact, the Soviets demanded exclusive, dominating privileges in the Persian Gulf area as an explicit condition for membership.

The strategic implications of the Soviet entrance into Afghanistan, therefore, are far-reaching but not new. They involve the puncturing of an American-developed strategic tier that was meant in the postwar era to shield the vital area of the Persian Gulf from Soviet intrusion. This tier once stretched from the northeastern frontier of Turkey across the northern frontiers of Iran and Pakistan, with Afghanistan serving as a neutral buffer. Developments in the last two and a half years have transformed that buffer into a potentially offensive wedge aimed at both Iran and Pakistan, with Baluchistan as the point of vulnerability. Furthermore, the former strategic pivot of that defensive tier, Iran, has been transformed into a political wreck. The political contest over Iran continues, but the current turmoil precludes that country from playing the role of pivot in the strategic tier. The second strategic zone thus suddenly appears vulnerable, just when this zone's importance to the economic well-being of the first and third zones—Western Europe and Japan—is most vital.

Many analysts perceive two prongs in the Soviet Union's southward push. The central prong, through Afghanistan, Iran, and the Persian Gulf, has recently been reinforced by intensified Libyan activity. Libya seems to be applying intense pressure on the Sudan through South Yemen and Ethiopia. This opens a backtheater potentially dangerous to Saudi Arabia.

Soviet involvement in Vietnam is viewed as the second prong. The Soviets have established closer ties with the Vietnamese for a variety of reasons. One involves the tense and very hostile Sino-Soviet relationship. Moscow may simply be exploiting an opportunity in order to put added pressure on a threatening adversary that has recently moved closer to the Soviet Union's principal rival, the United States.

Whatever the Soviet Union's subjective motivations, there are certain objective consequences of its involvement in Vietnam that have potential strategic implications. The gradual buildup in Cam Ranh Bay and Danang gives the Soviets the potential to interdict very important trade and energy resource flows through the Straits of Malacca. One might question whether this is aimed only at China, or whether the acquisition of this capability may be part of a larger strategic design.

This question also arises in connection with the overall buildup of Soviet forces in Asia. I will not dwell on the global strengthening and deployment of Soviet military forces. Their buildup in the Far East is critical, for it has implications for Japanese security and the U.S.-Japan bilateral relationship.

In 1965, just prior to full-scale involvement in Vietnam, the American Seventh Fleet was vastly superior to the Soviet Far Eastern fleet in both tonnage and quality: 900,000 tons for the Seventh Fleet versus 700,000 tons for a Soviet Pacific fleet that consisted mostly of aging vessels with limited operational capability.

The American Seventh Fleet's tonnage today has decreased to 650,000, and its vessels are not as modern as before. In addition, some of its key ships have been shifted to the Indian Ocean. In contrast, the Soviet Far Eastern fleet has been greatly modernized and now accounts for 1.6 million tons. There has thus been a very significant shift in the naval balance. Moreover, the Soviets have added some 300,000 tons of highly modern naval vessels to the fleet in just the last few years. This additional tonnage, incidentally, amounts to 50 percent more than the total Japanese fleet and about half as much as the existing U.S. Seventh Fleet.

We are all familiar with the buildup of Soviet conventional forces in the Far East from about twelve divisions in the early 1960s to about forty-five by the late 1970s and approximately fifty-one divisions today. Most of these divisions are directed at China, but one cannot ignore the recent increase of nine divisions in the three Far Eastern districts of the Soviet Union. If this is added to the naval and air capacity buildup and to the deployment and presence in Vietnam, wider strategic questions that bear on the interrelationship of the first, second, and third strategic zones become apparent.

In this context, what should our concerns be in the region? Three problems stand out. The first involves the still tenuous character of the American-Chinese connection. That connection is clearly a major asset for our national security. It has a diversionary impact on Soviet strategic planning, draining about 25 percent of the Soviet defense effort, roughly close to what NATO drains from the overall Soviet defense effort. This is a significant and major contribution to U.S. security.

The American-Chinese connection also imposes restraints on the Vietnamese. I was intimately involved in the discussions that took place prior to the Chinese attempt at giving Vietnam a "lesson." Although we were concerned about the potentially destabilizing consequences of that action, some of us perceived potential benefits as well. China's "lesson" certainly cost Vietnam severely: It forced Vietnam to redeploy its forces northward; it severely damaged Vietnam's economy; and it gave the Vietnamese food for thought in terms of any further ambitious operations beyond the frontiers of Cambodia. If I were a Thai, I would feel reassured by the Chinese move and by the deployment of sizable Chinese forces on the Vietnam-China border.

The American-Chinese military connection has contributed to a greater sense of security about Korea. The United States has been alarmed by the scale of the North Korean buildup. In the late 1970s intelligence information made it clear that the buildup was more ambitious and sizable than previously assumed or expected. The closer American-Chinese connection, coupled with a North Korean effort to steer a relatively independent course between the Soviets and the Chinese, reduces the danger of a massive North Korean attack southward. The North Koreans would be unlikely to undertake such an attack unless they were fairly confident of political and other support from both neighbors to the north. They would hardly undertake such an operation if they could count only on the support of one, and perhaps the opposition of the other, power.

I am very much concerned that the American-Chinese relationship may deteriorate in the near future. It may deteriorate largely because of the excessively rigid doctrinal preoccupations of some policy-makers in the new U.S. administration. After my visit to China, I reported my conversations with Deng Xiaoping and Geng Biao to administration officials. I was struck by the prevalence, particularly in the White House, of a hard-to-define sense of obligation to provide Taiwan with more advanced weaponry, for purposes that escaped me in terms of any tangible danger that needs to be met or any political benefit that would thereby accrue to the United States.

I am convinced, on the basis of recent discussions with the Chinese and extensive contact with them for four years, that the Chinese reaction will be serious, far-reaching, and damaging to the U.S.-China relations. They are not bluffing. This is a psychologically sensitive issue that touches a raw nerve in Peking. The Taiwan issue could potentially weaken Deng Xiaoping's power and affect not only his foreign policy but his domestic policies as well. The issue has the potential to disrupt a security pattern in the Far East that has up to now contributed to greater stability.

The second security issue that should be of concern to Americans is the problem of political stability in the Far East. This problem may not be as major as the Chinese-American question, but it is certainly germane to our security interests. There are several candidates for instability in the region. The first is the Philippines. It possesses a political order that has not institutionalized itself effectively. It is overly personalized and susceptible to major disruptions. This is significant for U.S. security because of American facilities there and because of the centrality of these assets to our strategic planning in the defense of the region.

Indonesia is a second candidate. In some respects, its situation resembles that of the Philippines, but it is enhanced by the combination of massive corruption and the insular decentralization of the government. Indonesians would have difficulty holding the government together in the event of major succession struggles. Suharto is likely to hold things together, if he maintains his health, since he will probably be renominated by the army. But it makes me uneasy to think that a major country of this size and importance in an area so proximate to the Straits of Malacca should be potentially vulnerable to political instability.

Thailand is also a possible candidate for instability, but the Vietnamese presence in Cambodia has had a consolidating impact on the character of the Thai body politic. Pressure from the north has a revitalizing impact on Thai political stability, producing a degree of cohe-

sion out of a sense of threat. In that sense, it may have dampened the rise of intense domestic political problems.

Finally, there is uncertainty about China. Taiwan's claim to overall Chinese sovereignty not only may precipitate American difficulties with Taiwan but also may cause strains in Washington-Peking relations. I suspect that many Americans would be sympathetic toward such a development as the fulfillment of Taiwanese national self-determination. But that would be a blatant negation of the Shanghai Communique and the commitments undertaken by three administrations in developing a more normal relationship with China. Any redefinition of Taiwan's status by the Taiwanese that seemingly met the criteria of national self-determination would have a disruptive impact on our relationship with the Chinese on the mainland.

The third U.S. security concern in the region is the Soviet military role, the scale of which I have summarized briefly. The danger is not likely to take the form of overt military activity but rather the emergence of a pattern that, over time, might repeat the European experience. Just as Asia has followed Western Europe in attaining an equal status in terms of its strategic importance for global stability, so too may Asia eventually follow Western Europe in its political evolution toward a direction often referred to as neutralist. That is, there is an increasingly pervasive feeling in Europe that the growth of Soviet military power necessitates the recognition of certain political realities. For moral or political—or idealistic or expedient—reasons, it would be better to distance oneself from the United States as the principal opponent of Soviet power in favor of a more independent position. I do not know if this is likely, but it does give me some concern. I sense a susceptibilty in the Far East to such a development, especially in Japan because of its tragic experience with nuclear warfare.

How can we enhance our security ties in the Far East? First of all, an American-Chinese security relationship is in the American national interest and contributes to both regional and global security. I have felt this way for some time and nothing has happened to change my mind. This is not to say that this security relationship should be pursued blatantly or aggressively. Far from it. It should be pursued steadily but cautiously.

This is how the Carter administration pursued relations with China. It moved gradually at first along two parallel lines: secret efforts to normalize relations and semi-open efforts to engage in strategic consultations, for which I was personally responsible. The administration then moved to the next stage, which involved actual normalization of relations and a very deliberate attempt to expand immediately the scope of the economic relationship to a level that equaled the treatment accorded the Soviet Union. Secretary of State Cyrus Vance referred to this as a policy of even-handedness; Secretary of Defense Harold Brown and I thought of it as a balance in our relationships with China and the Soviet Union. That is, we must recognize that China is more underdeveloped and weaker than the Soviet Union; therefore, the transfer of identical technology to both nations does not have an equal impact. The administration thus made China eligible for the transfer of advanced technology.

The next phase entailed the enhancement of an indirect security relationship in which the United States would give China dual-use technology while denying it to other communist countries. That is, we would supply technology susceptible to exploitation for military purposes.

The new administration has just embarked on the last phase by deciding to make China eligible to purchase American arms. The Carter administration would have taken that same step had it been returned to office, despite strong opposition from some quarters in the government. Harold Brown and I would have pushed for it, and, more importantly, President Carter leaned in that direction—in effect, he said as much during his recent trip to China.

The American strategic relationship with China is underway. It will grow over time, but Taiwan is the uncertain element. If that issue does not derail the relationship, I expect it to expand further, beginning primarily with overt defensive weaponry. The first step would be TOW antitank weaponry and weapons of that sort, followed by command and control systems and graduating to more advanced weaponry in time. I see no reason for the United States to refrain from this course of action. It enhances our security by imposing greater costs on the Soviet Union and therefore deflects the Soviet Union from a westward or southward orientation. It also makes the Chinese less susceptible to Soviet intimidation.

The more difficult question pertains to our relationship with Japan. On the one hand, one must be sensitive both to Japanese political realities that make the enhancement of the U.S.-Japan security relationship difficult, especially the potentially destabilizing consequences of demands for a greater Japanese defense role, and to the living legacy of history. These considerations dictate caution and restraint. They require delicate handling on the part of those Americans who raise the defense issue.

At the same time, one must also recognize a self-serving element in the Japanese reaction. These political, historical, and moral complications do serve as useful bargaining tools that make it easier for the Japanese to

East Asia and Global Security

avoid increasing their defense burden. They are motivated primarily by expedient economic reasons—that is, they are unwilling to pay the commensurate cost that increased defense efforts impose on overall productivity and profits.

There is no simple remedy for this problem, but I do feel that the American expectation that Japan should do more in the defense area is justified in terms of both strategic necessity and international equity. If the three central strategic zones are interrelated and of central importance to us, then the defense of the Middle East and the Persian Gulf, for example, is of direct benefit to both Japan and Western Europe. The security of the second strategic zone has practical application to Japanese interests.

What contribution could Japan make? Possible efforts fall into three broad areas. First, Japan can help contribute to greater stability in the Middle East and the Persian Gulf. This difficult strategic problem also involves social and political dimensions. Such an effort would entail, for example, greater assistance to Pakistan and the Sudan. We have encouraged the Japanese to be more responsive to the social and political needs of Pakistan. The Sudanese are very vulnerable, and if their country collapses, the threat to Saudi Arabia would be intensified with implications for the stability of the entire Persian Gulf. It would not be out of order for the United States to make clear to the Japanese that under the present American budgetary stringency, Japanese assistance to the Sudan would be viewed as a significant strategic contribution, rather than a case of more help to developing countries. There is some movement in this direction.

Second, Japan can assume more direct military responsibility by widening the perimeters of its air defense and sea patrols. This means assuming a greater defense burden, with the result of crossing that magic threshhold of 1 percent of GNP. That figure is to some extent mythical. If you calculate Japanese defense spending using American defense spending criteria, it is already about 1.4 to 1.8 percent of GNP. Perhaps the best way to cross this barrier is simply to recalculate. That way, no one must make a specific decision to cross the barrier, and once it is crossed, further increases may be easier.

The doubling of the Japanese defense effort is no doubt justified in terms of both need and equity. Movement toward such an increase cannot be rapid, but excessively lengthy deferral of it is likely to affect adversely not only the stability of the Far East but also Japan's relations with the United States and Western Europe. There are political considerations involved. As in the area of strategic aid, however, there is some movement in this direction by the Japanese.

The third area demands systematic attention, although only preliminary efforts have been made to date. Japan should share its increasingly sophisticated and advanced research and development with the United States for defense purposes. Japanese microelectronics and optics and lasers are very advanced and have military applications. The Japanese will have no defense application for this technology until they double the percentage of GNP devoted to defense. Such technology could therefore be transferred to the United States as a contribution to our common defense effort and significantly reduce our own research and development costs. This would give us the benefit of genuinely important frontier technology that has significant implications for our overall defense capability.

One cannot, on the one hand, say that Asia is a central element in American global policy of equal importance to Western Europe; that Japan is an equal

11

partner; and that stability in the Far East is critical to us, without acknowledging on the other hand that a redefinition of the Japanese defense role has become timely for the above historical and strategic reasons.

The question is not just one of doing more to please America. There is also the issue of participation in the creation of a more stable global environment, of which Japan is a key member. I do not know if psychological satisfaction is enough to compensate for the sacrifices that would have to be made, but the acceptance of responsibility is accompanied by status enhancement.

It is also true that nothing will ever be enough. It is like tending a garden: You fertilize, water, reap, harvest, and then start over again. Even if Japan increases its defense spending and helps Pakistan and the Sudan, the world will impose new obligations. We face the same dilemma. Americans for many years have been asking, how many more billions must be spent on defense? Can't we kill every Russian many times over already? Unfortunately, it is still not enough. That is the dilemma of the world in which we live.

Insularity, the Hiroshima experience, domestic political difficulties, self-interested expedience—these are all factors that the Japanese must consider. I do not know what the mix is for them, but I do not disregard self-interest. The Japanese are a very intelligent, hardworking people who know it is advantageous to spend less than 1 percent of GNP on defense if someone else is prepared to spend.

I believe that the five-year defense plan, adopted not long ago by Japan, is responsive to the need for Japan to do more in the security area. In strategic terms, I believe that Japan should assume greater responsibility for its own air defense and for an enhanced role in the protection of its maritime routes, particularly those north of the Straits of Malacca. The plans for the improvement of the Japanese navy contained in the five-year defense plan, do provide for a very considerable increase in Japanese capabilities. Furthermore, I have the impression that the Japanese have derived considerable satisfaction from their enhanced standing in world affairs, particularly from their role in the economic summit with top Western leaders.

I have proposed on several occasions that the international economic summit be expanded into what I call a *strategic* summit. The countries participating in that annual summit have major strategic concerns, their common interests are not only economic, and they could contribute a great deal to global stability and progress by enhancing their strategic cooperation. Moreover, such a strategic summit would provide a more flexible mechanism for the needed strategic consultations than, for example, informal links between Japan and South Korea on the one side and NATO on the other. In brief, the expansion of the economic summit into a strategic summit is needed and at the same time would be less controversial than some other possible solutions.

As an observer of the Japanese role in these summits for four successive years, I have noticed a qualitative enhancement in the degree of Japanese participation and assertiveness and a feeling of equality. The Japanese themselves know they are doing much more on the international scene and enjoy the international recognition.

A final note: I expect Prime Minister Nakasone to be careful but persistent. He has a defined strategic view, and in that respect he is ahead of the thinking of most Japanese. I consider him to be the first postwar Japanese prime minister who has a sense not only of Japan's international economic role but also of Japan's geopolitical responsibility.

Saburo Okita

JAPAN AND THE PACIFIC BASIN*

Over the years I have been involved in various capacities with Japan's postwar economic planning and with the problems of developing countries, particularly those in Asia. As a member of the secretariat of the Economic and Social Commission for Asia and Pacific (then ESCAFE) in Bangkok in 1952 and 1953, I was the first Japanese to serve on the staff of the United Nations. This background of work in Asia has resulted in my continuing interest in the problems of Asian countries. For example, I visit China once or twice each year to discuss economic policy problems. This past June there was a seminar in Bangkok convened by Thanat Khoman, the deputy prime minister of Thailand, on Pacific regional cooperation. Then in August I was asked to speak at a conference in Kuala Lumpur on Japan and Southeast Asia. Along with former Japanese Prime Minister Takeo Fukuda, I met with the prime minister of Malaysia, Mr. Mahatir, to discuss his "Look East" policy. Just recently I attended a Pacific Trade and Development Conference in Manila where I also had the opportunity to meet with President Marcos to discuss some of the issues confronting the Philippine economy. Subsequently, I met with a number of government leaders in Jakarta to talk about Indonesian development. Thus I try as much as possible to keep abreast of developments in Asia.

When I met with Dr. Goh Keng Swee, deputy prime minister of Singapore in August 1982, he expressed a sense of apprehension about the future of the world economy, particularly given the severity of the present world recession. Although Singapore has enjoyed a period of continued prosperity over the past ten years or so, the recession is making itself felt there as well. If the depressed state of the world economy does not improve within the next eighteen months, according to Dr. Goh, even the Singaporean economy may suffer substantial setbacks. Singapore and the other newly industrialized countries in Asia such as Taiwan and Korea, as well as the ASEAN countries, have experienced relatively high growth rates in the recent past, but the global recession has even cast its shadow over this dynamic region. The fall in primary commodity prices in Malaysia, for example, adversely affects the nation's balance of payments and the budget. Indonesia is now confronted with three major difficulties. First, the slump in oil prices has constrained economic growth, since 80 percent of Indonesia's foreign exchange earnings and 70 percent of the government budget are derived from oil sales. Secondly, this year's rice production is expected to fall below that of last year. And finally, Indonesia's non-oil exports are also declining somewhat. The Philippines is also suffering from heavy borrowing and falling prices of its export products. Korea's position is somewhat better, recovering from the period of negative growth experienced two years ago. Korea con-

---

*The following text is drawn from Dr. Okita's address to the Columbia University East Asian Institute Toyota Seminar meeting in February 1983 and from the discussion which followed. The Toyota Seminar is a series of meetings in which experts in business, government, and academia discuss current issues in American-Japanese relations.

tinues to enjoy foreign exchange earnings from the Middle East, where Korean construction and consulting projects have done very well.

In general, the growth rates of the East and Southeast Asian countries last year were half of what they were in earlier years. For the moment, because of the dynamism of the economies of the region, the countries are faring relatively well by global standards, but as Dr. Goh has said, a prolonged recession could take a heavy toll.

The rate of Japanese growth, which has dropped to around 3 percent, compares favorably with those of the United States and other industrialized countries, but is still very low for Japan. Despite the relatively weak yen exchange rate, the level of exports from Japan in dollar terms was 7 percent lower in the third quarter of 1982 and 14 percent lower in the fourth quarter than the comparable periods of the previous year. Japan has not been spared the effects of the downward spiralling world economy, including depressed commodity prices and reduced purchasing power in the industrialized countries.

But although there is some danger of a vicious circle gathering momentum even in the more dynamic regions of the world, I also see the likelihood of an upturn in the world economic situation before too long. Among the encouraging sign posts are the moderation of inflation in the United States and the gradual decline in American interest rates. If economic activity in the United States is thereby stimulated, the expansionary effect would be felt throughout the world via a strengthening of the commodity market and expanding trade. The financial burden would also be alleviated somewhat in Mexico and other Latin American countries that have suffered from the current weak demand for their exports. It is possible, then, that a virtuous circle instead of a vicious circle could emerge at some point this year or early next year.

Turning to longer-term prospects and problems, I still believe that the East and Southeast Asian regions form the most dynamic part of the world economy. If the economies of the industrialized world start picking up, these countries are likely to resume their high rates of growth and regain momentum in their economic development. We also see structural changes occurring in these economies. Some twenty years ago manufactured goods accounted for 20 percent of the total exports of South Korea and Taiwan. Today that figure has reached 85 percent. Over the same period, the share of manufactured goods has risen from 5 to 25 percent for the ASEAN countries excluding Singapore. Perhaps ASEAN exports will also be composed primarily of manufactured goods in another twenty years.

There is a strong likelihood that these Southeast Asian nations will become the next generation of newly-industrialized countries (NICs), following in the steps of first Japan, and now Korea, Taiwan, Singapore, and Hong Kong. Japan's high growth rate stimulated growth of other Asian economies in the postwar years as the current NICs will continue to do. Already Indonesia's textile exports have increased fivefold since 1978. Likewise, its rice production has more than doubled in the past fifteen years, increasing from 10 to 22 million tons. The Philippines has also recently become self-sufficient in rice, with improvements in irrigation techniques, fertilizers, and new high-yielding strains of rice. Thailand has not only managed to increase its rice production, but has evolved into a major rice supplier, exporting about 3.5 million tons despite the doubling of its population in the past twenty-five years.

Thailand, Indonesia, Malaysia, and China each receive about $250 million of Japanese Official Development Assistance (ODA), making them among the largest recipients of Japanese aid. But in 1981 Korea requested $6 billion in aid from Japan, and after lengthy negotiations and the intervening textbook controversy, the Japanese government finally agreed to provide Korea with $4 billion in loans over the next five years. Prime Minister Nakasone visited Korea in January 1983, before his Washington trip, to finalize the agreement. About $1.85 billion of the $4 billion are soft loans, despite Japan's implicit policy to reserve special low interest loans for developing countries unable to afford the market rate of interest. But this aid package, which now makes Korea the top recipient of Japanese aid, was granted with special bilateral political considerations in mind.

Taiwan has a chronic balance of trade deficit with Japan. As a result, the Taiwanese have placed import restrictions on about a thousand Japanese commodities. Korea similarly complains that Japan is not buying enough Korean products. Thus, the displeasure with Japan is also felt in areas outside the United States and Europe. Yet our overall current account surplus is actually quite small, because of our overwhelming trade deficits with Middle Eastern oil suppliers as well as with Canada and Australia, which are Japan's chief suppliers of raw materials and foodstuffs. Japan also has a large deficit in service trade. If trade figures with Taiwan were to include invisible items such as tourism, for example, Taiwan would probably show an overall surplus with Japan in spite of its commodity trade deficit.

Although various problems and issues arise between Japan and other Asian countries, relations are generally better now than they have ever been. It was only ten years ago when Prime Minister Tanaka was greeted during his Southeast Asian tour with widespread demonstrations against the alleged Japanese economic invasion. The rapid increase in Japanese capital investments in the region from 1971 to 1973 aroused apprehension about the potential danger of domination by the Japanese economy, before the 1973 oil shock forced a sharp cut in Japanese investment abroad. Greater sensitivity towards local communities on the part of Japanese businessmen and efforts to share the benefits of trade with host countries have also eased tensions.

Another significant factor in the improved relations between Japan and its Southeast Asian neighbors was the political change in Indochina. Since the fall of South Vietnam the region has been perceived as being more volatile. Ties with Japan have come to be regarded with greater importance for stable development. The size of Japan's official development assistance has also increased, as has the volume of two-way trade between Japan and Southeast Asian countries.

When former Prime Minister Fukuda visited the ASEAN countries in 1978, he announced Japan's policy towards those countries in what has subsequently come to be known as the "Fukuda Doctrine." Japan would never again become a military power; it would establish ties on equal footing with governments of the region and would strive to develop "heart to heart relationships" with Asian countries. In 1981 Prime Minister Suzuki reiterated Fukuda's statement, adding that Japan would place priority on assisting food production, energy production, human development, and small and medium-size enterprises in those countries.

The recent textbook controversy aroused new fears among Asian countries about the possibility of military rearmament in Japan. President Marcos and President

Suharto expressed a good deal of concern during their recent visits to Washington. China, although basically supportive of new U.S.-Japanese security ties, would take serious exception to an excessive Japanese military build-up.

Southeast Asian countries have also expressed misgivings about the possibility that Japan will take on responsibility for a one thousand nautical mile sea lane region. In general they do not object to Japan's strengthening its strictly defensive capability, but they do not wish Japan to extend its defensive perimeter into Southeast Asia. They would like instead for Japan to assist Southeast Asian nations to strengthen their own capabilities.

Timothy Curran, *Columbia University's East Asian Institute:* Dr. Okita, I wonder if you could comment on China's economic prospects, and particularly on the debate that is currently taking place in China over the future direction of its economic development.

Okita: Four years ago, in January 1979, I was invited by the Chinese government to discuss economic concerns, partly because they wanted to hear about the Japanese experience in economic growth and industrial development. I told Deputy Prime Minister Gu Mu and State Council members who were in the audience that I thought the ten-year plan they were promoting at that time was too ambitious. They later scrapped this ten-year plan and introduced an "adjustment period." The present five-year plan, which aims for 4 to 5 percent growth per year, is much more realistic, emphasizing the improved use of existing equipment and better management. A number of technicians and managers have been sent to Japan and elsewhere for training to absorb the experience of other countries. When they suddenly cancelled orders placed with Japanese and other companies in early 1981, I rushed to Peking as a representative of the Japanese government to discuss economic relations. The Chinese felt that their investment program was still too ambitious at that time and feared inflation would run rampant unless they cut back on heavy capital investment and military expenditures. They realized that China's infrastructure—transportation, energy supply networks, and so on—needed to be improved before introducing new modern equipment.

Now prospects are brighter; there have even been some foreign exchange surpluses. In 1979 Japan provided a soft loan of $250 million to improve railway lines connecting inland areas with ports. Similar amounts of loans have been extended every year since then. Agricultural policy makes use of incentives to encourage food production and has recently achieved growth rates averaging about 5 percent a year. Heavy industry suffered considerably in 1981 due to adjustment policies, but fared much better last year as the government attempted to restore some balance between light and heavy industry. The Chinese hope to quadruple their total industrial and agricultural output by the year 2000. The plan seems to be to continue the adjustment efforts for the next five years or so, after which growth will be expected to accelerate steadily. One statistical problem is that, because they measure gross rather than net production, there may be some double-counting.

Jagdish Bhagwati, *Arthur Lehman Professor of Economics, Columbia University:* If one took a longer view, might not the region's fear of Japan's increased military expenditures change? In the first place, the new generations coming to power will have no memories of World War II. Secondly, China's military capability may increase so as to seem threatening without Japanese power to serve as a counterweight in the region.

Okita: On the other hand, if we build up our military forces within the framework of continued friendly relations with China, the combined power may seem a serious threat to the smaller countries in Asia. But at least as far as Japan is concerned I think our military role must have certain limits. There is little possibility that the two-thirds Diet majority and national referendum required to amend the present constitution could be attained in the foreseeable future. Although Prime Minister Nakasone has called for open discussion of the issue, he has not actually advocated constitutional revision. Furthermore, the apprehensions of the Southeast Asian countries serve as a brake on any rapid military build-up. If China were to make advances in satellite or missile technology, this could perhaps set off repercussions within Japan. In 1979, for example, there was some opposition within the Liberal Democratic Party to proposed aid to China, because China produces nuclear weapons. This was a minority view, however, and the government has continued to provide China with economic aid.

Laurence Stifel, *The Rockefeller Foundation:* Over the next five to ten years, how do you project the development of ASEAN as a regional organization? It seems the economic measures of cooperation have been somewhat disappointing in terms of producing tangible results. There are also political differences regarding the role of China in the region. How do you see the organization evolving?

Okita: In ASEAN's early years there was little perceptible movement; it was even referred to as the "tea party of foreign ministers from five countries." Since the fall of Saigon, however, the climate of uncertainty has been more conducive to closer relationships among them. Subsequently, they have realized how ASEAN can serve as a means for dealing with the rest of the world, particularly in trade matters. Several years ago at an UNCTAD meeting in Nairobi, for instance, the ASEAN delegates invited me to dinner and requested Japanese support for the UNCTAD proposal on commodity agreements.

Within ASEAN, agreement has been rather slow in evolving, but they have arrived at some eight thousand items for preferential trade among themselves. Differences remain, of course, but the trend, however slow, seems to be towards economic integration. Despite disagreements over China and the Kampuchean issue, ASEAN's effort to maintain cohesion is significant. I do not expect to see spectacular accomplishments, but I do sense a certain degree of consolidation.

William Overholt, *Banker's Trust Company:* Dr. Okita, in your view how serious is the problem of the Third World debt in the vicious cycle of the world economy? Does the Japanese government have any proposals for emergency measures to deal with the problem? Is it possible that the idea of forcing Japanese banks to contract their loans will heighten the crisis in Africa and Latin America?

Okita: Our financial institutions have apprehensions about the solvency of some of the major developing countries. Japanese banks hold $10 billion of Mexico's $80 billion foreign debt. They would therefore suffer a severe blow should bankruptcy occur. The case of Brazil is similar. Private banks, concerned about country risks, have started accumulating reserves even without receiving special tax treatment. The government, for its part, is encouraging banks not to contract their loans excessively, lest they aggravate the existing problem.

In the final analysis, Japanese banks are in the same boat with American and European financial institutions. If the burden of handling the Third World debt problem is shared equitably among the major creditor nations, Japan will be willing to cooperate. Japan has supported a doubling of the IMF's resources, although recently only a 49 percent increase was agreed upon. But even if concerted action among the major industrial countries is able to stave off a crisis for the time being, it is important to keep in mind that international finance is only a reflection of the real side of the world economy, which consists of production and trade. As long as the real side of the economy does not recover, the financial sector will continue to face difficulties.

Howard Wriggins, *Professor of Political Science, Columbia University:* Could you elaborate on the debate to which you alluded within the Japanese government regarding Japan's role in defending the sea lanes?

Okita: Since I am not actually within the government, my remarks are not representative of official policy. A U.S.-Japan joint study group has been established to discuss this problem. The issues are complex and we do not know precisely how or to what extent we share responsibility for defense of the sea lanes. Under the terms of the U.S.-Japan Security Treaty, the United States is obligated to defend Japan in the event of a third-party attack on Japanese territory, but Japan has no reciprocal commitment to the United States. While this has led some to contend that this security treaty is one-sided, the counterargument, now as twenty years ago, is that Japan's contribution consists of supplying military bases for American forces in Japan. Prime Minister Nakasone expressed this latter view in his recent statement that Japan serves as a "large aircraft carrier." My view is that Japan should probably strengthen its surveillance capability, without moving into offensive weaponry or giving up its non-nuclear principles. So far, American defense experts have not requested us to abandon our "peace constitution" or to consider nuclear armament. Secretary Weinberger's recent remark may indicate a shift from that position on the constitution.

The question of whether or not a collective defense arrangement is permissible under the present constitution remains a delicate one. Under the current official interpretation of the constitution, an amendment would be necessary to permit any mutual or collective security arrangement. But defense of the sea lanes introduces another consideration, since it is difficult to conceive of Japanese forces remaining aloof if American forces were attacked while protecting Japanese carriers near the Japanese islands. The joint study group will have to clarify issues such as these.

James Morley, *Professor of Political Science, Director of Columbia University's East Asian Institute:* Dr. Okita, it has often been said that Japan has no obligation to defend the United States. But it is true, is it not, that under the terms of the Security Treaty, Japan has the obligation to defend Americans within the territory administered by Japan? In return, the only obligation of the United States is to protect the Japanese on territory administered by Japan. Legally speaking, then, questions about the sea lane and Japanese oil interests are beyond the treaty provisions for both countries.

Whether the United States indeed wishes to protect Japanese shipping and whether Japan wishes to protect Japanese shipping are similarly political questions in each country, rather than legal questions on either side. So there are actually two sides to these negotiations.

Okita: When Prime Minister Suzuki came to Washington two years ago, he stated explicitly at the National Press Club that Japan would try to defend the one thousand mile sea lane. But there still remain areas of ambiguity. Whether defense means surveillance or the use of military force against an attacking country remains unclear.

Richard Nations, *Far Eastern Economic Review:* Japan has long been in favor of arms control, but now that there is the prospect of some agreement emerging between the United States and the Soviet Union within the year, Japan is expressing concern that if the United States insists on the zero option and does not compromise with the Soviet Union, this could adversely affect Japanese security. And yet there seems to be a consensus emerging within the Atlantic community that the zero option is not feasible and that, as Vice President Bush put it upon returning from his trip to Europe, an intermediate stage may have to be considered. This is all bound up with the direction of politics in Europe over the next year. If it appears that the United States and the Soviet Union are moving towards some sort of compromise which would allow the Soviets to shift some of these missiles eastward, how do you feel the Japanese would react? Do you see this becoming an important issue in U.S.-Japanese security relations? How will it affect the debate within Japan about the constitution and security issues?

Okita: When Mr. Gromyko made his statement in Bonn, the Japanese Foreign Ministry protested to the Soviet government, stating that Japan could not tolerate the movement of SS-20 missiles to Asia. There are already some SS-20s located in central Siberia. Backfire bombers also have the capability of reaching Japan. The possibility of a Soviet attack on bases in Japan could not be excluded if a war between the Soviet Union and the United States were to break out. Indeed, some groups with Japan, notably the Japan Socialist party, argue that it is the very closeness of the military relationship with the United States that involves Japan in this dangerous possibility.

The Japanese government, however, holds that the U.S.-Japan Security Treaty is the critical deterrent against an outside attack and that this relationship is essential to Japan's security. But while there are conflicting views, many of us feel that if a U.S.-Soviet conflict were to begin, Japan would inevitably be involved, and therefore efforts should focus on preventing any such conflict. So our position is somewhat complicated. We feel that the security relationship with America is a necessary deterrent to any outside attack, and that to maintain that relationship it is incumbent on Japan to support the American defense position. But on the other hand, we have an internal political problem involving the constitution and the basic framework for our own defense.

Taking a longer-term view, survival on this planet may require adherence to the sort of non-offensive, non-nuclear, and ultimately non-military principles that Japan has attempted to adopt. This sounds unduly idealistic, perhaps, but looking into the next century, an increasing number of countries may find it prudent to renounce the use of force for the settlement of international disputes.

For the moment, we must expand our security efforts, particularly because of the American sentiment that Japan benefits from a "free ride." Granted, the present treaty was concluded in 1960 when Japan's GNP was only 10 percent that of the United States. Now, as Japan's GNP is approximately one-half that of the United States, Americans insist that Japan should spend more for its own security. In the longer term, however, Japan favors global disarmament, step by step.

Richard Sneider, *former U.S. Ambassador to Korea:* Part of the rationale for Japan's low defense contribution has been that you have a comprehensive security plan under which more of your resources go into economic aid to developing countries. I recall former Prime Minister Suzuki's statement that Japan would attempt to double its Official Development Assistance in five years, and certainly when we look at the current economic conditions in the Third World, the requirements for greater assistance are there. Yet, the recent statistics indicate that, if anything, Japan's ODA has declined in the last year or two.

Okita: As a matter of fact, the Fukuda Plan for doubling the ODA in three years was already surpassed by its 1980 target year. Prime Minister Suzuki then introduced an additional plan to double ODA in another five years. Despite this policy announcement, ODA declined from .32 percent of Japan's GNP in 1980 to .28 percent in 1981. But a breakdown of the figure shows that the major decline was in the contribution to multilateral aid, particularly to the International Development Association. Bilateral aid, by contrast, was increased in 1981 by 15 percent over the previous year. The reduction in multilateral aid of about 40 percent was in keeping with the concept that Japan's contribution to the IDA should be proportional to those of the major industrialized nations. Because the United States reduced its contribution to the IDA, Japanese financial authorities insisted that we should cut our contribution accordingly. This, in my view, was a mistaken decision, and I argued that we should instead step up our aid program. But partly because of our budgetary constraints, and partly because even countries like Germany took a similar position of proportional funding, there was a rather sharp decline in our multilateral aid in 1981. Nevertheless, there should be some increase in 1982, if not a return to .32 percent of the GNP, perhaps up to slightly over .3 percent. The government's basic decision to increase development aid has not changed. It may be noted, for example, that the only two items allowed to increase in the 1983 budget were defense expenditures, which rose by 6.5 percent and foreign aid, which rose by 8.9 percent.

Hugh Patrick, *Professor of Far Eastern Economics, Yale University:* Dr. Okita, what in your view will be the most serious problem Japan will face in dealing with its Asian neighbors over the next five years?

Okita: If the world remains at peace, there should not be any serious problems. Of course if the recession stretches out indefinitely, the economic repercussions in the Southeast Asian economies could lead to political problems, which could in turn have an impact upon Japan. So the two potential problems are the continuation of stagnation in the industrial economies and direct military confrontation, but I am optimistic that neither will materialize.

Robert S. Ingersoll

TOWARD A BILATERAL PARTNERSHIP:

Improving Economic Relations

U.S.-Japanese trade relations may not be at an all-time low, but the common sentiment around Washington these days is that we would rather "shoot ourselves in the foot" than grant Japan any further access to U.S. markets. Many legislators feel politically justified in taking punitive actions against the Japanese, even when these actions are counterproductive to long-term U.S. national interests.

The dockside inspection of every imported Toyota or Datsun, to take one example, would cost the U.S. government millions of extra dollars in additional inspectors and would cost American retailers millions of dollars in lost sales. But the resulting delays would harm the Japanese, and thus such policies are currently under serious consideration in Washington. There is at present so much anger, resentment, and hostility toward Japan that a shot in the foot may be seen as an acceptable price to pay for even a small measure of revenge.

The past few years have seen an extraordinarily intensive effort by Congress to limit imports from Japan. Fortunately, most of the reciprocity bills which have been enacted do not have the retaliatory force of some of the original proposals. But the fact that some legisla-

tors even advocate such pernicious protectionist measures goes against the traditional free trade policies long championed by the United States. It also indicates a misunderstanding of the basic issues.

The U.S.-Japanese trade imbalance is not just a function of U.S. imports and Japanese exports. It is, rather, the most visible manifestation of the need for the United States to strengthen its industrial base and revitalize its economy. An economically sound America should be the objective of even those legislators most concerned with the Japanese threat; the threat will diminish as the United States regains its competitiveness in world markets by retooling its industries, retraining its workers, and reordering its priorities.

Currently, the high rate of unemployment in the United States is the most pressing domestic problem, but in the long run inflation presents the single greatest obstacle to be overcome. The recent decline in the inflation rate is an encouraging indication that American faith in the dollar may once again be restored. If we believe the dollar will still be worth a dollar a year or ten years from now, we may be inclined to put some of that money in the bank. Moreover, if we believe that prices are fairly stable, we will be likely to spread out purchases over time. With incentives to save and more money available for capital investment in plants and equipment, the United States will be in a position to regain its comparative advantage without having to "take it out" on the Japanese.

There is no question that inflation has been an important factor in the U.S.-Japanese trade war. Take automobiles: in 1970 the average American car cost less than $3500; in 1982 it cost more than $10,000. In the case of compacts, Japan's cost advantage is close to $2000 per car. This clearly presents an attractive incentive for American consumers to think small—and to think Japanese. Before the "voluntary restraint agreement" on automobile imports went into effect, Americans who bought Japanese cars saved over $1 billion annually on the purchase price and millions of dollars on reduced gasoline consumption. It did not take long before Detroit manufacturers were motivated to make every effort to recapture the U.S. market by producing smaller, more efficient cars. There are, then, very real benefits from the competitive lessons of free trade.

There are, of course, also real benefits to be gained from protectionism, but they are mainly short-term. For example, the so-called trigger price mechanism, which helped the U.S. steel industry compete with Japanese imports, did not force American manufacturers to upgrade their plants and equipment but enabled them instead to buy oil fields. When this is the result of protectionist barriers, ultimately no one gains. The "time" bought by protectionism is only useful when applied to making structural adjustments and other preparations to deal better with future contingencies. A revitalized U.S. economy is not dependent on trade barriers but on upgrading domestic productivity. Political actions taken to redress immediate economic grievances do not address the underlying macroeconomic factors which form the real basis for trade imbalances.

But addressing the big factors is the hard part. The antagonistic nature of labor-management relations in the United States makes it particularly difficult to transfer employees between jobs, to introduce labor-saving machinery, or to retrain workers for new careers. Labor contract negotiations in the United States are not generally amicable or, ultimately, cost-effective. In addition, management in the United States is in most cases unwilling to make heavy investments in labor-saving equip-

ment or in retraining workers if it means forgoing short-term profits. Shareholders are more concerned with the bottom line today than with future growth potential, and chief executive officers are accountable from the moment they take charge.

High-leverage financing to promote long-term investment, easily available in Japan but not in the United States, presents another domestic obstacle to instant revitalization of the U.S. economy. The high interest rates of recent years have virtually eliminated most large-scale, long-term corporate borrowing necessary for capital improvement. If American industry has been "done in," it is inflation, not Japan, that has been doing it in.

None of this is to suggest, however, that there are no real problems between the two countries. There are. The situation is similar to that which a historian once noted existed between Carthage and Rome: "They were friends until they became equals." In some areas, of course, Japanese equality has been followed by superiority. Bilateral trade between the United States and Japan, totalling more than $60 billion annually, is very much in Japan's favor, with a trade surplus of close to $20 billion. While this figure in no way represents the entire picture of U.S.-Japanese relations—the United States, for example, has a considerable surplus in service industries and each country is the other's largest supplier of manufactured goods—its adverse effects are serious enough to trigger a bilateral trade war which could have a significant impact on the entire world economy.

International trade is vital to most nations of the world, approaching one-third or more of the gross national product in many countries. A certain amount of short-term economic dislocation is the inevitable cost of such extensive global intercourse, but it is important that the dislocation remain as limited as possible. The General Agreement on Tariffs and Trade (GATT) has regulated this enormous volume of exchange fairly well through a system of multilateral agreements accepted by most of the industrial countries. While measures to protect domestic markets from foreign competition are part of the trading system, they rarely occur on a large scale between major national economies.

Yet this is just what would happen if the United States and Japan were to intensify their protectionist tendencies. The result would be a diversion of both American and Japanese exports to third countries. This would lead such countries to erect barriers to Japanese and American products and would lead Japan and the United States to limit imports from the new protectionists. In fact, the voluntary restraint agreements on Japanese auto exports to the United States spawned immediate demands by Canada and several Western European nations for similar measures.

This highly simplified scenario is likely enough that one may be properly concerned with the eventual dismantling of GATT should a full-fledged U.S.-Japanese trade war actually occur, and with the threat of greatly increased protectionist measures by other trading partners.

Fortunately, there are many compelling reasons to believe that a full-fledged trade war is not imminent. For one, the United States is still the most productive nation in the world in terms of GNP and still dominates international activity, producing about 22 percent of gross world product. The United States also maintains its world leadership position in many areas, including computer software, construction machinery, commercial aircraft, photographic film, agriculture, and distribution systems. As the United States and Japan become more similar economically, the prospects for cooperation still seem to outweigh the potential for further deterioration of relations.

Japan's economic growth has not been as spectacular in the 1980s as it was in the 1970s, falling from an average of about 10 percent to approximately 5 percent, with further declines likely as the decade progresses. Even so, it will continue to grow faster than the United States and other industrialized countries. The fact is that economic maturity entails the same kind of slowing down as physical aging. The efforts and sacrifices made early on are made much less willingly when relative affluence is an established fact of life. Japan has begun to experience a decline in the "work ethic" and a popular desire for greater leisure. The "social" limits to growth which exist in the United States and much of Western Europe are becoming apparent in Japan as well, especially in terms of concern with the environment, industrial pollution, and social welfare.

But Japan also faces important economic limits to growth, primarily its lack of natural resources. The almost total reliance on imported oil, gas, and coal means that the economy will remain a precarious one as long as it is dependent on access to foreign energy and minerals. This being the case, it is vital for Japan to maintain or improve its competitive position in the world and to overcome the natural tendency toward a relaxation of economic efforts.

Japan's position will not be improved if it has to devote a great deal of time and attention to fixing, upgrading, downplaying, or rearranging its relations with the United States. And in fact, this should not be necessary since American and Japanese interests often coincide, the cases of automobiles, textiles, steel, and color television sets notwithstanding. As pointed out in

23

a recent article by David MacEachron in *Foreign Affairs*:

> Both favor a liberal economic world order, a world which is open to trade and capital movement. For both, open democratic societies are preferable to autocratic regimes with their inherent propensity to violence and sudden foreign policy changes. Both are eager for an end to Soviet expansionism and for a continuation of the evolution in the People's Republic of China toward moderation. Japan has been as supportive of the United States in the cases of Iran, Afghanistan and Poland as any of America's allies. Both Japan and the United States benefit from and support the growing prosperity of the Association of Southeast Asian nations. Expanding Japanese foreign aid has increasingly been directed to countries considered strategically important to the United States...
>
> A weakening of the close diplomatic cooperation which has developed between the United States and Japan in recent years would be serious for both. [1]

The political friction which often accompanies economic and trade disagreements can jeopardize many of these mutual interests. In an effort to reduce these tensions, President Carter and Prime Minister Ohira appointed a panel of eight private citizens, four from each country, to study the economic problems which could endanger good relations between our two countries. In January 1981 this Japan-U.S. Economic Relations Group, labeled the "Wisemen" by the Japanese press, issued its report and recommendations. The overriding consensus was that the public and private sectors of both countries have to look not only at their national needs and priorities but also at their international responsibilities and objectives.

Increasingly, issues which were once thought to be purely domestic concerns are having worldwide repercussions: transportation, health and safety, employment, welfare legislation, and so on. The effects of economic policy choices are especially likely to touch foreign sensitivities and must, therefore, be formulated with the greatest care. The task is for business leaders, policymakers, and the public at large to learn to view traditional domestic economic issues from a broader international perspective.

Considering the deep-rooted historical, social, and cultural differences between the United States and Japan, this is no small feat. For the Japanese especially, one of the most isolated and inward-turning societies in history, taking the interest of other nations into account is a totally unfamiliar way of thinking. Even after Japan opened its doors to the West, the "outside world" continued to be regarded as a hostile albeit important entity. Mainly, Japan's perception of itself was that of a small and unsure nation against the world. The only significant change in this attitude has come as a result of Japan's extraordinary economic achievements. Japan today still views itself as a small but more self-confident — some would say, bordering on arrogant — nation against the world. There is very little recognition of the need to assume an international role commensurate with its economic importance and global reach.

American attitudes have tended to change in the opposite direction. From a posture bordering almost on omnipotence, or at least invulnerability, the United States has suffered severe economic, political, military, and moral setbacks in the past two decades. While humility has not yet become a prevailing national characteristic, the easy generosity which was so evident when things were going well for the United States has been replaced by a much more "up tight" and nervous

---

1. David MacEachron, "The United States and Japan: The Bilateral Potential," *Foreign Affairs* 61 (Winter 1982/83): 404-5.

guarding of those competitive advantages it still enjoys. The American public and its representatives feel unable to make any further concessions to "Japan, Inc." Indeed, to avoid even the appearance of concessions it is deemed better to "shoot ourselves in the foot."

It is not easy to synthesize traditional values with new economic realities, but it is a good opportunity for both sides to make constructive adjustments. The United States ought to retool its industries to deal effectively with the increasingly competitive international environment of the future. Japan ought to actively try to change its image as a country with closed markets which does not play the international trade game fairly. Primarily, there has to be a bilateral approach which exhibits some consistency: the love/hate ambivalence of the U.S.-Japanese relationship only increases mutual distrust and suspicion. It will not do for the United States to encourage Japanese high-technology industries, for example, then decide to institute protectionist measures against them. As a basically reactive society, the Japanese are completely jolted by these kinds of shocks, which only reconfirm their basic fear of outsiders. Conversely, their economic structure, designed to increase Japan's competitiveness and preserve Japanese jobs, has outlived its usefulness in an international context. Japan is now strong enough to eliminate virtually all of its trade barriers. While this would not automatically reduce its trade surplus, it would immediately create a better psychological atmosphere.

To some extent, natural market forces will correct much of the trade imbalance that now threatens the U.S.-Japanese bilateral relationship. As noted, the limits which inhibit the continuation of rapid economic growth in industrialized countries are becoming apparent in Japan. Furthermore, Japan is in the first stages of phasing out its basic manufacturing industries and in the future will be turning more from products to services, where the United States still clearly has the advantage. The Japanese government's economic policy is likely to become more responsive to internal development needs, implying that national objectives will become more heterogeneous: But to the extent that bilateral trade problems will continue to exist, perhaps even intensify in the short run, the Wisemen report offers some suggestions which I think are worth noting here.

In particular, there must be a better understanding of the reasons for the current trade and account imbalances. Indeed, even if American goods had total access to Japanese markets and even if American economic policies were perfectly managed, there would still be a disequilibrium caused by structural differences. A singular and simplistic focus on the bilateral merchandise trade imbalance is detrimental to overall good relations. It is up to the leadership of both Japan and the United States to educate themselves and their colleagues on the broader benefits of world trade, the global nature of even bilateral trade and capital flows, and the necessity of trade-offs in a system of economic interdependence.

The concept of comparative advantage becomes especially relevant in a world where every nation has something to offer. Variations in the cost of labor and capital, changing patterns of consumption and demand, and technological innovations all contribute to economic dislocations. Neither Japan nor the United States consistently enjoys an advantage. But there often exist powerful political pressures to assist those industries which are presently suffering most. It becomes, then, a major responsibility of both countries to avoid protectionist temptations and to foster instead domestic adjustments which are consistent with the changing conditions of international competition.

The Austrian economist Joseph Schumpeter called this process of adjustment "creative destruction." Simply, the term means that innovation and progress often threaten, disrupt, or even destroy traditional values, institutions, and jobs. Ideally, the destruction creates a more efficient, cost-effective, and satisfying outcome. In the case of Japanese-American relations, the process of structural adjustment will benefit consumers through the creation of better products at lower prices and will open new export markets to domestic producers.

Changing international economic conditions also have a significant effect on exchange rate fluctuations. Shifts in the yen-dollar exchange rate increase or decrease the magnitude of the trade imbalance. With the yen's increasing international role, Japan should share the burdens of a key currency country by taking domestic actions to help maintain the stability of its currency, and therefore of the international monetary system. Similarly, the United States should strive to stabilize the dollar, a task to be accomplished mainly by a revitalization of the American economy.

Problems of structural adjustment as well as exchange rate fluctuations should be addressed through a coordinated bilateral approach. Indeed, probably the most complex issue in the U.S.-Japanese relationship is how to coordinate policy responses to cyclical economic problems. Tightly coordinated macroeconomic policies may be counterproductive or destabilizing. A better and more realistic solution might be to aim for close consultation and general agreement on economic conditions and future policy responses. Frequent working meetings of economic policy-makers from government, the private sector, and the academic community can ensure an ongoing dialogue on matters of current as well as long-range importance.

It is imperative not just for Japanese and American leaders, but also for the people of the two nations, to become more aware of what is happening in each other's country. Business and labor task forces, study groups, and conferences involving representatives from both countries should work to identify and treat trade problems before they reach the front pages of newspapers as "insoluble" or "intractable."

Official negotiations should concentrate on appropriate issues. Not all problems can be negotiated, and those which are not should be excluded from official trade talks. Bilateral government meetings should concentrate on those areas where direct intervention can make a difference, and where the private sector can follow up and implement decisions reached in the negotiations. The new international roles of both the United States and Japan can be sustained only by enlightened public and private leadership. Both countries must recognize their international responsibilities and carry them out according to their respective capabilities.

Japan, for example, is under increasing pressure to reduce both its formal and nontariff trade barriers. In 1980 Prime Minister Suzuki appointed a commission headed by former MITI Minister Esaki to investigate charges of restrictions on imports. Significantly, the commission endorsed the suggestion of the Wisemen report to establish an Office of Trade Ombudsman. The agency now exists to resolve the grievances of foreign businessmen, an important first step in recognizing Japan's vital interest in a free trade system. But Japan also needs a domestic agency which can initiate actions against trade restrictions as well as respond to complaints.

26

Improving Economic Relations

Japan has long had a problem with taking the initiative in the absence of outside pressure. This means that the United States will have to continue to apply pressure on Japan, but selectively—in areas and in ways where it can do the most good in terms of our own national interest. Specifically, the U.S. government should push for the faster liberalization of Japanese capital markets. Japan has made substantial progress in opening its market to manufactured products—very few quotas are still in place. Most foreign exchange and investment controls have been lifted. But the perception of a closed Japanese market remains.

Japan, then, not only has to continue the actual process of liberalization but must also work on changing foreign perceptions. One way to do this is for Japan to further expand the visibility of its governmental economic decision-making processes, and to permit greater private sector access to these processes. It is up to the United States to monitor Japanese actions in those areas where Japanese industrial development policies are likely to be most protectionist: their declining domestic industries, for example, and high technology. In some instances positive results may be achieved by pointing out that exclusionary policies might deprive them of access to U.S. technology. In others the most practical results may be achieved by creating incentives whereby the Japanese regard improved market access to be in their own interest.

The latter method proved successful in the dispute over airline traffic rights: the United States was able to secure concessions from the Japanese because the American negotiators could identify how such concessions would benefit Japan. Similar attempts by the U.S. cigarette industry have not been as successful, suggesting that some of the obstacles to a further opening of

Japanese markets are governmental (cigarettes are produced and distributed by a government monopoly) as well as private.

In the United States the primary obstacles to improving bilateral relations will continue to be inflation, poor productivity, and declining overall economic performance. Without an effective policy of positive adjustment to international competition, the temptation is always to resort to stop-gap protectionist measures. But as noted earlier, such political remedies only create economic disincentives to adjust.

> Take the case of the U.S. auto industry. "Temporary" and "voluntary" export quotas were agreed upon in 1981 specifically to buy time in which the U.S. industry might make adjustments during a period of short-term cyclical recession. Assuming management and labor were really able to make better cars (in terms of quality, price, and overall consumer preferences), continued quantitative restrictions on Japanese automobile exports, let alone the more intense protectionism represented by the proposed local content legislation, would actually tend to work against the U.S. industry's making further improvements. Such protection would tend to drive auto prices up for both domestically-produced and imported cars; in so doing, the restrictions would make U.S auto workers less inclined to accept wage restraints, perhaps in exchange for job security, and U.S. auto-industry managers less inclined to design cost-reducing production processes. Yet members of Congress might well want to maintain existing quantitative restrictions or impose new barriers precisely because they were a highly visible—if also economically counterproductive— way of dealing with their particular political problems. [2]

Yet in spite of such political "quick fixes," I believe that the desire to strengthen the international trading sys-

---

2. Jimmy W. Wheeler, Merit E. Janow, and Thomas Pepper, *Japanese Industrial Development Policies in the 1980's* (A Hudson Institute Research Report, October 1982), 62.

tem exists in both countries. The recent U.S.-Japanese agreement to accelerate tariff reductions on semiconductor products represents a constructive effort to strengthen the semiconductor industry in Japan as well as in the United States. Japanese producers will lose some protection but they will gain from the benefits of cooperation in research, development, and procurement programs.

The idea here is not to go through all the various issues and areas where the potential for improved bilateral relations exists. Rather, the point is to reiterate the importance of a more comprehensive partnership whereby each nation is cognizant of the interests and sensitivities of the other, even on issues that are not directly bilateral in nature. The economic relations between Japan and the United States are so important to the health of the international economic system that neither country can allow sectoral problems to undermine the essential strength and stability of the partnership.

That both nations benefit from an international system of free trade and capital flows is a fact which is not understood well enough in either country. There is a need for a continuing and constructive dialogue between Japanese and Americans at all levels to deal with difficult economic issues, resolving those which are soluble, pre-empting those which are avoidable, and preventing even those which seem "intractable" from threatening overall political and diplomatic relations.

Sadako Ogata

THE CHANGING ROLE OF JAPAN IN THE UNITED NATIONS

It is often said that the influence of Japan in the United Nations is not commensurate with the power it possesses.[1] Although states that possess great power do not necessarily exercise strong influence in international organizations, the case of Japan merits special attention. Japan is perhaps the only state in the UN with a predominantly economic power base that is beginning to wield its economic strength to gain political influence. The purpose of this study is first to examine the changes in the type of influence Japan exercises in the UN, and second, to relate Japan's objectives and actions in the UN to its overall foreign policy.

In considering the role played by Japan in the UN, it is important to examine the organizational structure and decision-making processes of this international institution. Japan's economic power is reflected most directly in the volume of its financial contributions. Japan's actual contribution to the UN system is now second only to that of the United States. Yet, in a world organization founded on the wartime alliance of the "United Nations," positions of influence, including permanent Security Council seats, were distributed to the five major victorious powers on the basis of their political and military power. Economic contributions as such were not perceived as legitimate grounds for granting special rights or privileges. Moreover, with decolonization, many new states have joined the UN, forming voting blocs and vying for influence as pressure groups within the organization. Constraints deriving from UN Charter provisions and postwar international relations have affected Japan in its bid to gain a position of importance in the UN proportional to its economic weight.

The significance of the UN in Japan's foreign policy must be examined in relation to the changing power relations within that organization as well as in terms of shifts in Japan's policy objectives. When Japan joined the organization in 1956, the UN was under the predominant influence of the United States. There was little incongruity between supporting the UN and maintaining close allegiance to the United States. However, beginning in the mid-1960s, the UN has come increasingly under the control of developing countries that demand changes in the political and economic *status quo*. Japan has often found it necessary to demonstrate its support for the developing countries' demands in the UN because these countries frequently possess vitally important natural resources. Aside from considerations of national interest, Japan's UN policy has also been affected by domestic opinion, which regards the UN with idealism and maintains high hopes for disarmament and social reform. Recently Japan has been showing renewed interest in realistically evaluating the importance of the UN for its foreign policy.

By examining Japan's policies and activities in the UN, this study tries to indicate possible areas in which

---

1. The terms "influence" and "power" are used in the sense defined by Robert W. Cox and Harold K. Jacobson, *The Anatomy of Influence* (New Haven: Yale University Press, 1974), 1-5.

Japan will attempt to exert its influence in international relations in general, and in the United Nations in particular.

Japan's Role in the UN System

In the UN, member states gain influence by mobilizing votes in support of their policies and proposals. The rights and privileges of the permanent members of the Security Council are prescribed in the Charter, and in the earlier days the five permanent members were also those most capable of mobilizing large blocs of votes in support of their respective national policies. Through rapid decolonization and extension of membership in the 1960s and 1970s, however, the numerical balance within the UN began to tilt heavily in favor of the newly independent states. These new nations organized themselves into political groups to coordinate and develop common positions with regard to issues of mutual concern. Today the group of non-aligned nations comprises approximately two-thirds of the total UN member states. The Group of 77 has become the most important institutionalized coalition for negotiation of economic matters vis-à-vis the industrialized market economy countries.

Japan is neither a permanent member of the Security Council nor of any of the political voting blocs. The only manner in which Japan's economic strength is recognized is in the assessment of its percentage contribution to the UN budget. From the initial assessed contribution of 2.19 percent at the time of its admission in 1956, Japan's assessment has increased rapidly in reflection of its growth in GNP. In the three years starting from 1983 Japan's assessment will be 10.32 percent, coming close to the Soviet Union, which is assessed at 10.54 percent. Combined with the voluntary contribution to the operational programs of the UN system, Japan provided a total of $347 million in 1980, surpassing the other permanent members of the Security Council except the United States (see Table 1). It is often said that the UN is based upon the incongruity of providing the same one vote to the United States, which assumes a 25 percent burden, as to the seventy states that contribute the minimum 0.01 percent of the budget. Obliging Japan to assume major financial obligations without enjoying any of the privileges accorded to the permanent members seems to be a similar absurdity. At the 23rd and 24th General Assemblies, Foreign Minister Aichi made statements that were interpreted to express Japan's aspirations to become a permanent member of the Security Council. At the 28th General Assembly in 1973, Secretary of State Kissinger expressed United States support for the permanent membership of Japan on the Security Council. In the Tanaka-Nixon Communiqué of the same year,

UN Contributions (in Thousands of U.S. Dollars)

	Assessed Contribution		Voluntary Contribution		Total	
	1979	1980	1979	1980	1979	1980
USA (25%)	(1)344,361	(1)370,872	(1)461,386	(1)562,597	(1)805,747	(1)933,469
USSR (11.10%)	(2)133,783	(3)134,785	7,822	8,760	(9)141,605	(9)143,545
Japan (9.58%)	(3)115,193	(2)136,237	(9) 80,055	(4)211,549	(7)195,248	(2)347,786
Germany (8.31%)	(4)102,946	(4)115,979	(4)158,688	(5)167,658	(2)261,634	(3)283,637
France (6.26%)	(5) 84,331	(5) 96,170	26,161	44,938	(11)110,492	(10)141,108
United Kingdom (4.46%)	(6) 64,910	(6) 70,645	(5)155,583	(9)119,925	(4)220,493	(7)190,570

Report of the Committee on Contributions A/36/11 Addendum

President Nixon's belief was included that "a way should be found to assure permanent representation in that council for Japan, whose resources and influence are of major importance in world affairs." In 1973, Japan's assessed contribution to the UN was raised from 5.4 percent to 7.15 percent. Surpassing France and the United Kingdom, Japan became the third largest contributor to the UN.

With the exception of the United States, however, no support has been forthcoming in favor of permanent representation for Japan on the Security Council. The Soviet Union, the United Kingdom, and France have been reluctant to take up an issue that might undermine the established power distribution. The People's Republic of China, though in principle in favor of revising the Charter, has not clarified its view on the desirable composition of the Security Council. Though some states have shown sympathy for Japan's aspirations, no one seems willing to take up an issue that might open up "Pandora's Box." In fact, many states have demonstrated their own designs on permanent membership on the Security Council. Latin American states feel that their region should be represented by a permanent member. The Organization for African Unity and the group of non-aligned nations expect to see their presidents *ex officio* serving permanently on the council. India feels it should represent the region of South and Southeast Asia. When an *ad hoc* committee was formed in 1974 to deal with the question of reviewing the Charter, Japan supported the move with the intention of seeking to gain permanent membership. By the time the committee was formally launched the following year, however, the mandate itself had been diluted so as to embody a general consideration of ways to strengthen the role of the UN.

At least in the foreseeable future, there is no likelihood that Japan alone will be granted permanent membership on the Security Council. Since Japan finished its two-year term on the council at the end of 1982, it will be interesting to see how long it will be able to restrain its urge to be represented once again on the council. Apart from the Security Council, Japan has been rather widely represented in the various organs of the UN. Japan has been a member of the Economic and Social Council almost continuously except for 1966-67, 1971, and 1981. It has also been serving on most functional commissions and on the governing boards of development assistance agencies. A Japanese judge sat on the International Court of Justice from 1961 to 1969, and again since 1976. Japan's representation in UN bodies is equal to that of the permanent members. Yet the one UN organ in which frequent representation is elusive is the Security Council. In the past Japan was able to follow an informal policy of running for election after short intervals.[2] With the number of aspiring candidates increasing in the Asian group, such a policy might no longer be possible, as its defeat in the 1978 Security Council election against Bangladesh amply demonstrated. Barring the possibility of becoming a permanent member, the recourses left for Japan seem limited. Japan could support such initiatives as taken by India in the last few years to call for an increase in the membership of the council, with the hope that in a larger council it would stand a better chance of being elected. Still, whatever role Japan might play would be necessarily limited, because an enlarged council could well turn into another General Assembly dominated by

---

2. Japan was a member of the Security Council during the years 1958-1959, 1966-1967, 1971-1972, 1975-1976, and 1981-1982.

the majority control of politically dominant groups such as the non-aligned nations. Japan could also attempt to demonstrate interest in issues relating to peace and security in order to impress upon the member states its ready concern. The initiative Japan took in the 37th session of the General Assembly, calling for the strengthening of the peace-keeping functions of the UN,[3] may be seen as an indication of the kind of style Japan might develop in the coming years.

Though much less direct and obvious, it is important to recognize that a country's representation in the secretariat may also be a useful source of influence in the UN. Being regularly present in all aspects of the organization's work, the secretariat controls the collection, processing, and distribution of information. It acts as an intermediary in informal contacts and negotiations. It stands to protect the general interest of the organization as embodied in the Charter and other public documents. The secretariat is allowed particularly wide latitude in its operational activities. Member states therefore attempt to exercise influence over the secretariat through various means, including the appointment of their own nationals to important posts. While successive secretaries-general have been selected from relatively small and neutral countries, other high-ranking posts have been distributed carefully among the major powers of long standing. In practice, for example, the undersecretary-general for political and General Assembly affairs has been given to the United States, that for political and Security Council affairs to the Soviet Union, that for special political affairs to the United Kingdom, and that for economic and social affairs to France.

Of the seventy-nine senior posts throughout the UN, consisting of secretary-general, director general, under-

secretary-general and assistant secretary-general, Japan only occupied the post of undersecretary-general for public information since 1972. Of the twenty-three agencies represented on the Administrative Committee on Coordination, not a single Japanese serves as head of an agency. The question of appointment to the UN has become a serious concern for the Japanese government in the last ten years.

The Charter provides that the secretary-general should appoint the staff taking into consideration "the necessity of securing the highest standards of efficiency, competence, and integrity," and with due regard to "the importance of recruiting the staff on as wide a geographical basis as possible."[4] In order to apply the principle of equitable geographical distribution, "a desirable range" is set up for each country by the secretary-general as a guideline for staff recruitment. Up to the present, assessed contribution has been used as the main factor in determining this range. As Japan's assessed contribution has nearly doubled in the last ten years, Japan's "desirable range" has also grown. Japan thus heads the list of countries that are considered to be "under-represented" in the UN secretariat.

The appointment of Japanese international civil servants has been difficult for many reasons. First, Japan's late entry into the UN prevented it from providing staff during the formative years of the organization. Secondly, Japan has been faced with new rivals from developing countries that also have demanded representation in the secretariat. During the 1970s, recruitment of women and nationals from developing countries became the main issue in the personnel policy of the various UN

---

3. UN General Assembly Resolution 37/67, 3 December 1982.
4. Article 101, UN Charter.

agencies. As a result, the post of director general for the development and international cooperation was created immediately below the secretary-general, with the understanding that it would be occupied by a national of a developing country so long as the secretary-general came from an industrialized country. A post of assistant secretary-general for social development and humanitarian affairs was also set up to facilitate the appointment of a woman to a senior position. The third and most important factor limiting rapid increase in the number of Japanese lies in the relatively limited availability of suitable candidates. To begin with, there are few Japanese who command several of the official UN languages. The pattern of lifetime employment practiced in Japan does not favor career interruption for lengthy periods of service in international organizations. Favorable employment opportunities at home do not cultivate incentives to seek work in international organizations. To work on the double task of pressuring UN organizations to recruit more Japanese and of allocating suitable candidates, the government recently has set up a recruitment center for international organizations in the Foreign Ministry and has appointed personnel officers at Japan's UN missions in New York and Geneva.

Although no new appointment has yet come through at the senior level, 1981-82 witnessed a sudden increase in the number of Japanese professionals in the UN. The number of Japanese staff had remained constant at approximately eighty for many years. A net addition of twenty-one took place in the course of last year. With a total of 101 professionals, Japan now ranks fifth in providing staff to the UN. Japan also sponsors about fifty "associate experts," primarily to the various field operation agencies. This substantial increase in personnel is undoubtedly the result of years of effort on the part of the Japanese government to improve its representation. This personnel expansion should be viewed as the secretariat's recognition of Japan as a major financial contributor.

Recent history has also witnessed a marked change in Japan's involvement in the operational activities of the UN. Although the percentage of Japan's voluntary contributions to operational programs does not match its assessed payments, Japan has continued to increase its share of voluntary contributions in the last several years. At a time when the traditional major donor states have been seriously affected by the world recession, Japan's contribution is given growing recognition. In particular, the programs for Indochinese refugees have turned Japan into a major donor with substantive interest in the administration of programs. The frequency of visits to Tokyo by heads of various UN agencies has also shown a notable increase in recent years.

In short, Japan's role in international organizations is beginning to take on a more substantive character. From a participant in international discussions, it has evolved into an active supporter of international operations, which in themselves have come to represent a growing feature of the UN. This examination of Japan's changing involvement in the UN suggests that Japan has expanded its influence in spite of the existence of considerable historical, legal, and political constraints.

The UN in Japan's Foreign Policy

The next question to be addressed is the importance of the UN in Japan's overall foreign policy. What objectives does Japan have in the UN? What changes might be observed in the future?

In 1956 Japan joined the UN with high expectations.

To the Japanese their admission symbolized Japan's return to an international society from which it had been isolated for some time. Aside from membership itself, Japan's single most important objective in joining the UN was to help guarantee its national security. At the time such a guarantee was considered particularly important, because Japan, under its postwar constitution, had abolished armaments and renounced the right of belligerency. Although a degree of *de facto* rearmament was taking place through the build-up of the Self-Defense Forces, the desire that Japan's security be guaranteed by the UN received widespread support from the people. After the voting that approved Japan's membership, Foreign Minister Shigemitsu made the following statement:

> We have determined to preserve our security and existence, trusting in the justice and faith of the peace-loving peoples of the world...We desire to occupy an honored place in an international society striving for the preservation of peace... Japan is gratified that together with the maintenance of peace, the United Nations places great importance on humanitarianism. It has taken up the problem of disarmament as a major task in the pursuit of its objective of maintaining peace...Being the only country which has experienced the horrors of the atomic bomb, Japan knows its tragic consequences...We earnestly hope that, under the leadership of the United Nations, the great task of disarmament will be successfully consummated.[5]

A highly idealistic perception of the UN as a guarantor of peace and security was to persist for a long time in the minds of the Japanese public.

The UN also occupied a focal point in the thinking of foreign policy decision-makers. Shortly before Japan's entry into the UN, the government proclaimed three basic principles of Japanese foreign policy: (1) it would be "UN-centered"; (2) it would cooperate with the free democratic nations; and (3) it would identify closely with the Asian countries.[6] The Japan-United States Security Treaty was already in existence, providing a substantive guarantee of Japanese security. However, there were strong domestic opinions opposed to security arrangements with the United States. The principle of "UN-centered" diplomacy both assured cooperation with the United States in a U.S.-dominated global forum and satisfied domestic aspirations to contribute to world peace.

The principle of "UN-centered" diplomacy, however, rapidly eroded in the next few years. Although prime ministers and foreign ministers continued to emphasize the importance of cooperation with the UN, references to "UN-centered" diplomacy as such disappeared from public documents by 1960. The immediate reason for the change was the increasing awareness of the UN's limitations as an effective collective security system. The frequent failures of the Security Council to act due to the use of the veto was enough to undermine trust in the UN as a guarantor of peace and security. More fundamentally, the growing influence of the developing countries, supported by the Soviet Union, gradually diminished the usefulness and effectiveness of the UN as an instrument for the United States and the Western industrialized democracies. These changes significantly affected Japan's policy toward the UN. "UN-centered" diplomacy, in the sense of expecting the UN to guarantee Japan's security, was no longer a realistic objective. Rather, the importance of the UN gradually came to depend upon the extent to which Japan could usefully

---

5. Statement by Foreign Minister Shigemitsu, 11th Session of the UN General Assembly, 18 December 1956.

6. Statement by Foreign Minister Kishi at the 26th session of the Diet, 4 February 1957.

resort to that body to promote cooperation with Western countries or with Asian countries in matters related to Japan's fundamental policy objectives.

Chinese representation was the first major issue that Japan pursued upon entry into the UN. Japan joined the United States to block the recognition of representation for the People's Republic of China, a move in direct accordance with its policy of defending the Nationalist government in Taiwan and of containing the spread of communism. After the question of Chinese representation was settled in 1971, and after the issue of Korean representation and unification was taken off the UN agenda in 1976, no vital Asian issue remained that called for close cooperation between Japan and the United States.

Then, in December 1978, Vietnam's military thrust into Kampuchea introduced a critical Asian issue into the UN. By then, as a leading Asian power, Japan was expected to take an active part in dealing with the Kampuchean situation, a role quite different from those it had taken in the past. At the 34th, 35th, 36th, and 37th Sessions of the General Assembly, Japan co-sponsored resolutions outlining various conditions required for the settlement of the problem, including the withdrawal of foreign troops from Kampuchea and self-determination for the Kampuchean people. It participated in the international conference on Kampuchea in the summer of 1980, joined the *ad hoc* committee established by that conference, and made various diplomatic efforts inside and outside the UN for the peaceful settlement of the Kampuchean situation. In addition to these political efforts, Japan undertook a major role in humanitarian relief measures for the Indochinese refugees. The government announced its readiness to provide approximately half the funds required for the United Nations high commissioner for refugees assis-

tance program for Indochinese refugees in 1979-80. Japan also continued to be a major donor to agencies such as UNHCR, WFP, and UNICEF, which are engaged in the relief of Indochinese refugees including affected Thai villagers. When the Afghan refugees poured into Pakistan in the winter of 1979-1980, Japan also responded to the appeal of the high commissioner to provide relief supplies and increased economic assistance to Pakistan. These acts were also intended to show Japan's readiness to cope with the security interests of countries adjacent to areas of conflict with strong East-West overtones.

Assistance to Indochinese refugees involved Japan in international cooperation for refugee resettlement. It was the first time that Japan had ever arranged for permanent resettlement of refugees on its own soil. From the initial quota of five hundred it expanded its quota to three thousand, and to date some two thousand refugees have been settled in Japan. Japan also operates processing centers within the country in cooperation with the high commissioner and provides economic and technical assistance to those in refugee centers in other parts of Asia. These relief activities have drawn Japan deeply into the web of international humanitarian activities. Japan's cooperative posture in regard to programs concerning the Asian region has turned Japan into a partner for the economic and humanitarian assistance programs of the UN.

The growth in the importance of North-South issues within the UN framework has further complicated Japan's policy in this organization. Japan's posture as a leading Asian country has obliged it to show a sympathetic and cooperative attitude toward the aspirations and demands of the developing countries of the region.

The 1973 oil crisis had a tremendous impact not only on the Japanese economy but also on Japanese diplomacy. Internally, there was a pressing need to readjust the domestic industrial structure. Externally, greater efforts had to be made to assure the maintenance of friendly relations with all countries, especially with those possessing resources of which Japan was in great need. "Being friendly with everybody" was the catch phrase of Japanese diplomacy in the wake of the oil crisis. Japan believed that it had to make vigorous efforts to assure a supply of essential goods from all countries, regardless of their location or political orientation.

This meant that in the UN context, Japan had to readjust its positions with regard to issues that were considered to be of vital importance to the developing countries. The Middle East question in particular proved to be a severe testing ground. Along with the United States, Japan had traditionally held the position that peace should be achieved through the early and complete implementation of Security Council Resolutions 242 and 338, which recognized the "sovereignty, territorial integrity, and political independence of every state in the area" including Israel. Japan had already shown understanding for the "inalienable rights" of the Palestinian people before the Middle East war of 1973.[7] But in the 1974-75 period Japan veered much closer to the Arab position by voting for the resolution that invited the PLO as the representative of the Palestinian people to the deliberations of the General Assembly[8] and by abstaining on others that supported the Arab cause.[9] In particular, Japan's abstention on the "Zionist" resolution[10] was widely noted, as the resolution was adopted against the opposition of the entire Western group of nations and was to cost the UN dearly in terms of governmental as well as public support in these countries. Furthermore, Japan went beyond support for Security Council Resolution 242 and endorsed recognition of

the legitimate rights of the Palestinians, including the right of self-determination, by voting for two Security Council resolutions that were ultimately vetoed by the United States.[11]

In upholding the principle of the right of self-determination for the Palestinian people, and in accepting the role of the PLO in the peace process leading to a lasting settlement in the Middle East, Japan made clear its support for the Arab position. Japan actively began to extend economic and technical assistance to the Islamic countries in the Middle East. In the UN, Japan increased its contribution to UNRWA by five times in 1974, and has continued to increase it, becoming the third largest contributor by 1981.[12] At the same time, Japan has exercised great caution in dealing with the PLO. Although it recognized the opening of a PLO office, Japan did not agree to grant the organization diplomatic status. Moreover, Japan gave full endorsement to the Camp David Agreement as the first step in

---

7. The term "inalienable rights" appeared in General Assembly Resolution 2443 XXIII establishing the "Special Committee to Investigate Israeli Practices Affecting the Human Rights of the Population of the Occupied Territories," and in a series of resolutions on the report of UNRWA to the 24th, 25th, 26th, 27th, and 28th General Assemblies.

8. UN General Assembly Resolution 3210 XXIX.

9. UN General Assembly Resolutions 3236, 3237 XXIX.

10. UN General Assembly Resolution 3279 XXX.

11. Security Council resolutions on the Middle East problem including the Palestinian question, 26 January 1976, and the report of the Committee on the Exercise of the Inalienable Rights of the Palestinian People, 29 June 1976.

12. Japan's contribution to UNRWA was less than $1 million until 1972. It increased to $5 million in 1974 and $7 million in 1979. In 1981, Japan's contribution was $10.6 million, ranking third. The U.S. contribution was $62 million, while the EEC donated $36.5 million.

reaching a comprehensive settlement of the Middle East problem. It has recently welcomed the peace initiative made by President Reagan and by Saudi Arabia at Fez. Over the years, the Middle East debates in the UN have proven to be excruciating experiences for Japan, which has to steer carefully through conflicting expectations without offending the sensitivities of any of the parties concerned.

In fact, the difficulty in the UN political process is that member states are required to take clear positions on divisive diplomatic issues. During the 1970s Japan found this process frequently to be at odds with its policy of "being friendly with everybody." A critical test faced Japan during the Iranian hostage crisis in November 1979. The Japanese attitude during the early weeks of the crisis in Iran was one of caution. It was a difficult situation involving the national pride and principles of an ally and the revolutionary fervor of a country that possessed vitally important resources. The press coverage consistently reflected concern over the future supply of oil to Japan and the fate of the giant Mitsui petrochemical project in Iran that was nearing completion. In a statement at a meeting of the Security Coucil on 2 December 1979, Ambassador Masahiro Nishibori expressed the "most profound concern" over the fate of the hostages and observed that the "present situation, regardless of the reasons involved, constituted a deviation from the well-established norms of international law concerning the inviolability of diplomatic personnel and property." At the same time, he was careful to add that Japan hoped that "solutions to the various problems which lie behind the present situation (would) be sought with greater earnestness and that, in so doing, the countries (would) act with utmost restraint and deliberateness."[13] Once the purchase of Iranian oil by Japanese trading firms became a serious bilateral issue between Japan and the United States, Foreign Minister Okita, on 12 December, was quick to announce that "the holding of hostages, for whatever reason, is a violation of well-established international law," and Prime Minister Ohira also confirmed Japan's support of the United States position. Thereafter, Ambassador Nishibori came out with a much stronger statement in the Security Council criticizing the Iranian action and expressing the belief that the "Security Council should take effective and appropriate measures in accordance with the relevant provisions of the Charter of the United Nations."[14]

Japan's decision to reaffirm its relationship with the United States as the cornerstone of its foreign policy was to characterize its UN activities in the following years. Increasingly, with the East-West conflict reappearing as the focal point of world politics, Japan turned to the UN to assert its position as a member of the Western industrialized democracies. At the time of the military intervention by the Soviet Union in Afghanistan, Japan was quick to urge the withdrawal of Soviet troops in respect of the Afghan people's right of self-determination and supported the resolution adopted at the emergency special session in January 1980 calling for the immediate, unconditional, and total withdrawal of foreign troops.[15] Japan also joined the United States and the Western European countries in undertaking sanctions against the Soviet Union and in providing

---

13. Statement by Ambassador Nishibori at the Security Council, 2 December 1979.
14. Statement by Ambassador Nishibori at the Security Council, 31 December 1979.
15. A/RES/ES-6/2, 14 January 1980.

relief supplies to the Afghan refugees through the UNHCR. When the Polish situation deteriorated and martial law was imposed in December 1981, Japan showed common understanding with the Western countries and judged that the current state of affairs in Poland was brought about under pressure from the Soviet Union, "urging the Soviet side to exercise self-restraint." Foreign Minister Sakurauchi announced Japan's intention "to take appropriate steps in concert with other Western countries at the United Nations and other international organizations,"[16] and shortly thereafter Japan joined the Western countries in an effort to pass a resolution in the Human Rights Commission that expressed "deep concern at the continued reports of widespread violation of human rights and fundamental freedoms in Poland" and decided "to request the secretary-general or a person designated by him to undertake a thorough study of the human rights situation in Poland."[17]

In line with the policy of clearly demonstrating solidarity with the Western industrialized democracies, a policy change that drew strong domestic criticism was Japan's vote with regard to the resolution calling for the "non-use of nuclear weapons and prevention of nuclear war."[18] This resolution was originally presented upon the initiative of India on the occasion of the tenth special session devoted to disarmament in 1978 and had been put to a vote at every General Assembly since the fall of that year. Western countries have consistently voted against it, as the resolution is considered to be in line with the Soviet peace offensive and is designed to undermine the nuclear deterrence strategy of NATO. Japan abstained at the 33rd and 34th General Assemblies but changed its vote after the Soviet intervention in Afghanistan to show solidarity with the

Western nations. It subsequently joined the Western countries in casting a negative vote. In the public eye, however, the Japanese government's voting position on this resolution was taken as a symbolic act that revealed its lack of sincerity in promoting nuclear disarmament.[19]

As stated earlier, Japan's admission to the UN was accompanied by widespread public expectation that world peace would be realized through this global forum. Disarmament was a special mission that the UN was expected to fulfill, and Japan's role was believed to be one of promoting world disarmament and of publicizing the tragic consequences of nuclear weapons. In fact the government accorded a high priority to the disarmament issue in the UN. Through persistent efforts, Japan became a member of the Conference of the Committee on Disarmament when it was expanded to twenty-six from the original eighteen in 1969. It became a party to the Nuclear Non-Proliferation Treaty in 1976 and has called widely for its universal acceptance. At the forum of the Committee on Disarmament, Japan has promoted an end to all nuclear test explosions in order to arrive at the early conclusion of a comprehensive test-ban treaty. In particular, Japanese efforts have been directed toward helping to establish an interna-

---

16. Statement of Foreign Minister Sakurauchi issued by the Foreign Ministry, 14 January 1982.
17. UN Commission on Human Rights resolution 1982/26, 10 March 1982.
18. UN General Assembly Resolution 33/71 B.
19. At the 37th General Assembly, Japan reverted to abstaining on the resolution concerning the non-use of nuclear weapons. According to the *Asahi*, the change signified an attempt to respond to public opinion that intensified throughout 1982. *Asahi Shimbun*, 7 December 1982.

tional seismic data exchange system in order to verify compliance with an eventual test-ban treaty. The practice in the General Assembly has been that disarmament resolutions are sponsored mostly by either the socialist or the non-aligned countries. Japan's voting record in general is considerably more positive than that of most Western nations. Japan even sponsors annually a resolution calling upon the negotiating nuclear states (the United States, the Soviet Union, and the United Kingdom) to resume their negotiations at the Committee on Disarmament to bring about the early conclusion of a total test-ban treaty.[20]

The special sessions of the UN devoted to disarmament that took place in 1978 and 1982 drew nationwide support and enthusiasm. Millions of signatures were collected and hundreds of delegates were sent to New York, representing various citizen action groups that organized themselves to form a national committee to demand the prohibition of nuclear arms and call for disarmament at the special sessions of the UN. The fact that the two special sessions drew such a great deal of attention to the disarmament movement proves that the UN continues to exert influence on the Japanese public. Prior to the departure of Prime Minister Suzuki for the special session in 1982, the two houses of the Japanese Diet unanimously adopted identical resolutions on the promotion of disarmament, particularly nuclear disarmament. The prime minister was fully aware of the domestic significance when he addressed the special session in the following moving terms: "I stand here today in this Assembly Hall, representing the collective will of the Japanese people, as expressed in those resolutions. I am convinced from the bottom of my heart that the common aspiration for peace of all peoples of the world is concentrated in this room. Our

mission here is to combine our efforts in response to this common aspiration of mankind and to move decisively together on the road to peace."[21]

In the same statement the prime minister proceeded to point out three aspects of the efforts required in order to reach peace through disarmament. These included the following: (1) "to reverse the trend of the ever-increasing arms race by promoting mutual confidence among states"; (2) "to utilize the human and physical resources released by disarmament to alleviate the poverty and social instability which breed conflict"; and (3) "to strengthen and reinforce the peace-keeping functions of the United Nations in order to promote disarmament."[22] The Japanese government has since followed up the third aspect of the prime minister's proposal and has taken several initiatives in the UN. It sent a working paper to the twelfth special session concerning the strengthening and expansion of UN peace-keeping functions.[23] At the 37th General Assembly, it took the initiative in preparing and passing a resolution by consensus, emphasizing the need to strengthen the role and effectiveness of the UN for the maintenance of international peace and security.[24]

Recent Japanese efforts should be carefully examined, not only from the standpoint of the content of the proposals but also in the wider context of Japan's evolving

---

20. UN General Assembly Resolutions 33/60, 34/73, 35/145 B, 36/85.
21. Statement by Prime Minister Suzuki at the twelfth special session of the General Assembly, 9 June 1982.
22. *Ibid.*
23. Note verbale dated 25 June 1982 from the permanent representative of Japan to the United Nations addressed to the secretary-general. A/S-12.1/45, 28 June 1982.
24. UN General Assembly Resolution 37/67, 3 December 1982.

role in the UN. In essence, Japanese proposals recommend strengthening two components: existing peace-keeping operations and the authority of the secretary-general. The fact that Japan has been advocating the need to re-examine the peace-keeping operations to enable speedy and sufficient deployment is in itself noteworthy. Peace-keeping operations constitute the one area in which Japan has not been operationally involved. Foreign Minister Sakurauchi, in his statement to the 37th General Assembly, elaborated the possible points for consideration that included "a system of prior registration and organization of the personnel, equipment, and materials which member states are ready to contribute to future operations; the holding by the United Nations of study and training exercises relating to peace-keeping operations; and the securing of effective financial backing." Moreover, the foreign minister affirmed the commitment that "Japan, for its part, is ready to cooperate more actively in the strengthening of the peace-keeping operations of the United Nations."[25]

It is too soon to tell whether Japan is itself prepared to participate in the program improvements proposed. Yet it may safely be said that the government is examining various means of dispatching civilian personnel to provide medical services and to supervise elections. The possibility of dispatching Self-Defense Force personnel for observer missions, after eventually revising the Self-Defense Force law, does not seem to be completely out of the question.[26] The issue of dispatching Self-Defense Forces for UN peace-keeping purposes has been a sensitive political issue for many years. Opponents have argued that such an action might result in military forces being sent overseas, which is prohibited by the Japanese constitution, or it might serve to legitimize the Self-Defense Forces as a regular military organization. With the realization that Japan should contribute more toward world peace and prosperity, and with the greater acceptance of the Self-Defense Forces by the general public, a fresh look at the issue of participation in UN peace-keeping operations seems to be in the offing. Opinion surveys carried out in the last few years report an increase in the percentage of those who feel that "Japan should cooperate more" with the UN. Among those who held that position in the 1982 survey, 44 percent stated that Japan should cooperate with the UN peace-keeping operations while 18 percent were opposed. The exact mode of cooperation was not specified in the questionnaire, but a further point of interest may be that among those who believed that "Japan should cooperate more" with the UN, as many as 68 percent supported cooperation in the field of the peace-keeping operations.[27] It may safely be said that Japan's final decision over dispatching personnel from the Self-Defense Forces will ultimately depend on three factors: (1) the nature of the international conflict and the UN mandate involved; (2) the intensity with which the secretary-general invites Japan's participation; and (3) the political judgment of the prime minister himself.

With regard to the authority of the secretary-general, Japan had for some time been advocating the strengthening of the fact-finding functions of the UN.[28] In the

---

25. Statement by Foreign Minister Sakurauchi at the 37th session of the General Assembly, 1 October 1982.

26. Statement of Foreign Minister Sakurauchi at the Budget Committee of the House of Councillors, 30 June 1982. "Kokuren ni yōin haken o," *Mainichi Shimbun*, 24 August 1982.

27. "Public Opinion on Foreign Policy," survey conducted by the prime minister's office, June 1982.

28. "Japan: Working paper on the strengthening of the fact-finding functions of the United Nations," A/AC, 182/WG/44/Rev.ol, 12 February 1980.

same vein Foreign Minister Sakurauchi, in the statement already mentioned, elaborated the overall functions of the secretary-general under the Charter and urged that they be fully utilized. He proposed, among other things, the strengthening of the role of the secretary-general in preventing international conflicts through initiating contact with the parties concerned, sending his representative to investigate the facts, and undertaking mediation and conciliation. In insisting on the strengthening of the role of the secretary-general, Japan was in fact criticizing the inadequacy of the existing Security Council. Japan was showing its support for the secretary-general's readiness to "play a more forthright role in bringing potentially dangerous situations to the attention of the Council" and "to develop a wider and more systematic capacity for fact-finding in potential conflict areas."[29] It was precisely for the purpose of urging the secretary-general to carry on his efforts to find ways of strengthening the peace-keeping functions of the UN that Japan took the initiative in passing resolution 37/67 concerning the "Report of the Secretary-General on the Work of the Organization."

It is worth noting that the particular initiative that Japan took at the 37th session of the General Assembly was independent of both the Western group of countries and the Asian countries. Japan in this instance was joined by Yugoslavia and Austria, each of which had prepared its own draft resolution. The circle of supporters expanded and the following states ultimately served as the drafting group for the final presentation of the resolution to the General Assembly: Japan, Egypt, Austria, Yugoslavia, Sweden, India, Guyana, Algeria, Mexico, and Sierra Leone. Later the number of co-sponsors increased to forty-four and the resolution was adopted by consensus. What, then, brought these countries together? The advocates of the resolution seem to have one thing in common. They are small or medium-size countries that have traditionally regarded the UN as an important instrument for their foreign policy, whether in relations with their neighboring states or in dealings with the major powers.

Concluding Observations

Is Japan reverting to its "UN-centered diplomacy" of the late 1950s? That would be a rather exaggerated view. Japan does not expect the UN to guarantee its national security. Internationally, there is increasing reluctance among the major powers to resort to the UN for settling disputes. In the last few years, the United States in particular has begun to express its disillusionment with the UN. The attitude of the United States toward the UN cannot help but influence Japanese thinking, especially at the policy-making level. Nonetheless, there seems to be a nascent realization on the part of those involved with the UN in the Foreign Ministry of the importance of the UN as an instrument for Japan's foreign policy. Japan has already become a major financial contributor to the UN system and an important participant in many of its operational activities. Japan may find that it is in its interest to strengthen the world organization on which it has now begun to make a considerable impact.

More fundamentally, Japan may be coming to view the UN as a useful instrument by which to promote its own foreign policy. With no close power bloc behind it, Japan's only direct ally is the United States, which, however, frequently conducts its global policy based on its own designs and interests. For Japan, economic

---

29. Report of the secretary-general on the Work of the Organization, September 1982. A/37/1, 7 September 1982.

power *per se* is hardly sufficient for wielding influence on the complex and confrontational stage of world politics today. The UN may very well prove to be a necessary instrument through which Japan can carry out a global diplomacy that, it is hoped, will eventually help produce international peace and stability. It would be an irony of history if, nearly forty years after the "United Nations" alliance was founded, Japan were to play a crucial role in helping the United Nations weather the stormy period through which it is now passing.

Toshihiro Tomabechi

THE U.S.-JAPAN CONNECTION IN THE CHANGING WORLD MARKETPLACE:

A Trader's Perspective*

Comparing today's world with what it was when my generation was coming out of school can easily become a gloomy exercise. While we have watched the technology of destruction advance by leaps and bounds, there is little evidence that modern civilization has learned from the mistakes of the past, or that progress in human relationships has kept pace with the growing sophistication of our weaponry. On the economic front, as in the thirties, the world is in a protracted recession, and we are seeing a rise in economic nationalism precisely at a time when nations need to be working together to find *international* solutions. Not surprisingly, there are few signs of resurgent optimism, either in government or in world business circles.

On the other hand, there are sufficient changes occurring in the laboratory, the factory, the marketplace, and in society at large, to raise the possibility of new approaches and new directions as we seek to build a more prosperous and peaceful world community. Government and business decisions made in the next several years could have crucial long-term implications.

For one, it appears highly unlikely that we can sit around and just wait for a normal cyclical return to growth to rescue the world economy from its present doldrums. Neither, as in the past, can we expect the United States economy to crank up on its own and then let the rest of the world ride its coattails back into prosperity. Just as the recession itself has been worldwide in scope, so too will the recovery have to be.

Today, world GNP growth and world trade are in a negatively reinforcing downward spiral. In the developed countries, low capacity utilization, high unemployment, and huge budget deficits have become the norm. In the Third World, soaring indebtedness poses a threat to the world banking system itself—a situation complicated by uncertainties over OPEC's future and the prospect of further decreases in petroleum revenues in countries such as Mexico, Venezuela, and Nigeria.

A crucial factor in prolonging the recession is the overvaluation of the U.S. dollar. The combination of high interest rates in the United States and worldwide political uncertainty has created a flow of capital from abroad, causing unacceptably large misalignments vis-à-vis other major currencies. The result has been a sharp loss of competitiveness for American goods—a loss unrelated to productivity, quality, or salesmanship, but one that is seriously retarding prospects for renewed growth.

Nor have the bloated dollar and the relatively undervalued yen necessarily been a blessing for Japan either. Last year, for instance, Japan's exports to the United States actually fell by almost 6 percent, as a result of recession and various constraints, some self-imposed.

---

*This article is the text of an address by Mr. Tomabechi on 24 February 1983 organized by the Japan-U.S. Association of Columbia University.

But the cheap yen *has* helped increase the cost of Japan's imports which now stands at more than $140 billion, double what it was just five years ago. Today, correcting the misalignment of currencies is in everyone's best interest.

Perhaps the most frightening aspect of the widespread recession and unemployment is the protectionist pressure that has been generated throughout the world marketplace. The developed countries want to increase exports as a way of fueling new growth while at the same time protecting jobs in their own ailing industries. Developing countries who face mounting fiscal troubles have to cut back on imports and increase exports in order to produce the revenues needed to service their debt. Coming at a time of recession and negative trade growth, these pressures, reinforced by the rhetoric of domestic politics, could eventually pose a threat to the GATT and our free trading system itself.

None of this is to say that the problems are not solvable. My own bias is to suppose that they will be solved, rocky as the road may be. After all, fiscal and monetary issues can be hammered out, in part, through international negotiations. Old trade barriers can be taken down and the voices of new protectionism held in check. But we also have to recognize that world industry itself is undergoing fundamental changes — changes that are reordering the way in which goods and services are designed, developed, produced, and distributed in the world economy. The process entails substantial risks and substantial opportunities; how the world deals with both may hold the key to the future.

It is clear, for example, that all the developed countries are moving more or less rapidly into the new technology-intensive, knowledge-intensive industries: telecommunications, aerospace, optic fibers, biotechnology, and others. The thrust of automation is already beginning to be felt in the workplace; in a relatively short period of time it will revolutionize both the office and the factory.

Demographics also support this trend. In the developed countries, projections show blue collar workers declining drastically as a percentage of the total work force. Perhaps by the start of the next century, in the United States, Japan, and Western Europe, the image of the "average working stiff" will be that of a highly trained technical specialist; people who "work with their hands" will more than likely have those hands wrapped around a set of computer dials.

This is going to mean more shifting of basic smokestack production to developing countries where, conversely, blue collar labor will abound. The result is likely to be a multinational integration of supply, design, production, and marketing that departs significantly from the traditional arrangements we have grown accustomed to over the past thirty or forty years.

Increasingly, multinationals will have to integrate several stages of operation in order to make a given product and bring it to the end-user. This could entail computer-assisted design and manufacturing in a developed country, production and assembly in one or more LDCs, and marketing of the finished item on a broad international basis. This scenario is quite different from that in which a giant corporation sets up an overseas subsidiary for the purpose of making and selling its product in that market.

In fact, there are those who believe that the core companies of tomorrow's multinationals will not necessarily be the industrial giants, but medium-sized companies with highly specialized technology and with the flexibility to enter into production-sharing and cooperative marketing arrangements with other independent corporations in other countries.

The trend towards internationalization is also reflected in the strategic planning of *sōgo shosha,* or integrated trading companies, such as Mitsubishi. For one, there is a definite shift away from bilateral transactions to off-shore trade involving countries other than Japan: Korean jogging shoes to the United States, American-built cooling towers to a Philippine power plant, Canadian pulp to Europe — and so on.

The *shosha's* product mix is also changing, with more stress on high technology and innovative new products to complement long-standing shipments of raw materials and other bulk items.

Perhaps most important, we have come a long way from being traditional commission merchants and today engage actively in resource development, project management, and international investments that seek to integrate up- and downstream manufacturing and trade activities with a range of international partners.

In general, the internationalization of business is going to mean not only new players and new rules, but a livelier game and, in the final analysis, better scores. Given the realities of the world marketplace today, it is my own strong conviction that the leading edge of this change is occurring in the Pacific rim. In this context, the U.S.-Japan connection offers the best hope for generating a new cycle of real growth.

In the first place, despite lingering barriers, Japan has been steadily liberalizing its marketplace for the past decade. It is perhaps the only major country engaged in such an effort today — at a time when its trading partners are setting new quotas on Japanese and other imports, demanding "self-restraint," and proposing reciprocity and local content laws.

In addition, Japanese industry itself has undergone some important structural changes. Years ago, Japan began investing in Southeast Asia and other areas in order to shift labor-intensive production that was no longer economically viable in its home base. Because of the sharp rise in labor costs that accompanied Japan's high growth through the early seventies, and because of Japan's vulnerability to imported energy costs, this was a matter of necessity.

Today, with the advance of automation in Japan, some of these arrangements have already been modified, and in the electronics industry and others, the foundation is being laid for the kind of production-sharing that could typify multinational partnerships in the future.

More generally, with the end of the high growth era, Japanese industries are looking to increase overseas investment as a way of broadening their base for future growth while reducing dependence on export *per se.* Where circumstances permit, partnerships and joint ventures with the right American partners remain far and away the most attractive option.

In this regard, the new agreement between General Motors and Toyota is a step of both practical and symbolic significance. Particularly noteworthy is the fact that the principals are neither small nor troubled companies scrambling for a toehold, but the two leaders in the industry.

Looking over a broad range of industries, prospects for similar U.S.-Japan cooperative arrangements seem well worth exploring. Despite the cries of alarm you may have been hearing, the United States remains the world leader in research and innovative technology. The strength of Japanese industry, on the other hand, has been in refining and applying new technology to the production line. In addition, Japan's social homogeneity and relatively peaceful labor-management relations have helped speed the development and deployment of industrial robots, a factor that could be critical for future competition.

All in all, the wisdom of joining forces, of combining the relative strengths of both sides to make the best product and market it most effectively, appears self-evident. Could not such partnerships some day create the basis for a broader Pacific economic community?

Ultimately, I think the answer is "yes," but in the short term we still need to deal effectively with the chronic strains in the U.S.-Japan relationship itself. In America, recession, unemployment, and record merchandise trade deficits have created a new round of recriminations against Japan. Many Americans ascribe the blame to an alleged "Japan, Inc." that monomaniacally promotes exports while insidiously keeping its own market closed to foreign goods. Some politicians with aspirations for 1984 have already based their campaigns on these resentments.

On the Japanese side, there is growing ill feeling over what is perceived to be a deliberate misconstruing of the trade issue and an attempt to make Japan a scapegoat for problems of America's own making. Others, including a number of government and business leaders, see the current friction as little more than a replay of past U.S. fulminations that will similarly subside when economic conditions improve. When I was in Japan recently, one government official told me: "It's like a typhoon; you just duck and keep your head down until it blows over."

Fortunately, Japan's new government under Prime Minister Nakasone seems more inclined to take American sentiments seriously and to recognize that the situation calls not for a low profile but for effective action.

In pursuing a course of action, however, both sides have to be able to separate the realities from the symbols, rhetoric, and misunderstandings. To begin with, let us consider the Japanese marketplace.

Here, a paramount issue has been agriculture—in particular, Japan's quotas on the import of oranges and beef. The truth is, however, that Japan has the lowest agricultural self-sufficiency of any developed nation, importing some two-thirds of all sources of nutrition from abroad. Annual agricultural imports from the United States now total more than $7 billion, a sum that exceeds the total productive capacity of all the Japanese farmland now under cultivation.

In the area of citrus products, Japan's purchase of American grapefruits, lemons, and limes accounts for more than half of America's export of those products. It is true that quotas on oranges and tangerines have reduced Japan's share of those export items—but it is also true that the Japanese *mikan*, our most popular citrus fruit, has been banned from all but six of the fifty states.

Japan already buys 59 percent of all the beef and veal exported from the United States, and it is not clear that removing the quota would substantially increase that figure. There are those who believe that the main beneficiaries of a relaxation of curbs would be the relatively lower-cost Australian producers. Also, to the extent that cheaper imported beef caught on in the Japanese marketplace, chances are that it would be replacing consumption of domestic chicken and pork, which are raised almost exclusively on U.S. grains. In other words, the net result could conceivably *add* to America's deficit.

I am not saying any of this in order to defend Japan's agricultural quotas. I strongly believe that all such restrictions should be removed tomorrow. I do want to suggest, however, that our discussion of the issue should retain some sense of proportion, especially in view of the way in which agricultural questions are bound up in Japan's domestic politics.

In the area of manufactured and consumer goods, where the bilateral deficit is largest, an issue receiving scant attention amid the howls over standards and inspection procedures is the saturation of many segments of the marketplace itself.

For many years after the war, Japanese had to live in very spartan circumstances. As the economy recovered, however, more goods became available and there were three items that the average Japanese dreamed to buy and own. Those were called *"sanshu no shinki"*—after the three sacred treasures believed to be owned by Japan's founding goddess, Amaterasu Omikami.

The "sacred" treasures sought after in those days were "a car, an air conditioner, and a color television." Today most Japanese think of themselves as belonging to the "middle class" and they in fact own almost everything they need for a comfortable middle-class existence. The only item which is out of reach for most is a house with land; most people in big cities live in rented apartments euphemistically called "mansions."

Today's Japanese consumers demand innovative products built to very precise specifications; shipments of production overruns or other goods not carefully tailored to consumer tastes are unlikely to produce sales. Identifying and manufacturing the right products, and promoting them through the right sort of marketing effort pose far greater problems to potential exporters than trade barriers *per se*. Of course, it can and is being done. The success stories in Japan of corporations such as IBM, NCR, Polaroid, and many others more than amply illustrate the kind of approaches that do work.

Again, I am not trying to deny the existence in Japan of non-tariff barriers in the form of cumbersome product standards and customs clearance procedures. As a trader actively engaged in the import of American and other foreign-built goods into Japan, Mitsubishi itself has run afoul of such regulations more than once.

The point is, however, that if Japan were to remove all alleged barriers to the marketplace, including agricultural quotas, the impact on the bilateral trade balance would be marginal at best. An optimist might see $2-3 billion lopped off America's $19 billion trade deficit with Japan—and personally, I am somewhat less optimistic than others on that score. As I have suggested, both sides have larger issues to deal with than oranges and baseball bats.

But from Japan's own perspective, surely the time has come to discard all lingering market barriers—if for no other reason than that they have become symbols of Japan's alleged unfairness, lack of sympathy for her allies, and disregard for the free trade system. In fact, no nation on earth is as dependent on trade for its survival; no nation would be as immediately and totally devastated by a worldwide protectionist war. Despite the costs in terms of domestic politics, it is in Japan's own interest to demonstrate by example that the way to common prosperity lies in cooperation and competition in a truly free world marketplace.

Ending beef quotas and senseless product inspections is hardly the answer to the bilateral and multilateral problems we face, although it would be one more step toward achieving the kind of productive partnership envisioned by Japan's late Prime Minister Ohira, among others. But at the same time, it is crucial for both sides to engage in a productive dialogue based on real issues. The cost of continuing to make short-term political profit at the expense of long-term economic considerations and of allowing the rising tide of emotionalism to dictate our respective national responses is frightening to contemplate.

As *New York Times* columnist James Reston recently wrote: "We have reached a turning point in history, with new industries, a wholly different workforce doing different work ... leading to new relationships between management and labor, parents and children, and teachers and students, requiring different studies in the schools and new training and compassion for the people left behind in the storm."

Reston was writing in particular about the United States, but I cannot think of a more apt description of the challenges faced by the international community as a whole. As I tried to suggest earlier, the way to meet those common challenges is to work together to find common solutions. Surely, if we put our minds to it, we can prove equal to the task.

Shinkichi Eto

EVOLVING SINO-JAPANESE RELATIONS*

In studying China, one must beware of falling into the trap of the seven blind men, who each felt only a part of the elephant but claimed to know the appearance of the whole. The purpose of this article is to investigate Sino-Japanese relations and to try to highlight the major factors which determine the course of the relationship.

Love-Hate Syndrome in Prewar Japan

Throughout the 1950s and 1960s, Japan was clearly a house divided against itself, not only in terms of defense questions but also in terms of Chinese affairs. Some vehemently supported the Nationalist Chinese government in Taiwan while others advocated the legitimacy of the People's Republic of China (PRC). In the 1960s, the author developed a *center-periphery model* to aid in analyzing the impact of this dichotomy on Sino-Japanese relations. Borrowing from the field of psychology, the idea was subsequently likened to a *love-hate syndrome,* which the author discussed further in talks at the Japan Society in New York in 1976 and at the Chinese University of Hong Kong in 1980.

Given Japan's history of foreign relations, one can only conclude that the Japanese are an extremely adaptable people. During World War II, the Japanese clamored for an Asian Monroe Doctrine and were inspired by their own sense of manifest destiny to fight the white men and expel them from Asia. Those Japanese who showed the slightest sympathy towards white war prisoners were bitterly condemned by their fellow countrymen. Shortly thereafter, in 1946, many Japanese schoolteachers in the Tokyo area volunteered to take their classes to General Douglas MacArthur's headquarters to celebrate his birthday by singing the American song "Happy Birthday"—just a few months after Japan's surrender. Although nothing came of it, a group of Japanese initiated a movement to construct a shrine to the supreme commander when General MacArthur was ousted by President Truman. Many Japanese people appeared more faithful to the supreme commander for the allied powers, an American white, than to his own subordinates in the Japanese government. The elasticity of Japanese emotions was surprising to anyone who had witnessed the war in Japan.

Many Japanese intellectuals are Francophiles, always dreaming of Paris and longing for French things. They memorize the city map of Paris and talk about the French capital with tears in their eyes. They look down on those who do not understand French, and they seem even more Francocentric than ordinary Frenchmen. Other intellectuals are Anglophiles, not only admiring British literature and political policies but also wishing to adopt the British aristrocrats' way of life. Despising the American accent, these Japanese make

---

*This article is based on a series of lectures given by the author as a visiting professor in the Department of History of the University of Hawaii in 1982. It was substantially revised during his recent visiting fellowship at the Department of International Relations of Australian National University. The author wishes to express his gratitude to the members of both departments for their comments and to the secretaries for their editing and typing assistance.

every effort to imitate the Oxford accent, but they seldom succeed.

In a similar vein, a Kyoto University professor of European history, Aida Yūji, was a great admirer of European civilization, and in particular, a firm Anglophile, who held the code of the "English gentleman" in great esteem. He was drafted during World War II and became a war prisoner in Burma. There he discovered to his great disillusionment that British officers and soldiers were just as crude and cruel as their Japanese counterparts. After repatriation he honestly and soberly described his own experiences in the war prisoners' camp, and since then he has become very critical of Western civilization.[1]

Japanese intellectuals were both irresistibly attracted to European civilization on the one hand, and repelled by their countrymen who submitted to it on the other. From the Japanese viewpoint, modern Europe is located in the center of civilization while Japan lies on the periphery. The effect of this center-periphery relationship in the Japanese mind is characterized by extreme sensitivity to differences between Japanese and Europeans and a strong love-hate syndrome,[2] a complex of both admiration and contempt. An extreme sensitivity to differences coupled with ambivalent feelings has created a psychological pendulum that swings between extreme admiration and extreme contempt. The Japanese have developed a "periphery minority complex" ever since modern Japan came under the sway of European civilization in the late Tokugawa Shogunate era.

By the same token, Japan has been located on the periphery of the Chinese sphere since the initial contacts of the two civilizations. The periphery minority complex is expressed by a love-hate syndrome. It was the Japanese Confucians of pre-Meiji Japan who developed the love factor of the complex, frankly expressing their adoration of Chinese civilization, while others developed a strong competitive spirit vis-à-vis China. For example, Zeami of the thirteenth century, who could be considered the founder of the Nō theatre, had a profound knowledge of Chinese classics, history, and literature. He wrote a play entitled *Haku Raku-ten*,[3] in which Bai Luodian, who was the best-known Chinese poet among the Japanese, was awed by Japanese poetry and dance. Zeami's play illustrates the unyielding

---

1. Yūji Aida, *Aron Shūyōjo* (Arlon Prisoners' Camp) (Tokyo: Chūō Kōron-sha, 1962). Mori Ōgai was a leading writer in prewar modern Japan and well-known for his extraordinary understanding of Western Europe. He wrote a short novel based on his own experiences, *A Great Discovery*, in which a young Japanese medical doctor was sent to Germany by the Japanese government in the 1880s. He made a courtesy call on the Japanese minister in Berlin and was asked what he planned to study. The young doctor answered that he intended to study hygienics. The minister laughed and said, "What? I'm surprised. What use is hygienics for people who put strings between their toes to walk and who often pick their noses?" The doctor was enraged with the minister for this insult to his country but could not say anything at the time. Afterwards, he began to search for evidence of sandals and nose-picking in European culture. He soon discovered a simple Roman sandal not very dissimilar from the Japanese *zōri*, but he failed to find evidence of European nose-picking for many years. One day while reading a novel by Gustav Wied, the Danish writer, he made a great discovery. The novel concludes with the following passage: "Oh behold, a sailor there, sitting at a counter, listening to a chat, and picking a gigantic pill-like something out of his nose. The Former Minister Plenipotentiary of the Japanese Empire to the German Empire, Your Excellency Viscount S.A., please note that Europeans pick their noses, too."

2. The author dealt with the love-hate syndrome in Shinkichi Etō, *Nihon o meguru bunka masatsu* (Culture Conflicts with Japan) (Tokyo: Kōbundō, 1980), 18-26.

3. Cf. Sukehiro Hirakawa, *Yōkyoku no shi to seiyō no shi* (Yōkyoku's Poetry and Western Poetry) (Tokyo: Ashai Shimbun-sha, 1975), 19ff.

and competitive psychology of Japanese intellectuals vis-à-vis Chinese civilization.

A second anecdote concerns a scholar of the Tokugawa Shogunate era, Yamazaki Ansai, who one day asked his pupils what should they do if Confucius and Mencius were to lead an expeditionary force to invade Japan. No one could answer. He finally smiled and said, "One should fight the expeditionary troops and capture Confucius and Mencius for Japan. It is as they themselves taught."

Before the Meiji Restoration some Japanese visited Shanghai. In the land of their admired sages, they encountered filthiness, offensive odors, corpses afloat in the river, and a civil war. In Shanghai, British and French soldiers behaved arrogantly and had things their own way. Seeing this, the Japanese admiration of China suddenly changed to disillusionment.

Kishida Ginkō, the first Japanese to publish a newspaper in Japan in the last year of the Tokugawa period, was an admirer of China. With Ginkō's aid, James C. Hepburn compiled his well-known Japanese-English dictionary. Hepburn had it printed in Shanghai because, at that time, Japan had no Western printing presses. Ginkō accompanied Hepburn to Shanghai as his assistant and lived there for about half a year. As soon as Ginkō arrived in Shanghai and began to observe the decline of China, his adoration was quickly replaced by contempt. In his diary,[4] Ginkō wrote about his disillusionment with the Chinese, seeing their "foolishness and selfishness" everywhere. Once he came to feel that the Japanese were superior, he became arrogant. Later, when Ginkō accompanied the Japanese military expedition to Taiwan in 1874, he wrote "Why not conquer China now?"[5] His attitude had completely changed in only a few years.

Japanese intellectuals, viewing the declining fortunes of the Qing Dynasty in the mid-nineteenth century, reasoned that China, having been victimized by the Western powers, was a poor example to follow. Still, Euro-American expansionism posed a common threat to the Qing Dynasty and to Japan; therefore, if the Qing Dynasty were to be subdued, Japan would necessarily be next. This view was current among Japanese intellectuals whose Confucian education had nurtured an admiration for Chinese civilization, but who became bitterly disillusioned upon witnessing the decline of the Qing regime. Thus, this sense of common destiny dates back at least to the period of the fall of the Tokugawa Shogunate in Japan in the mid-nineteenth century.[6]

Consequently, just after the Meiji Restoration in 1868, a common notion among Japanese youth was that Eastern peoples should cooperate with each other in order to stand up to the West. It was felt that China, with its glorious history, huge population, and vast territory, should be strengthened in order to defeat the West. Thus, an unusually deep concern for China developed among Japan's intellectuals. Opinion on this issue, however, was divided. Some Japanese thought that the Qing regime could be reformed, while others saw

---

4. Ginkō's diary during his stay in Shanghai is analyzed by the author in Shinkichi Etō, "Chūgoku kakumei to Nipponjin", (The Chinese Revolution and the Japanese), in Kimitada Miwa ed., *Nippon shakai bunka shi* (Socio-Cultural History of Japan), Vol. 7 (Tokyo: Kodansha, 1974), 214-65.

5. *Ibid.*, 257.

6. The Japanese expression for the state of close interdependency, "shin-shi-ho-sha"—in Chinese, "chun-chi-fu-che"; in English, literally, "lips-teeth-lower jaw bone-upper jaw bone"—conveys the perception quite graphically. Japan and China are to each other as lips are to teeth and as the lower jaw is to the upper jaw.

no future for the Qing Dynasty. The optimists felt that Japan should assist the Qing's reforms and urge governmental cooperation between China and Japan.

Most of the Meiji government leaders shared this opinion and supported reforms of the Qing administration within the imperial system. This explains why reformists such as Kang Youwei and Liang Qichao were able to take political refuge in Japanese settlements in China and on Japanese ships whe the coup d'état against them occurred in 1898, and were warmly treated by the government during their exile days in Japan.

Others were pessimistic. They saw no hope for the Qing's future. This posed two alternatives for Japan: conquest of China or fostering a revolution within China. Even Miyazaki Hachirō,[7] a civil rights activist and well-known writer, in 1874 advocated a Japanese occupation of Taiwan as a stepping-stone for the conquest of all of China. Arthur Smith, a Christian missionary, similarly disillusioned by the Qing regime, urged Christianity upon the Chinese people as the alternative[8].

In contrast to some Japanese, who urged the conquest of China, Ura Keiichi strongly advocated the need for a strong China to check the eastward expansion of Russia. He was certain that Russia intended to occupy Xinjiang and he planned to travel there personally to investigate Russian penetration. "It is unnecessary for Japan to colonize all of China," he wrote. "It would be sufficient to overthrow the Qing imperial regime and implement political reforms in order to revitalize the people and strengthen the state. Asia can only cope with the West if our country allies closely with China."[9] Giving up his honeymoon at home with his young wife in 1889, he went to Lanzhou and then set out for Xinjiang. No further word was heard of him. He was undoubtedly killed soon after his departure.

"Weak people become the victims of the strong," said Miyazaki Yazō as he formulated his idea that "those who advocate civil rights should consider how to strengthen the weak." In Yazō's view, "the best way to strengthen the weak is to strengthen China, with its vast territory and huge population. Should China be reformed and unified, it could restore yellow peoples' rights and further its leadership in world politics so that the moral way would spread throughout the world." But Yazō was not willing to sit by and wait for this to happen. In his mind, the ideas of Chinese revolution and Japanese conquest were closely related. "I have made up my mind to go to China to look for a hero who can implement my idea. If I cannot find this hero, I will assume the role myself."[10] Yazō died while enthusiastically studying the Chinese language and way of life at a Chinese merchant's home in Yokohama. His aspirations were taken up by his younger brother, Miyazaki Tōten, who later became Sun Yat-sen's most devoted Japanese friend. He trusted Sun so faithfully that he opposed every policy of the Japanese government to interfere with the revolutionary movement in China.

Unlike Tōten, many prewar Japanese grew dissatisfied with the progress of events in China during the late Qing and the Republican eras. They still believed in the sense of commonality and shared destiny, ardently calling for "participation," "commitment," and "assistance," all of which culminated in Japanese interfer-

---

7. Cf. Seishi Araki, *Miyazaki Hachirō* (Kumamoto: Nihon Dangisha, 1954), 62.
8. Arthur H. Smith, *Chinese Characteristics* (New York: F. H. Revell Co., 1894), 325ff.
9. Kunzō Hanawa, *Ura Keiichi* (Tokyo: Junpu Shōin, 1924), 81.
10. Miyazaki Tōten, *Sanjū-san-nen no yume* (Thirty-three Year Dream) (Tokyo: Heibon-sha, 1969), 22-3.

ence in the domestic politics of China. This explains why participants in Japanese reform movements, such as the *Jiyū Minken Undō* (Popular Rights Movement), which supported the 1911 Chinese Revolution, later became vehement advocates of Japanese expansionist policies. Yamaji Aizan, a socialist journalist during the late Meiji and Taishō eras, stated the case in a typical fashion:

> Looking at China as a politician, one naturally perceives the border between Japan and China. But as a Japanese, one recognizes no boundaries that separate our hearts. Japanese and Chinese are not strangers to each other. We are of the same flesh and blood . . . the Chinese are not considered foreign by the Japanese people. This vast area consisting of the combined territories of China and the Japanese islands ought to be the arena for our activities; it is here we should breathe deeply the air of harmony.[11]

Such an outlook afforded the Japanese government a pretense for staging frequent armed interventions and stimulated its policies of political interference in Chinese affairs. Nonetheless, the outlook reflected not hostility toward China, but rather a feeling of shared destiny, a desire to see China "stand up" in the world. This notion, moreover, enjoyed wide public acceptance in prewar Japan.

A genuine sense of commonality and of shared destiny may engender a relationship of collaboration and friendship. But if the differences in economic or military capability are too great, this relationship may promote intervention. Disillusionment with the late Qing administration stimulated Japanese interventionist policies in China in the name of a sense of commonality and shared destiny. The supremacy of the Japanese military emboldened the Japanese government to undertake military adventures in China. Adoration for the land of the Confucian sages was transformed into contempt for a weak China. The question of Sino-Japanese relations frequently provoked military actions and constituted one of the most controversial political problems in prewar Japan. This is demonstrated by the fact that nine of eighteen cabinets in the prewar Shōwa era, beginning with the first Wakatsuki cabinet, were overthrown because of their failure to adequately deal with the China question.

The author has thus far examined the pre-war Japanese attitude toward China. But the question now arises: Did the Japanese attitude change after its defeat? To a certain extent, it did—the mood of confrontation between Asia and the West certainly disappeared. But the periphery minority complex has not yet dissipated among some Japanese in terms of Sino-Japanese relations.

Love-Hate Syndrome in Postwar Japan

It was only after Japan's defeat in World War II that China lost its ability to affect the survival of a cabinet in Japan. No cabinet in postwar Japan has resigned because of a China-related issue. While still important, the China problem has been superceded by U.S.-Japanese relations. It is ironic that Japan succeeded in becoming a leading economic world power only after losing its interests in China and Korea.[12]

The failure of Japanese undertakings in China during the period before 1945 demonstrated conclusively that

---

11. Cf. Shinkichi Etō, "Nitchū mochiaji o sonchōsuru no ron" (A Discourse of Non-involvement for Sino-Japanese Relations), *Bungei Shunjū* (Tokyo: Bungei Shunjūsha, July 1981), 102.

12. Readers may find a similar precedent in British history: Britain became a world power only after she lost all her continental territory in France.

it was impossible to effect a modernization of China from the outside. In the years after the end of World War II, recognition of this fact, in addition to feelings of guilt over the depredations Japan inflicted upon the Chinese people during the 1931-45 period, caused many Japanese to respond positively to the accomplishments of the Chinese Communist party in unifying China and in enhancing the country's international status and prestige. The psychological pendulum of the periphery minority complex began its swing from contempt to adoration.

In 1937 a young Japanese newspaperman fabricated a report that two Japanese army officers had competed to see how many Chinese each could kill. His report, saying that each had killed over one hundred Chinese, appeared in a reliable Tokyo newspaper. As a result, after Japan's surrender, these two army officers were arrested by the occupation forces in Japan, sent to China, and executed as war criminals. The newspaperman is now working quietly in the office of a Sino-Japanese friendship organization as a faithful pro-China activist.[13]

To cite another instance, a young army captain was sent to Mukden from the Imperial Chief of Staff in Tokyo to stop the war in Manchuria, shortly after the Mukden Incident of 1931. Upon arriving, he quickly converted to expansionism, becoming even more dedicated than the Guangdong army officers. He ignored an order from the army headquarters not to escalate the battle in China's northeast region. When later promoted to commander-in-chief of the army air forces, he sent hundreds of young pilots on suicide missions in planes filled with explosives. But after the surrender, he quickly reconverted to a Sinophile and has been expressing admiration for China ever since.

During the Cultural Revolution, the Peking government and the Chinese Communist party put pressure on the foreign media and tried to stop undesirable reports on China. The media in America and Europe resisted. After the *Asahi Shimbun* initiated its submissive posture towards China, the rest of the Japanese press followed, jumping on the bandwagon of servility toward Peking.[14]

When the Japanese and Chinese governments were beginning negotiations for normalization of relations, a leading businessman in Tokyo, Okazaki Kaheita, questioned the Japanese posture towards China in the following terms:

> If we were to consider Japan still at her point of defeat and trying to make peace, then it would not be fitting that she should issue conditions, but rather it is obvious that the terms stated by the other side should become the basis for talks ... If we were to imagine that these last twenty-odd years had not passed and we were back at that moment of defeat, then [Japan's situation] would be identical to [that of] Percival when he surrendered to General [Tomoyuki] Yamashita in Singapore. We can imagine then that peace really [would be] possible.[15]

Okazaki was likening Japan in 1972 to Percival, a British general who commanded the defense forces of Singapore in 1942. On the eve of losing Singapore, Percival tried to negotiate with Yamashita, then com-

---

13. Cf. Akira Suzuki, "'Nankin daigyakusatsu' no maboroshi" (A Myth in the "Rape of Nanking"), *Shokun!* (Tokyo: Bungei Shunjū-sha, April, August, and October issues, 1972).

14. Cf. Osamu Miyoshi and Shinkichi Etō, *Chūgoku hōdō no henkō o tsuku* (On the Distorted Report from China), (Tokyo: Nisshin Hōdō Shuppan-sha, 1972).

15. The quotation is from a speech Okazaki delivered at a symposium which was later published in *Ajia* (August 1972): 42-3.

mander-in-chief of the Japanese army in Malaya. This infuriated Yamashita, who insisted that the British either surrender or fight. Percival quickly realized that he was in no position to negotiate. Okazaki himself labored during the war years in Shanghai to construct a financial system favorable to Japan, but thirty years later he advocated that Japan assume a very submissive position in the normalization negotiations with China.

Since the beginning of the 1970s, love and adoration have dominated Japanese attitudes toward China. When the Japanese feel that China is weak and incompetent, they accentuate the hate side of this love-hate complex by becoming arrogant. When the Japanese feel that China is stronger, they emphasize the love aspect, becoming rather servile. Neither of these extremes is desirable. Sino-Japanese relations can develop in a positive direction only within conditions of equality and equilibrium. The two peoples and governments must be extraordinarily careful to maintain a well-balanced relationship, otherwise the Japanese attitude will continue to swing back and forth.

Postwar Sino-Japanese Relations in Retrospect

In studying the modern history of East Asia, it is apparent that China opened up to the West more reluctantly than did Japan. China clung more tightly to its own culture than did Japan, and its break with the past engendered more agony and civil disorder. China lumbered along like a huge Spanish galleon while Japan plotted its course like a tiny British frigate. But once China started to move, it moved with vigor. From a feudalistic peasant society, China lurched towards a Communist regime. In contrast, Japan responded quickly to an aggressive West. In the early twentieth century, Japan strutted onto the world stage by defeating

Russia, the first time a European country had been defeated by a non-European power. Its imperialist course was halted by its defeat in World War II, but like the Phoenix, it rose from its ashes. Japan developed into a Western-style democracy with a mixed economy of private initiative and social welfare. No matter what similarities China and Japan have—ethnic similarity, geographical propinquity, chopsticks, or their ideographic writing systems—the course China has plotted in the second half of the twentieth century once again contrasts sharply with that of Japan.

Are these two neighbors, who have fought against each other and more recently moved toward a conciliatory relationship, destined to be friends or adversaries?

In order to examine contemporary Sino-Japanese relations systematically, one can divide them into eight periods. The periods are as follows: (1) 1949-1950; (2) 1950-1953; (3) 1953-1957; (4) 1957-1959; (5) 1959-1966; (6) 1966-1971; (7) 1971-1976; (8) 1976-present. They will be discussed in turn.

The first period begins with the founding of the People's Republic of China in 1949 and ends with the outbreak of the Korean War in June 1950. It was a time when Sino-Soviet relations were on a good footing. Although the Chinese Communist party must have had hidden reservations about the Soviet Union, it tried its best to improve relations. Mao Zedong, heading a team of more than one hundred Chinese, traveled to Moscow for negotiations which lasted from December 1949 through February 1950. The result was the Sino-Soviet treaty, which proclaimed "eternal friendship between China and the Soviet Union." Although Soviet and Chinese Communist party leaders felt somewhat at odds with each other, cracks in the relationship were successfully kept secret. Both parties made harsh statements in reference to Japan and advocated severe punishment for Japanese war criminals.

In terms of the American reaction to the revolution in China, the United States signalled its openness to the new government in Peking by leaving some of its diplomats in mainland China. Then President Truman elaborated this policy further in a controversial declaration on 5 January 1950, asserting that "the United States has no desire to obtain special rights or privileges or to establish military bases on Formosa at this time. Nor does it have any intention of utilizing its armed forces to interfere in the present situation. The United States government will not pursue a course which will lead to involvement in the civil conflict in China. Similarly, the United States government will not provide military aid or advice to Chinese forces on Formosa."[16] Secretary of State Dean Acheson stated in his testimony to the Senate Foreign Relations Committee on 10 January that "the U.S. defense perimeter runs along the Aleutians, Japan, and the Ryūkyūs to the Philippines." This carefully enunciated policy intentionally avoided mention of Korea and Taiwan, two bones of contention in U.S.-Chinese relations. The United States maintained its policy of non-intervention in Taiwan until the outbreak of the Korean War.

During this first period, the People's Republic of China adopted a flexible foreign policy with a view to consolidating the little international standing it had. The new Peking government thus gained recognition not only by communist countries but also by a majority of the nonaligned countries in Asia and Africa. In contrast, Nationalist China, exiled to the island of Taiwan, found itself not only internationally isolated but also in imminent danger of invasion by the five hundred thousand troops of the People's Liberation Army concentrated in the Fujian Province across the Taiwan Straits.

This initial period also saw a rise in Chinese concern with its Japanese neighbor. The Chinese Communist party launched a campaign against "Japanese rearmament," which was grounded in the twenty-nine point manifesto issued 7 July 1949. Of six points relating to foreign policy, three of them concerned Japan:

(1) A peace treaty should be concluded with Japan as soon as possible;
(2) Japan should be demilitarized and democratized;
(3) The peoples of China and Japan must unite in the struggle against the U.S. occupation of Japan.[17]

This declaration is significant for several reasons. First, it is clear that for the Chinese Communist party, an early conclusion of peace with Japan was merely a means to counter the U.S. occupation, which it feared might be permanent. Secondly, it expressed a serious fear about the possibility of a new military buildup in Japan. This fear led China to state explicitly in the preamble to the Sino-Soviet Friendship and Alliance Treaty of February 1950 that it considered Japan to be an enemy, and therefore aimed to prevent Japanese rearmament and the establishment of U.S. military bases. Thirdly, the twenty-nine point manifesto of 1949 reflected Peking's expectation of a revolution in Japan. The editorial in the Chinese *People's Daily* of 17 January 1950 supported the Cominform's criticism of the Japanese Communist party: "the Japanese people . . . should carry out a determined revolutionary struggle against American imperialism and the reactionary forces in Japan."

---

16. U.S. Department of State, *American Foreign Policy 1950-1955* (Washington, D.C.: Government Printing Office, 1957), 2448-9.
17. Ajia Seikei Gakkai (Japanese Society of Asian Political and Economic Studies) ed., *Chūgoku seikei sōran* (A General Description of Chinese Politics and Economies) (Tokyo: Hitotsubashi-shobō, 1954), 264-5.

The second period of postwar Sino-Japanese relations began with the outbreak of the Korean War on 25 June 1950 and ended with the ceasefire in June 1953. This period was marked above all by a radical shift in American policy toward China; the United States now opted for the neutralization of the Taiwan Straits, sending in the Seventh Fleet on the second day of the war. The Peking government thus lost any hope of "liberating" Taiwan.

During this period, Japan was incorporated into the American strategic system against the strong opposition of the Soviet Union and the People's Republic of China. While Japanese preparations for concluding a separate peace with the U.S. went on, the Chinese repeatedly asserted that "the U.S. occupation authorities' policy in Japan has been to preserve Japan's militarism and to prevent the democratization of Japan,"[18] that "the U.S. government and the Yoshida government in Japan are plotting together for the rearmament of Japan."[19] But it is interesting to note that as soon as the San Francisco Peace Treaty between the United States and Japan was concluded in September 1951, the Peking government recognized the impossibility of immediate revolution in Japan and began to take a more flexible view towards the Japanese government. As a sign of relaxed tensions, the Peking government issued visas to three members of the Japanese parliament, enabling them to negotiate the first Sino-Japanese Nongovernmental Trade Agreement. The accord was concluded in June 1952, more than a year before the Korean truce. In December of the same year, Peking again showed its willingness to negotiate with the Japanese over the question of repatriating those Japanese who had been detained on the mainland at the end of the war.

Meanwhile, the United States was urging Japan to recognize Taiwan as the sole government of China, and the one with which Japan should conclude a peace treaty. Treaty negotiations between Japan and the Nationalist government were conducted along the following lines.

First, the Nationalist government claimed that the forthcoming treaty should follow the lines of the Treaty of San Francisco, that it should be called a peace treaty, and that Japan should recognize the Nationalist government as the legitimate government of China. Japan conceded these claims. Secondly, it demanded reparations, claiming that Chinese national sentiment would not allow China, the chief victim of the war with Japan, to forego its claim for reparations. Japan, for its part, maintained that war damages suffered on the Chinese continent were outside the scope of the treaty. In the end, clauses relating to reparations were deleted. Thirdly, Japan insisted on inserting a clause limiting the application of the treaty to only those territories which were then under the control of the Nationalist government or which might come under it in the future. The Nationalist government objected to this, and it was omitted from the actual text of the treaty, but Japan's position was accepted in the exchange of notes. Japan relinquished the form but retained the substance of her claim.

The third period of postwar Sino-Japanese relations extended from 1953 to 1957. Shortly before the truce in Korea was concluded, China had begun to reorient its policy from one of wartime emergency to one of peacetime economic construction. This shift in domestic

---

18. Zhou Enlai's letter of 22 May 1951 to the Soviet ambassador which appeared in Kazankai ed., *Nitchū kankei kihon shiryō-shū* (Selected Basic Documents on Japanese-Chinese Relations) (Tokyo: Kanzankai, 1970), 15.
19. Zhou Enlai's statement on 15 August 1951 which appeared in Kanzankai, 22.

priorities reflected changes in China's external policy. China began to emphasize the development of state-to-state relations rather than world revolution. Peking's earlier stress on a revolution in Japan was replaced by China's growing desire to normalize relations with the Yoshida cabinet. This was the same Shigeru Yoshida whom China had recently accused of being just a running dog of "American imperialism."

There was a dramatic acceleration of this rapprochement, beginning with Ichirō Hatoyama's rise to power in December 1954, and continuing into the years of the premiership of Tanzan Ishibashi and Nobusuke Kishi. During this period, a nongovernmental agreement on trade was renewed four times, and an agreement on fishing was concluded without difficulty. In addition, governmental negotiations took place in Geneva. Peking, expressing the hope for an "independent, peaceful and democratic Japan," addressed itself quite seriously to the question of the normalization of relations with Japan.

At the end of 1957, China exchanged its policy of moderation for one of radicalism; this marked the beginning of the fourth period, which lasted until early in 1959, the period of the "Great Leap Forward," during which Chinese foreign policy, in line with domestic policy, became radicalized. It was during this time that the Nagasaki flag incident took place. A Japanese youth tore a PRC flag to pieces on 2 May 1958 in Nagasaki. Infuriated by this act, the Peking government discontinued its trade with Japan, maintaining that the radical socialization policies of the Great Leap Forward would accomplish a quick increase in production without external trade. It vehemently called for the downfall of the Kishi cabinet and a revolution in Japan.

The fifth period lasted from 1959 until the summer of 1966, the beginning of the Cultural Revolution. It corresponds to what the Chinese call the adjustment period, and Chinese foreign policy at this time may therefore be termed "adjustment period diplomacy."

As long as the Kishi cabinet was in office, Peking, for reasons of principle and to save face, refused to compromise with the Japanese government. But as soon as Kishi was replaced by Hayato Ikeda in September 1960, the Chinese government adopted a more conciliatory tone. Secret contacts were established between Chinese officials and Japanese conservatives in an effort to reopen Sino-Japanese trade. Finally, a Sino-Japanese trade agreement was concluded in January 1962.[20] Through this agreement, Japan became the only country in the world to trade both with Taiwan and with the Chinese mainland with substantial freedom.

The sixth period spans the era of the "Great Proletarian Cultural Revolution," from the summer of 1966 to the National Security Advisor Henry Kissinger's secret mission to Peking in the summer of 1971. There was little elaborate Chinese diplomacy or external policy during the period of great revolutionary zeal from 1966 to 1969. The Communist party as well as the Chinese government stridently called for world revolution and a struggle against imperialism and capitalism. It was only after the Ninth National Congress of the Chinese Communist party in March 1969 that the government in Peking gradually resumed diplomatic activities, culminating in the unprecedented Chinese rapprochement with the West and Japan.

Henry Kissinger's mission to Peking inaugurated the seventh period. Following Dr. Kissinger's visit in quick succession were the admission to the United Nations

---

20. It is known as the L-T trade agreement after the initials of the delegates, Tatsunosuke Takasaki and Liao Cheng-zhi.

of the People's Republic and President Nixon's visit to mainland China. The improvements in Sino-American relations, however, were not paralleled by smooth relations between China and Japan. During the last few years of the Eisaku Satō's cabinet, Peking vehemently attacked the Japanese leader, claiming a resurgence of Japanese militarism. Peking's reproaches were provoked further by the Satō-Nixon Joint Communiqué made public on 21 November 1969. These actions focused Satō's attention on the issue of Taiwan: "the maintenance of peace and stability in the Taiwan area is also a most important factor for the security of Japan."[21] Satō's reference to Taiwan was undoubtedly motivated by a concern for the reversion of Okinawa to Japan. The Nationalist government had consistently opposed this reversion. Thus, as a concession to Taiwan in the joint communiqué, this issue was dropped to bolster the Nationalist regime. At that time, the reversion of Okinawa to Japan was a primary policy goal of the Satō cabinet.

As expected, Peking reacted strongly, viewing the joint communiqué as interference in the internal affairs of China. Peking soon let loose with a vitriolic campaign against Japanese militarism. Every effort made by the Satō cabinet to settle differences with Peking was mercilessly attacked, not only by Peking but also by the Japanese media. In the early 1970s, the media in Japan was extremely solicitous toward Peking in an effort to diffuse Chinese criticism of the Japanese press.

Only two days after Satō was replaced by Kakuei Tanaka on 7 July 1972, Premier Zhou Enlai went out of his way to refer to that event in a speech welcoming a visiting delegation from the Democratic People's Republic of Yemen. "The Tanaka cabinet was inaugurated on July 7," said Zhou, "and with regard to foreign policy it has announced that it will endeavor to bring about a normalization of relations between Japan and China. This is certainly to be welcomed."[22] Zhou's speech, including his conciliatory remark directed toward Tokyo, was promptly broadcast by Radio Peking and widely disseminated in the Chinese Communist press.

Slightly more than a month later, the Chinese Communist party's central paper, *People's Daily*, devoted the entire top half of its front page to stories about the return to Shanghai of a Chinese ballet troupe which had just completed a highly successful and warmly received tour of Japan. Banner headlines played up the "enthusiastic send-off" given to the troupe by "friends from all spheres of Japanese society" and the "deep friendship between the Japanese and Chinese people."[23] But what was most significant about this unusual press coverage was that it marked the first time that the Chinese party organ had given such front-page prominence to an event involving Japan without any suggestion of antagonism toward the ruling Japanese government.

In response to the change in Chinese attitudes toward the Japanese government, the Japanese media along with the opposition political parties, pro-Peking businessmen, and ruling Liberal Democratic party politicians, promoted a movement to normalize relations between China and Japan. Foreign Minister Masayoshi Ōhira was so cool to Taiwan that he did not hesitate to proclaim his intention to abrogate the Japan-Nationalist China peace treaty of 1952 upon normalization. Taiwan

---

21. *Mainichi Shimbun*, 22 November 1969.
22. *New China News Agency International Service*, 9 July 1972. Also, *People's Daily*, 10 July 1972.
23. *People's Daily*, 17 August 1972.

was too weak to cope with the pro-mainland flood of sentiment in Japan.

Coming after years of unremitting abuse directed by Peking at the preceding Liberal-Democratic governments of Kishi, Ikeda, and Satō, Zhou's gesture of conciliation and the subsequent abrupt change in the tone of Chinese Communist press treatment of Japan were important signs of a profound shift in Peking's attitudes vis-à-vis Tokyo. Both governments subsequently moved with surprising swiftness to pave the way for a top-level meeting between their respective leaders. In late September 1972, these moves culminated in the visit to Peking of Tanaka, Ōhira, and other ranking officials in the Japanese government. There is no doubt that the visit marked a historic shift in the long and tortured course of modern Sino-Japanese relations. Normalization between Japan and the People's Republic of China was achieved, and Ōhira unilaterally abrogated Japan's 1952 peace treaty with Taiwan while he was still in Peking.

But the rapprochement between the two countries still had some rough spots. Political struggles among the leaders in Peking during these years hindered smooth expansion of Sino-Japanese relations. Lin Biao was ousted in 1971, possibly indicating a major shift from radical to moderate policies. Building on this change, Zhou Enlai spent a great deal of political capital in improving China's relations with the West and Japan. For this he was fiercely criticized by those who were later to be called the "Gang of Four." Except for mutual trade which increased from $1.1 billion in 1972 to $3.78 billion in 1975 as indicated in Table 1, Sino-Japanese relations fluctuated depending upon the current state of power relationships in Peking. Even trade decreased noticeably in 1976 when the "Gang of Four"

temporarily succeeded in grasping political power after the death of Zhou Enlai.

The final period began when the Gang of Four was arrested and the new leadership in Peking started the drive for the "four modernizations." This period is still in progress. The Sino-Japanese Peace and Friendship Treaty was concluded in August 1978, preceded by a long-term nongovernmental trade agreement in February of the same year.[24] Trade grew from $3 billion in 1976 to $10 billion in 1981, and Japan agreed in 1981 to supply the People's Republic of China with economic aid amounting to 300 billion Japanese yen or $1.3 billion. The allocation for the fiscal year ending in March 1982 was estimated to be 60 billion yen or $260 billion. Taking into account the Japanese government's budget deficit, this agreement represents an enormous commitment by Japan.

Another Factor?

Until recently Sino-Japanese relations have progressed relatively smoothly despite some minor difficulties, such as the Chinese interruption of negotiations on economic cooperation and trade with Japan in January 1979, their unilateral abrogation of major, long-term industrialization plans in December 1980, and the textbook issue in 1982. These actions shocked Japan and toned down unrealistic hopes to open up a vast "China market," an idea developed by the Japanese media and businessmen. Shedding their "China euphoria," they began to appraise China more critically. This has worked to make Sino-Japanese relations more stable.

---

24. A detailed analysis of this period up to 1979 made by the author appeared in "Recent Developments in Sino-Japanese Relations," *Asian Survey* 20 (July 1980): 726-43.

TABLE 1

Japan's Trade with Neighbors (million US $)

	People's Republic of China			Taiwan	Republic of Korea	U.S.S.R.
	Export to	Import from	Total	Total	Total	Total
1972	609	491	1,100	1,513	1,406	1,098
1973	1,039	974	2,013	2,533	2,996	1,561
1974	1,984	1,305	3,289	2,964	4,224	2,514
1975	2,259	1,531	3,790	2,632	3,556	2,795
1976	1,663	1,371	3,034	3,470	4,720	3,149
1977	1,939	1,547	3,486	3,842	6,194	3,356
1978	3,049	2,030	5,079	5,335	8,594	4,372
1979	3,699	2,955	6,654	6,813	9,606	4,373
1980	5,078	4,323	9,401	7,438	8,364	4,638
1981	5,095	5,292	10,387	7,834	9,047	5,280
1982	3,511	5,351	8,862	6,698	8,135	5,557

(Sources provided by China Room, JETRO, Tokyo.)

But if shifts in policy on the Chinese side occur too frequently, the Japanese may increasingly revert to the negative aspect of their feelings toward the Chinese. In addition, should the Chinese "modernization" fail, it would be taken by the Japanese as an indication of China's weakness. A weak China might create a strong temptation among the Japanese to intervene in China, as indicated by the foregoing analysis.

Furthermore, the preceding examination of Sino-Japanese relations over the past thirty years reveals an important fact—that the state of their bilateral relations reflects the domestic politics of China more than it does those of Japan. It was China which modified its policy from calling for a Japanese revolution to normalizing relations with Japan in 1953. It was China which shifted from moderation to radicalism in 1958. China returned to moderation after the Great Leap Forward and initiated the development of Sino-Japanese trade links in 1960.[25] China lurched again into radicalism in 1966 but later sought normalization with Japan in 1972. The Gang of Four pursued radical policies again in 1976—but only briefly.

In all spheres, China regulates the extent of its contacts with Japan, as with other countries. The number of Japanese visitors to China has constantly increased since 1972, as China has moved to liberalize the issuance of visas. In 1976, when the Gang of Four temporarily took over the political leadership of Peking for several months, the number of Chinese visitors to Japan was drastically cut back, as Table 2 shows.

25. For a detailed analysis of the alteration of moderation and radicalism in Peking's policy, see Shinkichi Etō, "Moderation and Radicalism in the Chinese Revolution" in James Crowley ed., *Modern East Asia: Essays in Interpretation* (New York: Harcourt, Brace and World, 1970), 337-73.

TABLE 2

Exchange of Persons between PRC and Japan

	Japanese to PRC	Chinese To Japan
1972	8,052	994
1973	10,238	1,991
1974	12,990	3,161
1975	16,655	4,441
1976	18,825	4,018
1977	23,445	4,039
1978	40,574	5,951
1979	54,096	11,622
1980	71,473	15,328
1981	109,977	17,550
1982 (by Nov.)	128,112	19,284

(Sources provided by China Section, Ministry of Foreign Affairs, Japanese Government.)

A substantial drop in trade between Japan and China took place in 1976, as indicated on Table 1 and Graph 1, while Japan's trade with other Asian neighbors increased smoothly in the same year. By 1980, however, the Republic of Korea was severely hit by the 1980 world recession, as was Taiwan in 1982. Economic recession in both South Korea and Taiwan was immediately reflected in their trade with Japan. The decrease of Japan's trade with China in 1982, however, should be attributed to different causes. The decrease in Chinese trade with Japan was due primarily to tighter political control over foreign currency spending in order to readjust the government budget.[26] These factors lead one to the conclusion that Sino-Japanese relations will continue to evolve in accordance with shifts in Chinese policy.

Students of contemporary Chinese affairs may introduce a third factor into the Sino-Japanese equation: What would be the effect of a Sino-Soviet détente on Sino-Japanese relations?

Efforts toward a relaxation of tensions between the Soviet Union and the People's Republic of China began with L. I. Brezhnev's speech on 24 March 1982 in Samarkand. The Soviet leader proposed a rapprochement with China in his speech, to which China responded favorably, if in a restrained manner. Prior to this, the Soviet Union had made a similar proposal, but in vain. China had officially defined the policy of the Soviet Union as "socialist-imperialism" at the Eleventh National Congress of the Chinese Communist party in 1975,

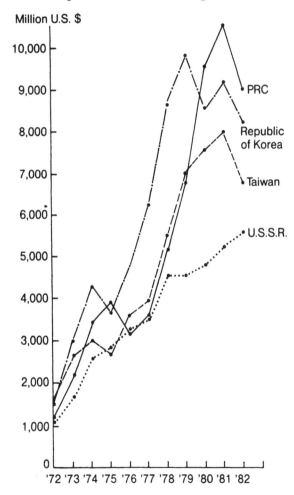

GRAPH 1

Japan's Trade with Neighbors

---

26. It is also interesting to note that Japan's trade with the U.S.S.R., another socialist neighbor, has increased steadily. The Soviet government during this era did not make any articulate change in domestic policy, resulting in no abrupt change in trade volume.

and the definition had been included in the 1975 constitution of the People's Republic of China. China had made tremendous efforts to induce Japan to enter into its anti-Soviet camp and urged Japan to join it in labelling the Soviet Union as a state of "hegemony." China had meanwhile allowed the Sino-Soviet Treaty of Friendship, Alliance, and Mutual Aid to expire in April 1980.

In April, Deng Xiaoping and Hu Yaobang made a secret visit to North Korea.[27] It is likely that the Chinese leaders wanted to diffuse any apprehensions Kim Il-song might have had regarding China's possible rapprochement with the Soviet Union as North Korea fears collaboration between its two giant neighbors. To this point, North Korea has successfully profited from the rift between its neighbors. In May, Kapitsa, director of the First Bureau of Far Eastern Affairs, visited Peking. In July, Yu Hong-liang, director of the Bureau of Soviet Affairs, visited Moscow. In September, Hu Yaobang, in his speech to the Twelfth National Congress of the Chinese Communist party, suggested that Sino-Soviet relations should be normalized. The word "socialist-imperialism" completely disappeared from the documents of the congress. In October, a series of vice-ministerial meetings between Ilyicher, Soviet deputy minister of foreign affairs, and Qian Qichen was held in Peking. In November, Huang Hua, then minister of foreign affairs, attended the funeral of Brezhnev and met with Soviet Foreign Minister Andrei Gromyko. Upon Huang's return to Peking he was replaced by Wu Xueqian, who received a cordial congratulatory telegram from Moscow.

To what extent will Sino-Soviet relations improve? The consolidation of Sino-Japanese relations has taken place in an atmosphere where the Sino-Soviet rift is taken for granted. Should the normalization of relations imply merely a reduction of tension between the two states, it should not have a serious impact on Sino-Japanese relations.

If, on the other hand, it were to result in a resurgence of close political collaboration or a military alliance, grave consequences might ensue for Sino-Japanese relations. An historical precedent can be cited: the Japanese astonishment at the German-Soviet Non-Intervention Treaty of 21 August 1939.[28] Kiichirō Hiranuma, then prime minister, resigned from office on 28 August. He stated that his firm conviction in moral diplomacy had collapsed and that international affairs was all too complicated and mysterious.[29]

Thus far, the recent changes in Sino-Soviet relations have not yet affected Sino-Japanese relations, but one cannot ignore their serious potential for affecting Sino-Japanese relations.

Conclusion

The three major factors which influence the course of Sino-Japanese relations have been analyzed above. First, there is the latent existence of the negative side of the love-hate dichotomy, which may be surfacing slightly due to frustrations with the stagnant Chinese economy. Second, the domestic side of Chinese politics reveals the emergence of more stable leadership accompanied by a shift of the political pendulum from liberalization toward tighter control. In accordance with this move, Peking is reorienting its course from openness to the West and Japan toward a more reserved stance. This

---

27. *Asahi Shimbun,* 17 September 1982.
28. *Asahi Shimbun,* 21 August 1939.
29. *Asahi Shimbun,* 29 August 1939.

swing of the pendulum creates cyclical shifts in Chinese policy toward the rest of the world. Finally, the present normalization of relations between China and the Soviet Union will be extremely limited. The two communist giants must make much greater progress toward closer relations than is anticipated at present before they will constitute a serious threat to Sino-Japanese relations. In sum, Sino-Japanese relations will continue to develop without serious difficulties in the foreseeable future.

William V. Rapp

INDUSTRIAL STRUCTURE AND JAPANESE TRADE FRICTION:
U.S. Policy Responses

The United States and Japan often appear to be mirror images. The United States has a large land area, many natural resources, including abundant energy supplies, a massive defense establishment, a low rate of savings, and a diverse economic structure. Conversely, Japan's land—especially arable land—is limited; its natural resources and fuels are largely imported; its defense commitment is restrained; and despite a high rate of savings, her export competitiveness lies across a narrow band of manufactured goods. Such structural differences are at the heart of U.S.-Japanese trade frictions, whether one is talking about the issue of access of U.S. agricultural commodities, manufactured goods, and services to the Japanese market, or the competitive pressures created by Japanese manufactured exports to the United States and the rest of the world market.[1]

Unfortunately, the frictions created by these differences are large and growing. High unemployment in the U.S. steel, auto, lumber, and other industries generates personal hardships and in turn, political pressures. Similarly, there is genuine concern over Japanese competitive "targeting" of U.S. high-technology industries, including aircraft, semi-conductors, computers, pharma-ceuticals, and automated machine tools.[2] Within this context, appropriate U.S. policy responses are both expected and required. Letting events take their course—having the market decide what will happen—is not a viable option. Such an approach ignores the impact of government actions and institutions on the market in both countries and the world as a whole. Furthermore, such policies are likely to increase bilateral tensions to serious, perhaps explosive, levels as important structural differences persist and frictions continue to escalate over time. Given the importance of Japan as an ally and trading partner to the United States and other Western countries, the American policy response must deal with the fundamentals of U.S.-Japanese competition as determined by these structural differences.

Such policies fall into two major categories: (1) specific industry- or product-related thrusts such as orderly marketing agreements (OMAs), access to the Japanese market, and government support for U.S. high-technology firms; and (2) general economic policy changes affecting monetary, fiscal, and tax policies in both the United States and Japan.

---

1. The impact of structural differences on U.S.-Japanese trade and economic relations are examined in more detail in William V. Rapp, "The United States and Japan: Competition in World Markets: Policy Alternatives for the United States," *Special Study on Economic Change, Vol. 9, The International Economy: U.S. Role in a World Market*, Joint Economic Committee (Washington, D.C.: U.S. Government Printing Office, 17 December 1980), 345-361, and in a forthcoming volume, William V. Rapp, "Re-evaluating Past Policy Approaches to U.S.-Japan Trade Problems," in *Northeast Asia and the U.S.: Changing Defense Partnerships and Growing Trade Rivalries*, ed. Richard Kosobud (Chicago: Chicago Council on Foreign Relations, 1983).

2. U.S. Department of Commerce staff report, "An Assessment of U.S. Competitiveness in High Technology Industries," unpublished (Washington, D.C.: October 1982).

Reprint rights reserved by the author.

So far, American initiatives have focused largely on the first area, especially on what the Japanese government can do to limit exports or open the Japanese market to American imports. However, these policies, while clearly necessary, would be much more effective if supplemented by targeted initiatives aimed at improving the competitiveness of key U.S. industries and by changes in general economic policies. More specifically, the United States needs to protect and foster its own basic and high-technology industries while increasing its overall rate of savings to improve real economic growth and industrial competitiveness. At the same time, Japan should be encouraged to lower its savings rate, increase consumption, and reduce its use of of oil for power generation.[3] In this way the United States can begin to address the fundamentals behind its persistent trade friction with Japan, while improving the strength and competitiveness of its economy.

American and Japanese Structural Dynamics and General Economic Policies

Both the American and Japanese economies are evolving toward a post-industrial or "tertiary" economy. Production of primary and manufactured goods accounts for a declining proportion of GNP while the services sector is growing. This appears to be a natural process of economic evolution.[4] However, due to Japan's high savings rate, this evolution is proceeding in a more orderly manner there than in the United States. The reason for this lies in differences in Japanese and U.S. postwar development. After World War II, Japan had to develop a competitive manufacturing sector to provide employment and pay for necessary energy and raw material imports. Achieving this objective along with non-inflationary growth required a high rate of investment supported by a high rate of savings. To facilitate

this process, the Japanese government encouraged savings by refraining from any capital gains tax, promoting tax-free savings accounts, and even establishing a special directorate within the Ministry of Finance (MOF). At the same time, the government sought to channel these savings into investments in key industrial sectors by means of the Bank of Japan's rediscounting policies, tax and fiscal incentives, and direct loans from the Japan Development Bank. These "target" sectors changed over time as the leading edge of the economy shifted from power, iron and steel, and shipbuilding, to autos and machine tools, and finally to high technology. That is, the beneficiaries of protectionism and supports changed as the economy moved toward producing higher value-added, more sophisticated products.[5]

The success of these economic policies is well known.

---

3. The idea of substituting capital for oil by phasing out existing oil-fired power generation capacity more rapidly and building coal and nuclear power stations instead is discussed in detail in William V. Rapp, "Re-evaluating Past Policy." Also see William V. Rapp, "Supply Management: A Key Element in Japan's Economic Policy," *The Morgan Guaranty Survey* (New York: Morgan Guaranty Trust, September 1975), 10-15.

4. The natural evolution of economies toward higher value-added, service-oriented societies has been analyzed by many writers including Herman Kahn and Anthony J. Wiener, *The Year 2000* (New York: Macmillan Company, 1967); Hollis B. Chenery, "Patterns of Industrial Growth," *American Economic Review* 50 (September 1960): 624-654; William V. Rapp, "A Theory of Changing Trade Patterns, Under Economic Growth: Tested for Japan," *Yale Economic Essays* 7(Fall 1967): 69-138.

5. A thorough discussion of Japanese industrial policy can be found in *OECD, The Industrial Policy of Japan* (Paris: Organization for Economic Cooperation and Development, 1972). Also see William V. Rapp, "Japan: Its Industrial Policies and Corporate Behavior," *Columbia Journal of World Business* (Spring 1977): 38-48. For shifts in Japan's protectionism, the following recent article is also relevant: William L. Givens, "The U.S. Can No Longer Afford Free Trade," *Business Week* (22 November 1982): 15.

Japan has for years had the highest economic growth rate of any major industrial nation, and the cutting edge of its industry has become increasingly more sophisticated. In addition, productivity and income have risen steadily. Yet, 1972-73 clearly marks a break in this progression. Rising energy prices, domestic and export market maturation for several major products, political pressures from the other advanced countries for a reduction in exports, and LDC requests to process more raw materials, all effectively reduced demand for Japanese production as well as demand for investment. In turn, this reduced investment demand was replaced neither by growth in the less capital-intensive service sector nor by greater consumption. Incentives to save remained intact, however, resulting in an economy generating excess savings relative to domestic requirements.[6] This kind of economic environment by its nature is quite deflationary as excess capital tries to find an outlet in (1) modernization and rationalization of productive processes, (2) new product development, (3) lower capital costs (lower interest rates and higher price-earnings ratios), and (4) more exports.

These developments are of course interactive, but appear to be limited by policy exigencies. Lower capital (interest) costs put downward pressure on the yen as investors seek higher returns elsewhere. A weaker yen encourages exports, helping to use the excess savings through transfer of physical capital abroad. However, as already noted, protectionist pressures have prevented exports from rising too dramatically, while accusations of "rigging" the yen have been running between Tokyo and Washington. In response, the MOF has tried to limit interest rate declines, thereby limiting one potential stimulus to the economy. Since the MOF also has resisted large budget deficits (negative savings by government) to take up the slack in investment, the economy must deflate or grow below its potential in order to bring about the necessary equality between investment and savings. Unfortunately, slow economic growth exacerbates the budget deficit problem.

These deflationary pressures have lessened the impact on the economy of the shift toward a post-industrial society. Japan's base manufacturing companies have been able to remain competitive, in many cases gaining a global market share in terms of exports and foreign investment. Also, the non-inflationary economic environment has supported the competitive development of Japan's high-technology industries, particularly for products such as computers, semi-conductors, automated machine tools, and video tape recorders. The capital to modernize basic industry has been readily available at relatively low cost. Pollution control equipment, energy-saving investments, and automated production facilities are now in place.[7] Today Japan has about twice as many installed industrial robots as the United States. Even pollution control devices, which have put a strain on many American industries, have actually benefited Japan in terms of growth, as firms made investments they otherwise would not have made, and have become leaders in a new technology.[8]

---

6. The issue of excess savings was first raised in a major way by Professor Gary Saxonhouse, University of Michigan, at a conference held by Columbia University's East Asian Institute, May 1980.

7. In a recent *Fortune* article it is reported that presently only 18 percent of Japanese machine tools are over 20 years old and 61 percent are less than 10 years old, compared to 34 percent and 31 percent respectively in the United States. See also Gene Bylinsky, "The Race to the Automatic Factory," *Fortune* (21 February 1983): 52-64.

8. Given Japan's higher savings rate, government-mandated investments of all kinds, which account for about 1.5 percent of GNP in both countries, take a higher percentage of the savings available for new productive investment in the United States than in Japan. This puts a greater burden on what is available for U.S. growth relative to Japan.

This emphasis on modernization and rationalization in turn created substantial domestic demand for automated devices, thereby promoting Japanese leadership in this area and building the base for an export thrust into the United States and other markets. A weak yen and the availability of finance further promoted this competitive development. Similarly, the trend toward greater automation and capital intensity in the production of high-technology items like semi-conductors has played to Japan's advantage. Not only has the lower cost of capital translated into a direct cost advantage, but its impact via the exchange rate has lowered the effective cost of all Japanese inputs. Exchange rate effects not only frustrate American desires to remain competitive in existing and new product areas, but can in fact create a policy dilemma with regard to opening Japanese markets to products where the United States retains an overwhelming advantage due to availability of raw materials, energy, and economies of scale. Such industries include aluminum, pulp and paper, and petrochemicals. Any increase in Japanese imports of these products can only further weaken the yen, while also reducing Japanese investment demand in these industries. The weaker yen then makes Japanese exports in other areas such as steel, autos, and high technology even more competitive.

The flow of these competitively priced goods towards the United States is inevitable. Unlike Japan, the United States is not generating enough savings, as indicated by its persistent inflation, growing trade deficit, and high interest rates. The first two developments should generate savings by reducing consumption or importing capital. The last shows the rising cost of capital as demand exceeds supply. In contrast to Japan's excess of savings, which has kept inflation and capital costs relatively low, the U.S. capital shortage has accelerated the decline in capital-intensive basic industries and promoted the shift toward a post-industrial economy. As recent articles have noted, American industry is far behind in automating its factories and modernizing its machinery because of high interest costs and uncertain demand.

Additionally, the greater capital intensity of new plant and machinery, pollution control equipment, and energy-saving devices has affected basic industries, such as steel, automobiles, non-ferrous metals, and chemicals more severely than the service and high-technology sectors. For the latter, the cost of major input, skilled labor, is fully tax-deductible in the year paid, productivity increases have been rapid, and major retrofitting for pollution and energy control have been much less of a factor. All this has drawn resources, especially scarce capital resources, away from basic manufacturing at a more rapid rate than would have occurred if more savings had been available. Improved Japanese competitiveness compounded these industries' natural decline as Japanese firms captured global market share, making new investment for their U.S. competitors more difficult both to justify and to finance. The economy's inflationary adjustment to a low rate of savings, which should have caused a decline in real consumption, merely added to industries' problems when they found it difficult to pass on cost increases by raising prices. This process accelerated the U.S. economy's shift toward a post-industrial society. The adjustment for the U.S. basic manufacturing sector was very difficult, because it was trapped by rising cost inflation and increased capital requirements on the one side and increased price competition from abroad on the other. The impact of "general" monetary and fiscal policy was quite specific.

While services and high technology continued to grow, steel, housing, and the automobile industry declined.

However, while this shift in comparative advantage and the relative decline of the basic manufacturing sectors are clearly explicable, their declining viability is neither inevitable nor desirable. Even in Japan, which has promoted the idea of giving up its declining industries more than any country, the policy is only one of decreasing an industry's *relative* contribution to GNP.[9] In some cases, such as coal, paper and pulp, aluminum, caustic soda, and petrochemicals, the industry will be protected as older capacity is abandoned. In other cases, such as textiles and shipbuilding, the government will work out arrangements, including government subsidies, to phase out production, retrain workers, and upgrade productivity while still permitting imports. The net objective is almost always the same: to retain some modern competitive capacity that is viable, particularly in the high value-added, more technically advanced end of the market. For example, Japanese textile and apparel manufacturers have made major efforts in high fashion and have steadily improved productivity, while cheap textile imports from Korea, Taiwan, Hong Kong, and Southeast Asia have grown enormously, sometimes as a result of Japanese investments in those countries. Thus, while textile production has remained steady and employment has gradually declined, the remaining facilities and companies are viable.

American basic manufacturing, although declining, remains quite considerable in absolute terms, directly and indirectly accounting for about 30 percent of GNP. It is critical to our overall defense needs and is a large employer of minority workers. Thus, we are not in a position militarily, politically, or economically to rely totally on imports of these goods while exporting food, raw materials, services, and high technology. In addition, the success of our service and high-technology sectors is partially dependent on demand from these basic industries. A more practical strategy would be to keep a modern competitive industry, as in Japan, whose contribution to GNP and employment would gradually decrease. This would require an increase in the U.S. gross savings rate and a targeted transfer of the expanded capital resources to support modernization of industry. It may also require some limited form of protectionism while these new plants and equipment are being purchased and installed. To successfully reduce trade frictions with Japan, U.S. policies must go beyond specific commodity proposals for opening the Japanese market, and deal with fundamental U.S. tax, fiscal, and monetary policies that adversely affect the industries most hurt by Japanese trade. Such policies should be coupled with targeted policies to reestablish the productive manufacturing base of the firms in these industries over a limited time period. In theory, the discounted economic benefits flowing from a more competitive industry and fuller employment should compensate for the higher prices paid during the time required to install more productive facilities. In reality, political considerations will probably predominate.

Relying on the projected 1983-84 recovery to solve our trade friction problems is unrealistic. Already forecasters are expecting that any recovery will maintain inflation in the range of 5 percent and will freeze long-term interest rates close to current levels of 12 percent

---

9. This point is covered in detail in William V. Rapp, "The United States and Japan," "Japan: Its Industrial Policies," and "Japan's Industrial Policy," in *The Japanese Economy in International Perspective*, ed. Isaiah Frank (Baltimore: Johns Hopkins University Press, 1975), 37-66.

as the Federal Reserve Board tightens monetary policy to avoid any resurgence of inflation. However, at this level of interest and inflation, demand for housing, consumer durables, and capital goods is not likely to be very strong. Furthermore, Japan's basic capital and manufacturing cost advantage will persist and even widen. Indeed, it will improve precisely in those capital-intensive, interest-sensitive industries that are likely to be lagging behind the economic recovery because of both high interest rates and international competition. Under these conditions, trade friction could actually increase rather than decrease if Japan is seen as denying the benefits of the economic recovery to important U.S. industries, especially in areas of continuing high unemployment.

Domestic U.S. Policy Requirements

Given the above, a logical set of U.S. policy initiatives would include the following:[10]

1. Tax and fiscal policies should be shifted to aggressively promote savings. These initiatives would comprise a mix of substituting some specific tax incentives to save for the tax cuts implemented in 1981 and by instituting taxes on consumption. The latter could substitute for some existing personal income or corporate taxes that penalize savings, such as double taxation of dividends. Taxes on consumption could be commodity-specific, such as an additional hike in the gasoline tax to take advantage of current oil price declines and to encourage conservation. Or they could be general, in the form of a value-added tax, or a tax on income when it is withdrawn for expenditure purposes. In all cases, tax deferral is only realized if people consume less or save. Furthermore, as these taxes are only a fraction of the total amount consumed, a small tax deferral can have a large impact on savings.

2. These specific incentives to save should focus on offering tax deferrals out of future tax revenues in response to actual increases in savings or net assets rather than merely assuming people will save more at higher after-tax incomes. The package should seek to improve real after-tax returns to savings in the form of financial assets and penalize consumption of earnings on invested capital. Proposals similar to Heinz's personal investment account bill, setting up tax-free investment accounts, represent one such possibility. Under these proposals, withdrawals are treated as earnings, capital gains, or principal recapture, in that order, and are taxed at current, capital gains, or zero rates accordingly. One advantage of this approach, as with the consumption tax approach, is that there is no immediate reduction in tax revenues as there has been with individual retirement accounts (IRAs), for example. A transfer of assets, unlike IRAs, does not by itself create a tax deduction. It is *after-tax* income that forms the investment base; only income and capital gains accumulate tax-free until withdrawn. Furthermore, the program could be designed to shelter only financial assets that represent a net increase in savings so that only true monetary savings from income or the

---

10. These policy recommendations have been made several times in various articles and speeches but remain quite valid in the current context. In addition to the articles cited in footnote one, for example, see William V. Rapp, "National Economic Policy and U.S. Export Competitiveness," Testimony to U.S. Congress (Joint Economic Committee, 29 July 1980) and "Industrial Policy and Economic Survival: The Japanese Case," Testimony to U.S. Congress (Interstate and Foreign Commerce Subcommittee, 26 June 1980).

sale of non-monetary assets would be eligible for tax-exempt investment accounts.

3. These approaches to stimulating savings should lower interest rates as savings increase. This will have a doubly beneficial effect on reducing the budget deficit as the cost of servicing the government debt falls and as lower interest rates promote greater economic activity. A reduced deficit, of course, also increases the flow of available savings, further promoting lower interest rates. Therefore, this tax incentive package for savings should not have the negative effect on the budget that the 1981 tax package did.

4. Federal expenditure growth should continue to be contained to keep savings growing. Given a 4 to 5 percent desired long-term real growth rate, a gross savings rate of around 25 percent of GNP seems necessary. An increase in desired investment and net exports will in turn substitute for the relative decline in government expenditures and consumption as a percentage of GNP, though absolute consumption will be larger given a higher economic growth rate. This will be the direct result of lower interest rates, a less overvalued dollar, and eventually, a more productive manufacturing sector.

Policies to promote savings, and in turn, more non-inflationary investment are therefore essential in order to improve U.S. competitiveness in industries heavily affected by Japanese competition. More savings and investment are absolutely necessary for solid growth, productivity improvement, low inflation rates, international cost competitiveness, and a strong currency based on trade performance rather than on high interest rates. However, some changes in the attitudes behind U.S. economic and trade policies are also necessary in order

to build on this foundation. This is true both for generating commodity or industry-specific proposals and in approaching the Japanese for specific concessions. These revised international competitive policy perspectives should incorporate an understanding that:

1. Growth and economic change are beneficial. Economic policy should thus seek to cushion the adverse effects of growth on specific economic sectors and to maximize its positive developments by promoting rather than opposing economic forces. Therefore, modernizing declining industries would keep firms competitive at a lower economic cost to the nation as a whole than would merely setting up protectionist barriers, which raise prices to consumers on a continuing long-term basis.

2. A successful macro-economic policy must take account of sectoral and industry differences. It also requires a dynamic long-term perspective, because economies, industries, and markets are constantly changing over time. Therefore, a dynamic disaggregative economic analysis is an important aspect of successful policy formulation. For example, energy policy is an integral part of economic strategy. Developing alternative energy sources to oil and conserving energy require higher levels of investment and structural shifts, which must be supported by a higher rate of domestic capital formation, i.e., more savings.

3. Markets are multinational and interactive. Therefore, policies must encourage international competition by rewarding competitive success both domestically and overseas. They must also recognize that competitive successes in one area may create problems in another, as countries shift resources and as varying exports and imports affect foreign exchange rates.

4. Because various countries have different institutional and regulatory environments, one's own policies and regulations must be flexible and one should consider their impact, as well as the impact of other governments' policies, on competition, world markets, and changes in comparative or absolute advantage. Some government interference in a complex pluralistic society is inevitable. At the same time, U.S. policies should be limited, emphasizing direction rather than control, and should be based on cooperation with business and labor. Government officials should not disregard the impact of their policies on the market and economic behavior.

A policy program aimed at coping with Japanese competition and trade friction would be based on increased capital generation—perhaps a logical conclusion for a "capitalistic" economy. In turn we should target strategic industries such as steel, non-ferrous metals, automobiles, machine tools, chemicals, pharmaceuticals, energy, aircraft, computers, semi-conductors and financial services, which are under competitive pressure and which represent a large proportion of U.S. manufactured output, have military importance, or are on the leading edge of technology. Other parts of the economy would benefit from their improved economic performance and would not be discriminated against in terms of growth opportunities. But we still need to recognize that some industries are tremendously important to the economy and to our economic future. Therefore their competitiveness must be maintained in some way. I would suggest that the government work with business and labor to assess these industries' economic structure, factor inputs, competitive environment, and long-term requirements. For declining or mature indus-

tries, incentives to modernize or phase out some capacity over a defined time period should be established with additional incentives given to those who rebuild at existing plant sites.

At the same time, as business must see the likelihood of recapturing its investment, it will probably need some limited protection until the new investments are in place and operating. This protection could take the form of orderly marketing agreements, government procurement preferences, and local content legislation. Though the latter has been much maligned in the press and in administration policy statements, some moderate local content legislation, with standby authority for the president to raise it if there is no progress in trade negotiations, is appropriate. This would send a signal to Japan that the United States is not a "paper tiger" and will take action if necessary to maintain or bolster its key industries. Credibility is important in our negotiations with Japan since many Japanese businessmen and policy-makers believe the U.S. administration is split between adamant free traders and supporters of protectionist legislation. In addition, they feel professional lobbyists, import interest groups, and consumers can be mobilized to put opposing pressures on Congress. Given this situation, the Japanese believe they need not give way substantially in any of the major areas under negotiation. This is a high-risk approach for both the Japanese and the American administration and could lead to passage of a "Christmas Tree" protection bill, rather than a more limited and well-targeted version in which the administration retains a large degree of flexibility in negotiations.

If even limited protectionism is pursued, however, it must have a sunset provision, and it must be coupled with policies stimulating savings and targeted investment noted above. Otherwise, U.S. industry will not be able to take full advantage of this competitive respite to modernize. Protectionism will also be likely to last longer, and its costs will not be recouped in improved competitiveness and productivity in the future. Finally, foreign investors who overcome these trade barriers with modern plant and machinery investments in the United States, financed primarily by debt issued under parent guarantees and special local benefits, will have an unfair competitive advantage vis-à-vis established U.S. firms with obsolete plants, union opposition, and deteriorating cash flows. This has already happened in the television and tire industries and may soon prevail in the auto and steel industries as well.

Moreover, pure protectionism is clearly costly to the national economy and counterproductive, particularly in mature industries. A declining industry is much larger than an infant industry, so that any protectionist measures represent large costs to be reduced as soon as possible through improved productivity and greater cost competitiveness. Secondly, raising the cost of a particular product reduces the competitiveness of the industries that use it, such as the effect of higher-cost steel on the auto industry. There must be a program to make these inputs competitive over time.

The Japanese will, of course, argue that any protectionism is bad, and that the world should avoid falling back into the protectionist whirlpool of the thirties. However, what we are discussing here is not an across-the-board hike in tariffs, but a selective and temporary policy to resuscitate important U.S. industries. Indeed, this program could be viewed as merely just compensation for Japan's past protection of its key industries. The fact that they are not protecting their auto, steel, and machine tool industries now does not detract from their past policies. U.S. firms were kept out of the Japanese market until Japanese industry had grown and captured most of the home market, had begun to export to the LDCs under various export incentive programs (replacing American and European products), and eventually, had developed the competitive strength to enter the American market.

This association between protection of infant industries and development is well-documented. Japanese economic success has been based on a combination of a high savings rate and strategic use of protectionism and fiscal policy to ensure competitive development. The policy proposed now for the United States can thus be seen as compensation for the success of Japanese protectionism, since existing laws cannot protect U.S. industries from competition with the Japanese, who do not need to resort to dumping or other "predatory" practices when they finally enter the U.S. market.

In the case of new industries such as high technology, where the United States desires to maintain or improve both its competitive advantage and market share, supports will likely be based on more procurement and tax-specific incentives such as the research and development credit or lower capital gains taxes on venture capital. These industries would also be among the greatest beneficiaries of the general economic impact of a higher savings and investment rate. Less protectionist support is probably needed in these cases and in any case is less costly than for mature industries. However, some protection may be necessary in industries such as computers, telecommunications, and semi-conductors in exchange for access to the Japanese market. This might convince the Japanese we are serious not only about negotiating, but also about supporting our key industries and competing in world markets.

Convincing Japan to negotiate trade issues more seriously is particularly important because to achieve our long-term objective of promoting trade, we need Japan to take specific actions along with our own initiatives. So far they have not done so.

U.S. Requests for Japanese Policy Action

The current U.S. trade initiatives with Japan focus on the following goals: (1) opening the Japanese market to U.S. goods and services; (2) restricting Japanese exports to the United States in certain commodities such as textiles, steel, televisions, and automobiles; (3) maintaining our lead in the high-technology industries. The U.S. policy program examined above would certainly help to accomplish these objectives by improving U.S. overall growth and competitiveness. However, these policy prescriptions will be insufficient to reduce trade frictions with Japan if the Japanese economy remains relatively depressed. This situation will occur as long as desired savings in Japan continue to exceed desired investment. Under depressed economic conditions, Japanese negotiators will remain extremely reluctant to open markets to U.S. exports of citrus, beef, aluminum, fertilizers, petrochemicals, pulp, and lumber if they have nowhere to transfer the workers who will be displaced. Moreover, any large increase in U.S. imports would strengthen the dollar against the yen, making U.S. high-technology exports more expensive and Japanese products less expensive, adversely affecting our high-technology strategy. There will also be an increase in the natural flow of resources to these growth industries as opportunities in other sectors are reduced due to stiffened U.S. competition. This latter development is particularly likely if the United States and the European Economic Community (EEC) con-

tinue to restrict current major Japanese exports like automobiles, televisions, and steel, and if Japanese foreign investment increases as a substitute for exports. These exports, then, will not rise in tandem with the increase in Japanese imports.

To deal with these developments, American negotiators will need to persuade Japanese policy-makers to reduce the current incentives to save, to lower interest rates, to phase out oil-fired power-generating capacity, and to promote retail demand for credit. These actions would complement the commodity- or industry-specific requests the United States already has on the table. Under these circumstances, U.S. goals could be trade-promoting rather than trade-diverting.

Examining each proposed request in turn, a reduction in excess savings is the most critical element. Whereas a high rate of savings was extremely important to Japan after World War II to realize a non-inflationary, rapid investment, high-growth strategy, it has become counterproductive when domestic and export demand in many industries is mature, when the economy has shifted to a high-technology, service sector base, when the world is unwilling to accept massive export outflows from Japan, and when the Japanese government is unwilling to run massive budget deficits. Under these conditions, in order to accommodate a high savings rate, the economy must adjust in order to equate savings and investment, thus inhibiting growth, demand, interest rates, wages, and yen appreciation. A logical solution is to reduce savings by policies such as introducing the green card, imposing taxes on capital gains transactions, and the spending of any tax revenue increases.

Although lowering interest rates would present some unusual difficulties in Japan because of its postal savings system,[11] it would stimulate demand for housing and consumer durables. At the margin, it would also reduce the incentive to save. Both these developments would clearly stimulate demand and growth, given the current excess savings environment. Income growth would then raise tax revenues, which could be used for more demand-stimulating monetary and fiscal policies—even lower interest rates and tax cuts. Since the domestic economy is considerably larger than the export economy and the external economic environment is depressed, the initial impact of such a domestic economic expansion based on lower interest rates would be to increase imports more than exports. In any case, the MOF can make use of the current fall in U.S. interest rates and in oil prices, which have strengthened the yen, to allow Japanese rates to fall without any real fear of American and European trade officials becoming greatly concerned over "yen rigging," especially if the import benefit of greater economic activity is stressed.

With respect to further reductions of oil imports, Japan could, over time, help itself and the rest of the world by more rapidly constructing new coal and nuclear power plants while phasing out oil-fired facilities. This would also create substantial new investment demand to use up part of the excess savings without increasing the government deficit. The power utilities would borrow more to fund the program. There would also be few siting or engineering problems in accomplishing this, as several approved projects have been postponed or scaled down due to the current recession and disappointing economic growth projections for the 1980s.

To achieve this conversion, the government will have to provide the utilities and the oil industry with sufficient incentives to undertake such a program. However, in cooperation with the industries, a suitable package

of low-cost or even tax-exempt loans, tax incentives, rate adjustments, and supply contracts could be devised to accomplish the goal. But once enacted, this policy would help to stabilize world oil prices in the 1980s as economic activity revives. An equally important U.S. objective will also be realized, because reducing oil imports allows U.S. commodity imports to increase without depressing the yen and thereby undermining U.S. goals in high technology.

The final recommendation, though at odds with Japan's postwar institutional policy of channeling savings into productive investment, is that the change in economic realities necessitates the direction of more savings into consumer credit. The ratio of Japanese consumer credit, excluding outstanding mortgages, to personal disposable income in 1980 was only 7 percent compared to 22 percent in the United States.[12] There is a great deal to be done here, but one very beneficial step would be the formation of a nationwide credit bureau to pool consumer credit information, a move that the MOF has not promoted thus far. This action would both reduce the cost of credit and free it to fuel consumption demand. Also, the government should move to stimulate the demand for new housing, a major element of new investment demand sensitive

---

11. Japan's postal savings system is a huge source of funds for the government trust accounts, and competes directly with the banks for consumer deposits. As the banks cannot lower interest rates on loans without lowering them on deposits, the MOF must negotiate with the Postal Ministry to lower their rates if depositors are not to withdraw funds from the banks. This is always a political issue focusing on the benefits to the economy from lower rates versus the need for savers to receive an adequate real rate of return.

12. For a good discussion of consumer credit in Japan see Japan Economic Institute, "Japan's Consumer Credit Market," *JEI Report* (Washington, 22 October 1982).

to interest rates with multiple benefits for the rest of the economy. This could be done by offering a five-year tax deduction for interest paid on mortgages for new housing. Furthermore, to avoid renewed land speculation, only the proportion paid for the *house* would be tax-deductible. As the economic activity generated by a rise in new housing demand would be substantial, the potential loss in tax revenues from the deduction should be largely offset by the rise in revenues resulting from this economic stimulus. The net result would depend on the average tax rate, the current mortgage rate, and the GNP multiplier.

Conclusions

U.S. policy objectives should logically include a low rate of inflation and unemployment, a policy mix that has been elusive in recent years. In addition, the United States should have industries that are competitive in the markets they choose to serve, nationally or globally, while maintaining certain key industries that are deemed vital to the national interest. A critical element in achieving these seemingly contradictory goals is a significantly higher rate of savings coupled with a target set of policies that would favor key industries but would also give them the resources to improve competitiveness. Achieving these economic objectives would provide a firm economic foundation for funding other national goals, including more defense and social services, through a higher real growth rate. It would also reduce unemployment as a basis for many of the trade problems with Japan. But it will require a major effort to stimulate savings since current projections indicate that U.S. government deficit financing could consume 60 to 90 percent of available personal net savings in the 1980s, compared to 10 percent and 20 percent respec-

tively in the 1960s and 1970s. This would leave little or no resources for new productive investment.

At the same time, while such a U.S. program is required to take advantage of a more open Japanese market, it is not sufficient to solve the trade friction problems with Japan. In this regard, the United States must keep pressuring Japan to open its markets to goods and services in which the United States remains competitive and to monitor their compliance under agreements such as the one for Nippon Telephone and Telegraph (NTT) procurement and the recent high-technology accords. For example, the United States should push for the proposed Japanese-depressed industry bill covering areas such as aluminum, paper, and petrochemicals, to accommodate large increases in U.S. imports over time while modernizing Japan's capacity. It should not formalize existing non-tariff barriers. The role and objectives of the Japanese Fair Trade Commission (FTC) in this area are probably similar to those of its American counterpart. In any case, the United States must avoid pressing for Japanese trade concessions when they have no meaning, for example, opening a market when domestic competitiveness is overwhelming or when other non-tariff barriers are used instead.

However, the United States must recognize that a significant opening of the Japanese market, especially in basic commodities, will tend to weaken the yen and domestic demand unless an offsetting policy can be found. Excess savings have already had a depressing effect on the yen and on economic activity, leading to pressures to export in areas where Japan is already competitive, e.g., steel, automobiles, and consumer electronics. More pressure of this sort is not necessary, especially as an undervalued yen is likely to make the

Industrial Structure

United States less competitive in the important area of high technology. Because the United States does not just want to substitute a new set of trade tensions for the old, a way of improving domestic Japanese demand and reducing potential exchange pressures from increased imports is called for. The logical complementary Japanese policy requirements are therefore a reduction in interest rates, a substitution of capital for oil, reduced savings incentives, and expanded consumer credit.

Through the above combination of American and Japanese policies, long-run benefits from economic expansion and trade flows can be enjoyed. The alternative is a continuation of trade tensions with Japan. In addition, if the administration does not come to grips with U.S. domestic competitive problems on a long-term basis, it faces the real possibility that extreme protectionist legislation could be enacted. This would only intensify the economic divisiveness which already faces the country in the midst of a major recession. States are actively trying to draw industries away from other states, and are offering incentives to foreign businesses to relocate. Meanwhile, the industrialized East and Midwest continue to lose resources and employment to the South and West. All this aggravates the political and economic environment, including relations with Japan.

The overall U.S. policy goal is therefore to successfully manage these developments while establishing negotiating credibility and improving U.S.-Japanese trade relations. The United States should not allow its free trade idealism to be used against it, nor should it forget that the maximum benefits of free trade are best realized in a full employment environment to which all parts of the world economy contribute efficiently. A balanced and well-targeted policy approach, dealing with the shortcomings and the economic realities of both countries, thus appears not only the best way, but perhaps the only way, through the eye of the policy needle that has proved so elusive thus far.

Hiroshi Kimura

THE SOVIET PROPOSAL ON CONFIDENCE-BUILDING MEASURES AND THE JAPANESE RESPONSE*

Soviet foreign policy under the new leadership will follow the same course as that set out under Leonid I. Brezhnev. This seems to be the message that Yuri V. Andropov wanted to convey in his maiden speech to the Central Committee of the Communist Party of the Soviet Union (CPSU) on 22 November 1982, which particularly underlined "the continuity"[1] of Soviet foreign policy. The new general secretary stated that "Soviet foreign policy has been and will be as it was defined by the decisions of the 24th, 25th and 26th Party Congresses."[2] Needless to say, no serious student of Soviet foreign policy would take these official statements literally. Given the nature of foreign policy, official comments are rarely implemented in their original form, but must instead be interpreted, modified, or even abandoned, depending upon the situation. Furthermore, actual Soviet conduct of foreign affairs frequently deviates from the goals formally enunciated, at times to such an extent that one comes to think that words and deeds are two completely different things in Soviet foreign policy.

On the other hand, regarding Soviet policy toward Japan, there has been no change since the ascendance of the new Kremlin leadership. While Japan surely does not occupy a very high place on Andropov's list of foreign policy objectives, the Soviet government must still clarify its position toward Japan on a day to day basis. In fact, since the death of Brezhnev, there have already been significant actions[3] and statements[4] by Moscow toward Tokyo. Careful examination reveals that, first, there is fortunately not a very large discrepancy between official Soviet pronouncements and their actual engagments; and more importantly, there is no indication of a shift in their foreign policy vis-à-vis Japan

---

* This paper was completed under the auspices of the Arms Control and Disarmament Program of Stanford University during the 1982-83 academic year.

1. *Pravda*, 23, XI, 1982.
2. *Ibid.*
3. To mention a few, the rather indifferent treatment of the Japanese delegation, headed by Prime Minister Zenko Suzuki, to Moscow to attend the funeral of Leonid I. Brezhnev (14-16 November 1982), the Soviet-Japanese fishing negotiations in Tokyo (15 November-4 December 1982), the meeting between Soviet Foreign Minister Andrei Gromyko and his Japanese counterpart Yoshio Sakurauchi, which lasted only thirty minutes (14-16 November, 1982), the Japan-USSR symposium in Tokyo (4-6 December 1982), and a courtesy call by Soviet Ambassador to Japan Vladimir Pavlov to the new Japanese prime minister, Yasuhiro Nakasone (6 December 1982).
4. To mention only those which are relevant to the main topic of this paper, T.B. Guzhenko, "Sovetsko-iaponskie otnosheniia," *Problemy dal'nego vostoka* (No. 3 [43], 1982), 9-20; Vsevolod Ovchinnikov, "Druz'ia i nedrugi molodykh gosudarstv," *Pravda*, 18 XI, 1982; Yuri Afonin, "The Soviet Union's Principled Foreign Policy Toward Japan," *Foreign Broadcasting Information Service, Daily Report (Soviet Union)* —hereafter cited as *FBIS(SOV)*, 22 November 1982, c1.

Reprint rights reserved by the author.

away from that of Brezhnev's days.[5] More concretely, what the Kremlin has been pressing the Tokyo government to do, both before and after the leadership change, is the same: to respond positively to any one of several Soviet "peace proposals"[6] — such as a peace treaty resolving the territorial issue (over the "northern islands"), a treaty of good-neighborliness and cooperation, an accord on confidence-building measures (CBMs), or an agreement on the non-use of nuclear weapons. Yasuhiro Nakasone, who assumed the top political position in Japan about the same time as did Andropov in the USSR, flatly rejected all these Soviet proposals and stated clearly that, continuing the policies of his predecessors, his government would accept nothing short of a peace treaty including the reversion of the four disputed islands to Japan.[7] The question that immediately arises, then, is why Moscow and Tokyo differ so sharply and why each has been so adamant in pursuing its own proposal. In order to answer these questions, it is necessary to examine the current state of Soviet-Japanese bilateral relations, since these proposals have not been made in a political vacuum. That is to say, without a proper examination of the context in which these proposals have been made, one cannot fully appreciate their significance, nor the tenacity with which each government has pursued them. The answers clearly go beyond the change in leadership.

This essay will focus on the proposal most recently made by the Soviet Union to Japan concerning confidence-building measures (*mery po ukrepleniiu doveriia*). I will first examine the function of an agreement on CBMs in the specific context of Japanese-Soviet relations; and secondly, attempt to provide the reader with a general sense of current diplomatic relations between Japan and the USSR.

Are CBMs Applicable in Asia?

Confidence-building measures (CBMs) were first agreed upon by thirty-five participating states at the 1975 Helsinki Conference on Security and Cooperation in Europe (CSCE), though the idea of strengthening confidence through bilateral or multilateral arrangements predates Helsinki by many years.[8] The CBMs included in the Helsinki Final Act consist of specific steps to reduce tensions between potential adversaries, such as prior notification of major and smaller-scale military maneuvers and inviting observers to attend maneuvers.[9] Of interest here is the applicability of European CBM arrangements to other parts of the world. In its first resolution on CBMs in 1978, the United Nations General Assembly, on the initiative of the Federal Republic of Germany,[10] recommended that "all states should consider, on a regional basis, arrangments for specific CBMs, taking into account the specific condi-

---

5. A Moscow Radio commentator Yuri Afomin stated in his comment entitled "The Soviet Union's Principled Foreign Policy Toward Japan," which was aired on 19 November 1982: "Statements by Soviet leaders and their talks with the chief of states and government leaders in Moscow in the past several days have demonstrated to the world *the complete continuity of the Soviet foreign policy* and the USSR's resolve to follow the path pointed to by the decision of the 26th CPSU Congress ... It also reflects the keynote of Soviet policy *toward Japan.*" (emphasis added) *FBIS(SOV),* 22 November 1982, c1.

6. *Ibid.*

7. Prime Minister Nakasone's maiden speech to the Japanese Diet, *Yomiuri Shimbun* (Evening Edition), 3 December 1982.

8. Jonathan Alford, ed., *The Future of Arms Control, Part III: Confidence-Building Measures,* (London: The International Institute for Strategic Studies, 1979), 1.

9. *Conference on Security and Cooperation in Europe: Final Act* (London: Her Majesty's Stationery Office, 1975), 9-11.

10. Kalevi Ruhala, *Confidence Building Measures — Options for the Future* (IFSH — Forschungsberichte Heft, 18 August 1980), 47.

tions and requirements of each region."[11] Since that time, there have been two schools of thought on the application of CBMs to other regions: one school advocates the usefulness of extending CBMs beyond Europe[12] while the other is more cautious about the transferability of CBM parameters to other regions with different "political, military, and geographical circumstances."[13] The Soviet Union has made it clear that it is eager for similar arrangements in the Far East, particularly on a bilateral basis with Japan, whereas in marked contrast, Japan has responded coolly to the idea.

In general the Soviets are not as original in their conduct of foreign policy as outside observers are tempted to imagine. They tend to apply automatically the same policies, methods, and tactics which were successful in the past to vastly different situations. This is illustrated by Moscow's recent proposals to Japan, almost all of which have precedents in Europe or elsewhere. An example is Brezhnev's scheme of collective security in Asia, which is nothing but an Asian version of the European collective security system.[14] A treaty of good-neighborliness and cooperation between the USSR and Japan would be similar in both name and content to the agreements which have been concluded by the USSR with Egypt, India, Iraq, Turkey, Iran, Afghanistan, Vietnam,[15] and other countries.

Against this general background, it is not at all surprising to discover that the Soviet idea of CBMs in the Far East stems from the USSR's experience in Europe, more specifically from the inclusion of CBMs in the Helsinki Final Act. In other words, Brezhnev's offer of confidence-building measures in the Far East at the 26th Party Congress is nothing more than a simple, mechanical application of the CBMs outlined in the Helsinki Declaration. In his address at the final stage of

the CSCE in Helsinki on 31 July 1975, the general secretary of the CPSU clearly stated, "We view the CSCE as a joint success for all participants. *Its results can also be of use outside Europe.*"[16] (emphasis added) The words of the general secretary were confirmed by the Politburo of the CPSU Central Committee, which

---

11. *Confidence-building Measures, Report of the Secretary-General* (A/34/416), 3; *Comprehensive Study on Confidence-building Measures—Report of the Secretary General* (A/36/474), (New York: United Nations, 1982), 2.

12. Ruhala, 47-49; Alford, 1.

13. *Confidence-building Measures,* 29.

14. Mikhail S. Kapitsa, then head of the First Far Eastern Division of the Soviet Foreign Ministry and now deputy foreign minister under Yuri Andropov, made no secret and, on the contrary, even argued publicly, that the Soviet Union should follow the model of the European collective security system in its appeal for a collective security scheme in Asia. "The successful completion of the European Conference on Security and Cooperation and the experience of strengthening security in Europe underscore the possibility and necessity of additional measures in which all the states of the continent would join with the aim of strengthening peace and security in Asia and ensuring friendly international cooperation in that area. There is, certainly, no question of copying or automatically transferring the European collective security system to Asia. The situation in the Asia continent is different, more complex than in Europe. At the same time, there is no doubt that the peoples of Asia, which is one of the cradles of human civilization, will be able to find correct answers to the vital problems facing them, problems crucial not only for the present but for the future." M. Kapitsa, "Bor'ba SSSR za mir i sotrudnichestvo v Asii," *Problemy Dal'nego Vostoka* (No. 1 [29], 1979), 52-53; for an English translation of "The USSR's Struggle for Peace and Cooperation in Asia," see *Far Eastern Affairs* 2 (1979): 49-50.

15. As for the Soviet proposal on the treaty of good-neighborliness and cooperation between the USSR and Japan and the Japanese response, see Hiroshi Kimura, "Japan-Soviet Relations: Framework, Developments, Prospects," *Asian Survey* 20 (July 1980): 715.

16. *Vo imia mira, bezopasnosti i sotrudnichestva* (Moscow: Politizdat, 1975), 8.

declared on 6 August 1975: "The decisions of the [Helsinki] Conference have great meaning not only for Europeans, because the right to peace belongs to every human being on our planet."[17] Soviet bureaucrats and specialists on Far Eastern affairs, arguing that a large portion of the Helsinki agreements can be applied to Asia and the Far East, have embellished on the official line set by the highest authorities in the Soviet foreign policy establishment. For instance, Soviet commentator Vladimir Kudriavtsev wrote in *Izvestiia* that the principles adopted at Helsinki were "universally applicable to Asia."[18] In 1977, V. N. Berezin (a pseudonym for high-ranking Soviet Foreign Ministry officials in charge of Japan) stated: "If we pay attention to the Final Document which was worked out at the [Helsinki] Conference, we find in it many conditions pertaining to those problems that currently confront the states in the Far East."[19] Application of CBMs to the Far East is justified by another Japan expert, N. Nikolaev, who wrote in 1981: "There is no need to say that the situation in Asia is particularly distinct from that in Europe. Nevertheless, the experience of European states in developing and employing CBMs may undoubtedly prove useful in Asian countries."[20]

Official Reasons for Japanese Reluctance

Japan has publicly endorsed the idea of CBMs. A booklet issued by the Japanese Foreign Ministry states: "The CBMs may not be regarded as an arms control arrangment *per se*. Yet our country considers that, provided specific political and military conditions of each region are sufficiently taken into account, CBMs can serve as an important element in the development of arms control. CBMs have made some achievements in

Europe, and now various proposals for making CBMs more effective are being discussed."[21] But when the Soviets approach Japan with regard to CBMs in the Far East, the Tokyo government's response suddenly takes a negative turn. The reason provided by Tokyo for its refusal is that "situations in the Far East are so different from those in Europe that automatic transfer of the CBMs from Europe to the Far East is unrealistic."[22] Naturally, regional disarmament and arms control should be left to the initiative of the countries concerned. Moreover, nobody expects that CBMs in Europe can be transferred to other regions without being tailored to the "specific conditions" of a given region. This reservation is stated not only in the recommendation of the UN General Assembly cited above but even by the Soviet Union.[23] Thus the question to be asked is what, in the view of the Japanese government, would consti-

---

17. *Pravda,* 7 VIII, 1975.

18. Quoted from Golam W. Choudhury, *Brezhnev's Collective Security Plan for Asia* (Washington: Center for Strategic & International Studies), 1.

19. V. N. Berezin, *Kurs na dobrososedstvo i sotrudnichestvo i ego protivniki* (Moscow: Mezhdunarodnye otnosheniia, 1970), 112.

20. N. Nikolaev, "Zigzagi politiki Tokio," *Mezhdunarodnye otnosheniia* 10 (1981): 46.

21. *Gunshuku-mondai to Nippon (Arms Control Question and Japan)* (Tokyo: Information and Culture Bureau, Japanese Ministry of Foreign Affairs, 1982), 29.

22. *Gunshuku;* Muto Toshiai, "Saikin no nisso-kankei to taiōshū, taiyōshū gaikō (Recent Japan-Soviet Relations and Japan's Policy towards Europe and the Pacific)," in *Saikin no kokusai-jōsei (Recent International Situations)* (Tokyo: Information and Culture Bureau, Japanese Ministry of Foreign Affairs, 1981), 49. For a similar remark by a high Japanese Foreign Ministry official, Yoshio Ōkawa, the former Japanese ambassador to the UN Disarmament Committee at Geneva, see *Asahi Shimbun,* 8 January 1983.

23. *Confidence-building measures,* 55.

tute "the specific conditions" in the Far East; and whether they are unique enough for Tokyo to categorically reject the transfer of CBMs into the region.

First, one must consider the geographical factors. Japan is separated from its potential adversary, the USSR, by water. This particular geographical (hence strategic-military) circumstance lessens the urgency of a Japanese-Soviet agreement on land forces, which is the chief issue covered by the CBMs in the Helsinki Act.[24] Toshiaki Muto, director general of the European and Oceanic Affairs Bureau at the Japanese Ministry of Foreign Affairs, concluded in 1981 that "differences in geographical situations make the idea of automatically bringing the CBMs in Europe to the Far East unrealistic," arguing that "even if the USSR gives prior notification of its military maneuvers in Siberia, it will not be of much use to Japan."[25]

Mr. Muto may have deliberately overlooked the fact that the Helsinki CBMs, obviously a by-product of particular environmental circumstances, are certainly not meant to be a formula to be automatically followed by other states in different regions. In particular, he appears to miss the point that CBMs can also be applied to naval and air forces, an idea that even predates the Helsinki Act.[26] The 1972 American-Soviet Agreement on the Prevention of Incidents on and over the High Seas[27] is one of the most relevant examples of naval CBMs. The Helsinki Final Act also covers certain "amphibious and/or air-borne troops." In addition, it is worth recalling that a proposal was made at the CSCE, though it did not materialize, to include in the Final Accord measures dealing with naval and air exercises such as "maneuvers in border zones, the flying of fighter planes close to border zones, and the navigation of warships in the vicinity of the territorial waters of other

states."[28] Moreover, there is no reason to assume that the CBMs in the Final Act will not be altered, even enlarged further in the near future. As a matter of fact, considering as "the salient anomaly"[29] the fact that current CBMs (agreed on at Helsinki) do not extend to naval forces, Western specialists who are in favor of extending confidence-building measures[30] strongly urge that CBMs be extended to both air and naval maneuvers.[31] Brezhnev also promoted naval and air CBMs in his speech at the 26th Party Congress, when he contended: "We have already said that we are prepared to go further—to also provide notification on naval and air exercises."[32] Strongly endorsing Brezhnev's idea of extending CBMs to naval exercises, Timofei Guzhenko, chairman of the Soviet-Japan Society and USSR minister of the maritime fleet, reminded the Japanese in an article published since Andropov became general secretary that, precisely because of its vital dependence upon ocean communication lines, Japan must consider more seriously than any other nation

---

24. Richard Haass, "Confidence-Building Measures and Naval Arms Control," in Alford, ed., 24.
25. Muto, 49.
26. Haass, 24.
27. Text in *World Armament and Disarmament, SIPRI Yearbook 1973* (Stockholm: Almqvist & Wikseel, Humanities Press, Paul Elek, 1973), 36-39.
28. Luigi Vittorio Ferraris, ed., *Report on a Negotiation: Helsinki-Geneva-Helsinki 1972-1975* (Geneva: Institut Universitaire de Hautes Etudes Internationales, 1979), 183.
29. Johan Jorgen Holst and Karen Alette Melander, "European Security and Confidence-building Measures," *Survival 79* (July/August 1977): 149.
30. Holst and Melander, 152-154; Alford, 1, 5; Ruhala, 52-73.
31. Alford, 5.
32. *XXI s'ezd Kommunisticheskoi partii Sovetskogo Soiuza: stenografisheskii otchet*, T. I. (Moscow: Politizdat, 1981), 46.

the security of sea lanes, which alone "can assure the security of Japan."[33] Guzhenko continued:

> Such initiatives must be of a special interest to Japan, which has been making an effort to assure security for sea transportation. Japanese leaders have already expressed more than once the apprehension that supply routes of energy and other industrial resources to this country pass along waters which can be seized in the fire of any military conflict, if it breaks out in the northwestern part of the Pacific Ocean or in the Indian Ocean.[34]

This statement may be dismissed as another attempt by Moscow to check the recent Japanese effort to take on its share of the defense of the so-called "1000-mile sea lanes," but at the same time it helps to recall the undeniable fact that the areas surrounding Japan have been made increasingly uneasy by frequent air and naval reconnaissance exercises and other military activities by the USSR, the United States, and other states. According to a white paper by the Japanese Defense Agency, the number of flights by Soviet military aircraft in the area around Japan is about 240 per year, and the number of passages of Soviet warships through three straits (Tsushima, Tsugaru, and Soya) is approximately 430.[35] As a result, a number of incidents have taken place—the Soviet MIG-25 jet aircraft landing at the Hakodate airport, the Soviet TU-16 *Badger* crash into the Sea of Japan, and a Soviet nuclear submarine breakdown within Japanese territorial waters, among others. In order to prevent these kinds of tensions from growing to such an extent that it becomes difficult to distinguish a simple exercise from a real military action, the concerned states must seriously discuss some sort of CBM arrangement. This line of argument sounds rather difficult to resist.

Second, there are negotiating circumstances. The CBMs constituted only one aspect of the whole package deal at Helsinki. In Europe the agreement on CBMs was reached not in isolation from, but closely connected with political and security issues in the form of "baskets," such as the affirmation of the East European *status quo*, non-intervention in the internal affairs of other nations, the improvement of economic, scientific, and technological cooperation, and the free movement, contact, and interchange of ideas, information, and people between East and West. In other words, the Helsinki Final Act was a product of compromise among the participating states, each of which recorded some gains in one or a few areas but only in exchange for concessions in other fields. The Soviet Union, for instance, agreed to Basket III, dealing with "cooperation in humanitarian issues," only reluctantly and only after it became clear that this was the necessary price for Western acceptance of the political and security commitments contained in Basket I.[36] It must be kept in mind that this is at least the official understanding of the Soviet Union on the Helsinki Final Act, although it has in fact been quite selective and arbitrary about carrying out each provision of the final accord. One Soviet specialist on international affairs put forward such an official position in an article entitled "The European Conference: Experience and Significance," in *International Affairs* in 1976:

---

33. Guzhenko, 18.
34. *Ibid.*
35. *Defense of Japan: 1982* (Tokyo: Defense Agency, 1982), 34-35.
36. G. D. Loescher, "Human Rights and the Helsinki-Belgrade Process," in *The Year Book of World Affairs 1981* (London: The London Institute of World Affairs, 1981), 62.

The Final Act is an *integral document* embracing the entire spectrum of questions related to the security of, and cooperation between, the participating states. This signifies that it must be put into effect in its entirety, with all its provisions as they have been agreed upon and provisions formulated in the Final Act. To single out individual provisions, to oppose them to the others, to secure priority for fulfilling some and ignoring other, similarly essential, provisions would mean to act in contravention of the spirit and letter of the Final Act, to break the fundamental balance of interests embodied in it. (italics in original)[37]

Moreover, the CSCE itself was the result of bargaining. For instance, the United States conditioned the convening of the CSCE on that of a conference on force reduction in Central Europe known as the Mutual and Balanced Force Reduction talks (MBFR).[38] Mr. Muto of the Japanese Foreign Ministry must have been familar with the circumstances under which CBMs were agreed upon at the CSCE when he said: "CBMs were adopted as a result of a variety of bargaining. Being under different circumstances in the Far East, therefore, we cannot easily say, 'Yes, indeed. We will make the same arrangement.'"[39]

Particularly disturbing to the Japanese is the inclusion in the same Helsinki Final Act, together with CBMS, of the provision for the "inviolability of frontiers," by which the West gave *de facto* recognition of those borders that the Soviet Red Army had drawn at the end of World War II.[40] This was the last thing the Japanese ever wanted to do. Theoretically, agreements on CBMs and a border settlement are two completely different things and yet can be very easily linked because, strictly speaking, the former assumes the latter. It is between neighboring states that one easily succumbs to misperceptions, misunderstanding, uncertainty, and fear about military maneuvers and movements of potential adver-

saries. As a matter of fact, according to the existing Helsinki Final Act, it is not the entire territory but only "an area within 250 kilometers *from a frontier* of each participating state" (emphasis added) that the provision on prior notification of military maneuvers is to be applied to. Therefore, it is not an exaggeration to say that without first settling borders, it is almost impossible to even discuss CBMs and expect them to work. One episode which demonstrates the necessity of having the borders clearly defined prior to discussing military affairs is provided by the following case of inconsistent behavior by the United States in 1968. When a Vietnam-bound Seaboard World Airways jet filled with U.S. military personnel was forced to land on Etorofu after trespassing into Kurile air space, Washington apologized to Moscow for infringing on Soviet territory, forgetting that the United States' official position regards Etorofu as not Soviet, but Japanese territory, thus putting itself in the awkward position of apologizing to Tokyo for apologizing to Moscow.[41]

---

37. M. L'vov, "Obshcheevropeiskoi soveshchanie: opyt i znachenie," *Mezhdunarodnaia zhizn'*, 3 (1976), 47.

38. William I. Bacchus, "Multilateral Foreign Policy Making: The Conference on Security and Cooperation in Europe," in David A. Caputo, ed., *The Politics of Policy Making in America: Five Case Studies* (San Francisco: W.H. Freeman and Company, 1977), 136.

39. Muto, 48.

40. Strictly speaking, the Helsinki Final Act was nothing but a confirmation by the West of what had been already recognized by the Federal Republic of Germany in its treaties with the USSR and Poland concerning normalization of borders. For more details, see Harold S. Russell, "The Helsinki Declaration: Brobdingnag or Lilliput?" *American Journal of International Law* 70 (April 1976): 249-253.

41. *New York Times*, 5-7 July 1968, quoted by John J. Stephan in "The Kurile Islands: Japan versus Russia," *Pacific Community* 7 (April 1976): 327-328.

Consequently, it is understandable that the Japanese have been insistent on negotiating the territorial issue before discussing CBMs, regarding the former as a precondition for the latter. In contrast, the Soviet Union officially takes the position that the territorial issue has already been resolved, but unofficially, it is well aware of the fact that there *is* a territorial problem between the two countries.[42] It intends to exploit a possible agreement on CBMs with Japan as a useful opportunity to let the Japanese accept formally and finally the presently existing borders, which were drawn by the Soviet military forces at the close of the Second World War. The Japanese seem very wary of this strategy, particularly because they have just experienced similar Soviet advances in a different area. In the 200-mile fishing zone negotiations between Japan and the USSR in 1977, the Japanese strongly refused to accept the demarcation line drawn unilaterally by the Soviet government, since this would have legitimated the *Soviet* view of the national boundary between the USSR and Japan. The Japanese correctly suspected that once they gave way on fishing rights, it would mean implicit or even explicit acceptance of *de facto* existing borders. After only ninety days of heated negotiations with the Soviets — it was then called "the 200-mile fish *war*" — the Japanese barely succeeded in winning Soviet consent to insert a compromise formula into a new fishing zone agreement: the separation of the fishing zone issue from other questions. The most important issue from Tokyo's perspective was that of the national borders, as shown in Article 8 of the final agreement, which stipulates:

No prescription in this agreement shall be taken to violate the position or opinion of either government with respect to ... issues in the (two nations') mutual relations.[43]

The negative attitude of the Japanese government toward the Soviet proposal for an agreement with Tokyo on CBMs can be viewed against the background of this agonizing experience in 1977.

Third, there are psychological factors which constitute "specific conditions." Japanese distrust of the Soviets is so profound that the proposal by the Soviets on confidence-building is unlikely to be considered worth examining. Among other things, the Japanese are disturbed by the very word "confidence-building," especially when uttered by the Soviets, since most Japanese see Soviet actions as falling far short of building confidence. The government of former Prime Minister Zenko Suzuki argued that if the Soviets ever wish to build confidence among the Japanese, there are other things for them to be engaged in before advocating CBMs, including "a withdrawal of their military troops from the northern islands claimed by Japan, or the reversion of these islands to Japan, or the removal of SS-20s from the Far East."[44] As long as the Soviets are

---

42. Stephan, "Asia in the Soviet Conception," 42.

43. Roger Swearingen, *The Soviet Union and Postwar Japan: Escalating Challenge and Response* (Stanford, California: Hoover Institution Press, 1978), 287.

44. *Nihon Keizai Shimbun*, 27 March 1982. Muto has made exactly the same kind of argument. See Muto, 49. An editorial in *Mainichi Shimbun* on 26 March 1982 also expressed a strikingly similar view to that of Prime Minister Suzuki: "It is a fact that one must doubt that the Soviet proposal [calling for an agreement with Japan on CBMs] lacks the concrete deeds, which underline their seriousness ... The proposal to talk on CBMs cannot in itself be said to be meaningless. The point is, however, that there is not much confidence [between the Soviets and Japanese] ... We have repeatedly written that the largest problem which has prevented us from building confident relations [between Japan and the USSR] is the northern territorial issue ... The invasion of Afghanistan has strengthened distrust of the Soviet Union." *Mainichi Shimbun*, 26 March 1982.

not ready to take these actions or even to discuss them with the Japanese government, the Japanese wonder how they possibly can take the Soviet suggestion on CBMs seriously. Pointing out such a sharp contradiction between what the Soviets are saying and what they are actually doing, the 1982 version of *Asian Security,* an annual report issued by the Research Institute for Peace and Security in Tokyo, states: "they can hardly help being skeptical of Moscow's sincerity in proposing to discuss confidence-building while also building up its forces in the region."[45] Thus what the Japanese want to say to the new Soviet leader Andropov seems to be similar to the message given to Brezhnev by the British weekly, *The Economist,* which wrote in 1982: "You can't shake hands with a clenched fist."[46]

However, the Soviets and some vigorous West European and Japanese advocates of CBMs[47] criticize the Japanese government for not trying to, or perhaps pretending not to correctly understand the preliminary and modest nature of CBMs in the military realm, and for attaching to its acceptance of the Soviet proposal preconditions clearly unacceptable to the Kremlin. After all, they argue, the existence of mistrust and lack of confidence among states is unfortunately normal in the current international system, the cold reality on which any international agreement must be based. Precisely where there is relatively little or no confidence, there is an urgent need for CBMs to be seriously considered.[48] This line of logic seems to the author of this essay somewhat appropriate, although not totally convincing.

When discussing confidence-building measures, one ought to be very careful about the meaning of the term "confidence," a vague and subjective word that allows different people to draw different interpretations. As already indicated, "confidence" in the CBMs agreed upon at the Helsinki CSCE has a very narrowly-defined, special meaning, i.e., confidence in the purely military field[49] which can be obtained by exchanging information on military activities between states. This type of narrow confidence is certainly of "an initial character and of a limited scope"[50] and yet, advocates of CBMs believe it should be pursued by as many states as possible as a precedent to be followed by others later on. The advocates of CBMs firmly believe in the correctness of the so-called "gradual approach,"[51] that confidence-building is by nature a process which should be carried out on a step-by-step basis,[52] and that any positive experience may lead to the development and enlargement of measures aimed at the further strengthening

---

45. *Asian Security 1982* (Tokyo: Research Institute for Peace and Security, 1980), 172.

46. *The Economist,* 6 November 1982, 17.

47. For instance, Reinhard Drifte, "Disarmament and Arms Control in Japanese Politics," (unpublished paper, September 1981) 25-26, 29-30; *Asahi Shumbun,* 8 January 1983; Takeshi Igarashi, "Nisso-kankei o dakaisuru michi" (The Way to Break the Deadlock in Japan-Soviet Relations), *Sekai* 8 (August 1982): 100. A majority of the Japanese participants in the first session of the third Japan-USSR roundtable, held in Tokyo on April 20-22, seem to take a positive attitude toward CBMs, judging from the final summary of that subcommittee, which states: "The subcommittee recognized that there is a need to establish a security system in Asia, and the Soviet proposal on CBMs is worth discussing . . ." *Jiyū* 7 (July 1982): 49. However, the important point to be remembered is that the Soviets regarded only the *official position* of the Japanese government as relevant.

48. *Comprehensive Study on Confidence-building Measures,* 4.

49. *Ibid.,* 3; *Confidence-building Measures,* 26.

50. *Confidence-building Measures,* 12.

51. *Ibid.,* 31; Ruhala, 49.

52. *Comprehensive Study on Confidence-building Measures,* 4; *Confidence-building Measures,* 20.

of confidence. Nevertheless, the Japanese government does not seem much interested in such narrowly-defined CBMs, particularly when it comes to concluding an agreement with the Soviet Union. By refusing the Soviet proposal to even discuss the institution of CBMs in the Far East, Tokyo appears to be deliberately adopting a broader interpretation of the term "confidence," as illustrated in the above statement by Prime Minister Suzuki. The remarks by Prime Minister Suzuki and other high Japanese officials confuse, whether intentionally or unintentionally, two closely related yet distinct concepts — confidence-building measures and arms control. Arms control aims at limiting military *capabilities,* but CBMs, by focusing on the parties' *perceptions* of each other's intentions, try to reduce unintended tension among neighboring states arising out of misunderstandings about their military maneuvers and movements.[53] Although the ultimate goals of CBMs may coincide with those of arms control, the immediate objective of CBMs is, as noted above, relatively modest. The preconditions attached by Prime Minister Suzuki to Tokyo's return to the negotiating table with Moscow, such as the "withdrawal of Soviet military troops from the northern islands" and "the removal of SS-20s from the Far East," fall into the category of arms control measures, thus making Suzuki's rationale seem inappropriate. Another precondition — the return of the northern islands to Japan — also does not appear to be properly linked to the issue. Only when a certain level of confidence and friendly relations has been developed between the countries concerned, some advocates of CBMs in Japan argue, can the return of the territory become possible, as was the case in the reversion of Okinawa[54] to Japan from the United States. Dal'nev warns that "to push confrontational and incompatible elements to the front is simply to further sharpen relations and make consensus-building not close but rather remote."[55] Based on this sort of "first-things-first" logic, Georgi Arbatov, supposedly one of the most influential advisers to Andropov, tried hard to sell the idea to the Japanese public in his interview with the *Yomiuri Shimbun* on 3 January 1983, claiming a need for "starting from the field which is possible at the present, leaving difficult problems for later."[56]

So far the argument of the Soviet, Western, and Japanese advocates of the CMBs sounds fairly convincing, but not overly so. Among other things, one important point that they overlook is the possibility that the initial step will not be followed up by any further measures. This has unfortunately often been the case in negotiations with the Soviet Union, as demonstrated by the past record. In other words, CBMs may at some stage give rise to further developments, but a process of continuing development cannot be taken for granted. Most likely, a process of developing genuine confidence would not only be impaired but even halted by a premature initial agreement. This seems to be what the Tokyo government really fears. Why then should it be fearful of such a situation? What would be wrong with a Japanese-Soviet agreement on CBMs, which might fall short of arms control or disarmament, but still be better than nothing as a form of preventing accidental war? The remainder of this article will be devoted to answering these questions.

---

53. Ruhala, 4.
54. Igarashi, 100.
55. V. Dal'nev, *Nekotorye problemy sovetsko-iaponskikh otnoshenii* (Japanese translation: *Nisso-kankei dakai no michi — Soren wa dō kangaeru ka)* (Tokyo: Asia-shōbō, 1981), 88.
56. *Yomiuri Shimbun,* 3 January 1983.

Japanese and Soviet Perspectives of Current Bilateral Relations

Soviet-Japanese relations have never been in good shape in the postwar period, and yet no other period has witnessed a worse situation than that of the past several years. As officially admitted by the Soviet side,[57] the deterioration of bilateral relations, though still "in isolated actions"[58] according to a Soviet observer's words, started in the latter half of 1970s. A series of events[59] contributed to the decline of the relations: the MIG-25 incident in 1976, in which a Soviet pilot landed at the Hakodate airport, seeking asylum in the U.S. and delivering into Western hands one of the most advanced Soviet aircraft, which was, by the decision of the Tokyo government, disassembled and thoroughly examined in cooperation with U.S. Air Force technical experts (1976); the lengthy and heated negotiations over fishing rights in the newly-established Soviet and Japanese 200-mile fishing zones (1977); and Japan's signing of a Treaty of Peace and Friendship with the People's Republic of China (PRC) containing an "anti-hegemony" clause, apparently directed against Soviet expansionism (1978).

At the threshold of the 1980s Soviet-Japanese relations drastically deteriorated, as admitted again by Soviet official pronouncements and writings.[60] The major cause of the deterioration at this time is the following series of events: Soviet direct or indirect intervention into other countries such as Afghanistan and Poland; Japan's participation in the West's sanction measures (freezing the exchange of high government officials, boycotting the Moscow Olympics, and limiting Japan-Soviet economic relations to a minimum); growing buildup of Soviet military forces in the Far East (e.g., deployment of 108 SS-20s, about 70 supersonic *Backfire* bombers, the

Kiev-class aircraft carrier, the *Minsk*, etc.) and redeployment of approximately division-sized ground troops on the northern islands; the rebirth of a national security consciousness among Japanese, and the revitalization of the campaign for the reversion of the northern islands (e.g., the establishment of Northern Territorial Day, Prime Minister Suzuki's inspection tour to the Nemuro city closet to the disputed islands, and so forth). As the above list of events and incidents shows, actions and reactions by both countries have become so complicated and intertwined that nobody has been able to clearly distinguish a consequence from a cause. Perhaps the best example of this is the recent move by the Soviet Union—deployment of a squadron of ten to twelve supersonic MIG-21 fighter-bombers on the island of Etorofu. The explanation for this move, according to American analysts,[61] is that it responds to Tokyo's acceptance of the Pentagon's proposals for deployment of forty to fifty advanced F-16 fighter-bombers capable of carrying nuclear weapons at the Misawa air base in northern Japan in 1985. But according to the judgment of Tokyo and Washington, this move is nothing but an inevitable response to Soviet deployment of

---

57. *Pravda*, 15 X, 1981; V. Dal'nev, "Chto meshaet razvitiiu sovetsko-iaponskikh otnoshenii," *Mezhdunarodnaia zhizn'*, 1 (1981): 51.

58. Dal'nev, *Ibid.*

59. The following three events, i.e., the MIG-25 incident, the fishing negotiations in 1977, and the signing of a Sino-Japanese Peace Treaty, were also listed by M. Kapitsa in his recent article. See Kapitsa, 45.

60. *Iaponia 1981*, 63. In his speech to the Central Committee at the 26th CPSU Congress on 23 February 1981, Brezhnev also noted that (in Soviet relations with Japan) "negative factors are becoming stronger." *XXVI s'ezd*, Vol. I, 42.

61. *New York Times*, 30 December 1982.

the *Backfire* bomber and SS-20, which can hit any part of Japan.

Against the recent decline in bilateral relations between the USSR and Japan described above, it is particularly notable that Moscow looks more interested than Tokyo in the improvement of the relationship. Japan does not, of course, regard the present situation as ideal. The Japanese government, however, contends that the undesirable situation presently prevailing between these two countries is nothing other than a product of inappropriate policy and actions of the Soviet Union in international affairs and in its relations with Japan. This posture relieves Japan of any responsiblity to take an intiative to correct the situation. "In the final analysis, what has made Japan-Soviet relations so cold? This ought to be the basic question, when one thinks about bilateral relations," said the Japanese ambassador to the USSR, Masuo Takashima, before briefing Prime Minister Yasuhiro Nakasone in December 1982. Answering the question himself, he argued that "the cause lies not with Japan at all, but simply with the Soviet Union. In the postwar period the whole responsibility lies consistently with the USSR." The Japanese ambassador continued:

> Thus, only when the Soviet Union comes to regard Japan as important, respects Japan, and hence amends its current attitudes, can Japan respond. Japan is not in a position to bow to the USSR or to seek good relations with this country.[62]

Surely the Japanese have not failed to notice the increasing Soviet military buildup in their immediate vicinity. At the same time, however, the Japanese government knows that the Soviet Union under Yuri Andropov is a sort of sick giant, which apart from its military muscle, has many weak spots and problems, both domestic and international. This would make it almost out of the question for the Soviet Union to become involved in another Afghanistan in the Far East. In other words, so long as Japan maintains its own "denial force"[63] to repel limited and small-scale military aggression, to make such aggression costly, and to prevent the invasion of Japan from easily becoming a *fait accompli*,[64] and as long as it continues to enjoy U.S. nuclear deterrence as a means of checking Soviet aggression, Tokyo need not worry too much about the threat from "the North Pole Bear." Further expansion of trade and economic relations between the USSR and Japan may still be desirable as a possible outlet for the stagnant Japanese economy. In Tokyo's view, such forthcoming moves must take into consideration other political and economic factors. These include Japan's international obligation as a member-state of the Western community to participate in sanctions against Soviet international adventurism; the overwhelming importance of the United States as a major trade partner, with which Japan has been conducting ten times more trade than with the Soviet Union; the USSR's own economic difficulties such as shortages of labor and foreign currency; and a possible Soviet shift in development priorities toward western Siberia and away from eastern Siberia and the far eastern region

---

62. *Nihon Keizai Shimbun,* 9 December 1982.

63. *Report on Comprehensive National Security* (English Translation) (Tokyo: The Comprehensive National Security Study Group, 2 June 1980), 9, 42. This concept is believed to have been borrowed from Glenn H. Snyder's article, "Deterrence by Denial and Punishment," in Davis B. Bobrow, ed., *Components of Defense Policy* (Chicago: Rand McNally & Company, 1965), 209-212.

64. *Report on Comprehensive . . . 42; Defense of Japan 1982* (Tokyo: Defense Agency, 1982), 81.

of the Soviet Union. Finally, psychological elements are not irrelevant. It has been observed lately that, rightly or wrongly, the Japanese have remarkably increased their self-confidence. This has especially been the case since Japan terminated the state of war with China by concluding a peace treaty with the PRC in 1978 and since it achieved the status of an economic giant second only to the United States. On the whole, Tokyo seems to have concluded that at present there is no particular reason for Japan to make a diplomatic initiative to Moscow in order to break the current deadlock in relations with the Soviet Union.

In contrast, although Moscow publicly attributes the chilled relations to the misconduct of Tokyo, Washington, and Peking, in practice the Soviet Union now seems to consider it necessary to improve bilateral Soviet-Japanese relations to a much greater degree than does Tokyo. The Soviets' increasing recognition of Japan's importance must be indeed regarded as a significant departure from previous Soviet attitudes and policies toward Japan. Since the end of World War II, Soviet political leaders have shown a tendency to underestimate Japan as a state and the Japanese as a people. They have retained their earlier image of the Japanese—particularly as submissive and easily intimidated—which they had formulated through their experience with Japanese prisoners in Siberian camps immediately after the war period. This tendency has been further reinforced by the Soviet inclination to assess the power of a state largely in terms of presently existing military might. However, though belatedly and still insufficiently, Soviet political leaders have become gradually aware of the significance of the Japanese power-potential which stems from specific geopolitical, diplomatic, military-strategic, and economic roles that Japan can play in the world, particularly in the Asia-Pacific region.

Japan's geopolitical and strategic importance has increased as the USSR desires to become a more and more influential power in the Asia-Pacific region. For instance, the USSR can now launch sea-launched ballistic missiles (SLBMs) from its military complex around the Sea of Okhotsk to any target in the United States except the Florida peninsula. But if its strategic chokepoints (i.e., the Tsushima, Tsugaru, and Soya straits) were ever to be closed by Japan, the Soviet Pacific Fleet would be confined to the Sea of Okhotsk and the Sea of Japan, making its passage into the Pacific difficult if not impossible. This would also permit it to be easily detected by American or Japanese radar.

Tokyo's diplomatic posture and foreign policy nowadays greatly affect those of Moscow. The best example is Japan's decision to improve relations with the PRC. At present, Tokyo does not have any intention whatsoever of allowing Sino-Japanese diplomatic relations to evolve into a military alliance, despite strong pressures from Peking in that direction. Should Japan decide for any reason to join in the formation of a military alliance together with the United States and the People's Republic of China, Soviet strategy would be greatly affected, not only in the Asia-Pacific region, but in the world at large. Japan's economic potential, the second largest in the world, is certainly becoming an ever larger attraction for the ailing Soviet economy. This is especially true since the economic development of the eastern part of the country has become crucial to expanding the Soviet economy. The geographical proximity of the two countries makes Japan a more natural economic partner than the West European countries to provide the capital, technology, and markets for Siberian resources, especially given the problems of rising transportation costs. In these respects, Tokyo now has an important card to play vis-à-vis Moscow. What is to be noted here is that the role that Japan plays vis-à-vis the USSR is largely of a potential nature. What Japan will or will not do (e.g., re-arm, move closer to the PRC, cooperate with the USSR in Siberian economic development, and so on) greatly affects the Soviet Union. Some Japanese political scientists argue that power in a potential form is more influential and effective.[65] At any rate, the Soviet political leaders have at last come to realize, albeit to an insufficient degree, the significance of the actual and potential power of Japan.

Moscow's Strategy and Tokyo's Counter-Strategy

Just because the Kremlin leaders have increasingly recognized the significant role of Japan, it does not necessarily follow that they are more likely to make concessions to Tokyo. The situation is not that simple for a variety of reasons. To begin with, perceptions and policy decisions are usually quite different things, the former being only one of many factors determining the latter.[66] Second, Tokyo's terms still seem to Moscow too extreme to be met. The return of territories once occupied by the Soviet Union and the removal of its military forces there are actions that the Kremlin is not willing or able to undertake. Above all, there is a possibility that in the perception of Kremlin leaders Japan has not yet become so important as to justify such major concessions as those requested by Tokyo. In any case, the core of the Kremlin's current Japan policy appears to lie in its stated intentions of improving relations with Tokyo on its own terms, without yielding at all.

In order to achieve this objective, the Kremlin has recently been pursuing a strategy dedicated to achieving a breakthrough in bilateral relations by reaching some sort of treaty agreement with Japan. However, Tokyo is intent on a peace treaty, which not only the Japanese, but sometimes even the Soviets[67] assume must include a clause on the settlement of the territorial question. But the Kremlin would be satisfied with any kind of legal document which could somehow substitute for a peace treaty in terms of its political and symbolic functions. Both public pronouncements and private remarks made recently by Soviet officials dealing with Soviet-Japanese relations almost always conclude with a strong assertion of the need to have such a legal document with Japan, since, as V. Dal'nev, a Soviet specialist on Japanese relations, believes, "the placing of their (Soviet-Japanese) relations on a firm legal basis would be an important and useful thing."[68] The conclusion of any legal document between the Soviet Union and Japan would serve two important functions in the present context. One is a political function, that is to

---

65. Believing that "in a potential form a negotiating power is most effective," Professor Yonosuke Nagai at the Tokyo University of Technology argues that Japan's bargaining power with the Soviet Union has such potentialities. See Yonosuke Nagai, "Moratoriamu-kokka no boei-ron" (The Defense Theory of the Moratorium State), *Chuo-Koron* (January 1981): 104-106.

66. Charles Gati, "History, Social Science, and the Study of Soviet Foreign Policy," in Erik P. Hoffman and Frederic J. Fleron, Jr., eds., *The Conduct of Soviet Foreign Policy* (New York: Aldine Publishing Co., 1980), 8.

67. In most cases, when the Soviets speak of a peace treaty with Japan, they have in mind a peace treaty which excludes the territorial issue, which in their view has already been resolved. In general, however, even in the Soviet understanding, the peace treaty also deals with the territorial question, as rightly admitted by Brezhnev in his interview with Shōryū Hata, editor-in-chief of the *Asahi Shimbun* on 5 June 1977, when he stated: "There is no need to say that a peace treaty usually includes questions dealing with broad matters, including the border issue." *Pravda,* 7 June 1977.

68. Dal'nev, *Mezhdunarodnaia zhizn',* 52.

say, a legal document can serve as a useful lever to artificially build a "solid treaty basis" [*prochnaia dogovornaia osnova*][69] on which the road to further development of Soviet-Japan relations can be paved. Such a document could help "to bring the bilateral relations up to a higher level and render them stable."[70] N. Nikolaev, another Soviet specialist on Japanese relations, does not conceal his expectations that a treaty would serve a sort of creative function, claiming that "such a document would *create* the atmosphere of deep confidence necessary for the development of good business-like relations between these two countries."[71] (emphasis added)

Interestingly enough, the Soviet approach provides a marked contrast to that of the Japanese in terms of what ought to be done first to improve Soviet-Japanese relations. The Soviets clearly deem it necessary to secure a written document in order to build confidence, whereas the Japanese proceed in exactly the opposite way. In order to illustrate this marked contrast, it is worth citing part of the debate between Dimitrii Polianskii, then Soviet ambassador to Japan, and Nobutaka Shikanai, the president of *Sankei Shimbun*:

Polianskii:	Thus, we are proposing a conclusion of a treaty with Japan to develop friendly relations. Such a treaty can be a peace treaty, or a treaty of peace and friendship, or a treaty of non-aggression, or a treaty of non-use of the military weapons.
Shikanai:	In the light of world history, conclusion of a treaty does not necessarily mean that everything is then completed and solved. A treaty becomes meaningful only when it is accepted and observed by the people of both signatory nations. Accord-

ingly, we should first make efforts to build the national feeling on both sides in order to bring about good results.[72]

In any case, in a booklet particularly aimed at the Japanese audience, and thus safely taken as an authoritative Kremlin view on the matter, Dal'nev expresses why the Soviets need a *political* treaty: "If we two countries can conclude an appropriate *political* treaty, it can serve not only to stabilize all positive factors that we have achieved in Soviet-Japanese relations but to determine the basic orientation of peaceful and mutually beneficial development of long-term future relations between the two countries. A treaty of friendship and good-neighborliness, a draft of which was given by Andrei Gromyko to the Japanese side, will be a treaty of such *political* character."[73] (emphasis added) A different yet related reason for concluding a legal document is its potential propaganda role. Once a treaty is concluded between Japan and the Soviet Union, it would symbolize a major breakthrough out of the current impasse, thereby announcing the improvement in relations to the entire world.

Whatever function a legal document with Japan may be intended to serve, nobody can deny the fact that the Kremlin has recently been doing its utmost to sell the idea of such a treaty document. Brezhnev's

---

69. *Ibid.* N. Nikolaev, "Dobrososedstvo i sotrudnichestvo—v interesakh SSSR i iaponii," *Mezhdunarodnaia zhizn'* 1 (1978): 52; S. Modenov, "Tokio v farvatere politiki Vashingtona," *Mezhdunarodnaia zhizn'*, 5 (1981): 71; *Pravda*, 14 IV, 1982.

70. *Mezhdunarodnaia zhizn'*, 52.

71. Nikolaev, *Nekotorye problemy*, 52.

72. *Sankei Shimbun*, 3 January 1981.

73. V. Dal'nev, 68.

proposal for an Asian collective security system is obviously one of this series of attempts. The idea of establishing an Asian collective security system was first posited in 1969 by Brezhnev, who stated that "such a system is the best substitute for the existing military-political groupings."[74] Most Western observers interpreted the Soviet proposal as a military alliance aimed at isolating the PRC and undermining the Western position in Asia.[75] Faced with indifference, coolness, and even suspicion in Asia, Brezhnev in 1972 decided to revise his scheme by making an initially vague proposal more concrete through a set of normative principles. The principles on which the proposed collective security system would be founded were renunciation of the use of force, respect for sovereignty and inviolability of borders, non-intervention in internal affairs, and the broad development of economic and other cooperation on the basis of full equality and mutual advantage.[76] They are almost the same principles as those incorporated into the Helsinki Final Act of the CSCE, from which the idea of the Asian collective security system itself was derived. Japan, supposedly a principal target of a Soviet-sponsored collective security initiative,[77] ignored the Soviet proposal, mainly because of its anti-Chinese and military implications.[78] For Tokyo, an especially disturbing aspect of the Soviet scheme was that the principle calling for "respect for inviolability of national borders" would serve, as it in fact did in Europe, to consolidate Moscow's view of the territorial *status quo* and undermine Tokyo's claims to the northern islands.[79] Encountering rather cool responses among most Asian nations, the Kremlin in 1973 started to emphasize that its idea of collective security in Asia could not necessarily be realized overnight, but had to be approached gradually by accumulating a series of

selective bilateral treaty arrangements between the USSR and the various Asian states as building blocks for an eventual edifice of *collective* security embracing all of the states in the continent.[80]

It is quite accurate to regard Moscow's 1978 proposal of a treaty of good-neighborliness and cooperation as one of these bilateral treaty arrangements, as similar to the Soviet treaties of peace, friendship, and cooperation with Egypt, India, Iraq, Outer Mongolia, Afghanistan, and Iran. It is thus clear what kind of function the newly proposed treaty is expected to have for the Soviet Union: to serve the Soviet Union as an artificial lever to break its deadlock with Japan and to pave the way for new developments. This intention is

---

74. *Pravda*, 8 VI, 1969.
75. Victor Zorza, "Collective Security," *Survival* 11 (August 1969): 248; Peter Howard, "A System of Collective Security," *Mizan* 11 (July/August 1969): 199-201, 203; Hemem Ray, "Soviet Diplomacy in Asia, *Problems of Communism* (March-April 1970): 46; Ian Clark, "Collective Security in Asia," *The Round Table* 252 (October 1973): 477-478; Alexander O. Ghebhardt, "The Soviet System of Collective Security in Asia," *Asian Survey* 13 (December 1973): 1076; Arnold L. Horelick, "The Soviet Union's Asian Collective Security Proposal: A Club in Search of Members," *Pacific Affairs* 47 (Fall 1974): 269; Howard M. Hensel, "Asian Collective Security: The Soviet View," *Orbis* 19 (Winter 1976): 1564, 1579; Alfred Biegel, "Moscow's Concept for Collective Security in Asia," *Military Review* 57 (February 1977): 3, 7, 11.
76. *Pravda*, 21 III, 1972.
77. Ghebhardt, 1084.
78. For instance, Nobuhiko Ushiba, Japanese ambassador to the United States, was quoted as saying that "the Soviet proposal aims at encircling China, and it will not be easily accepted by the United States." *Asahi Shimbun* (evening edition) and *Mainichi Shimbun* (evening edition), 23 May 1972.
79. Ghebhardt, 1579; Horelick, 282; Biegel, 10.
80. Horelick, 274; Horelick, "Soviet Policy Dilemma in Asia," *Asian Survey* 17 (June 1977): 511.

clearly evident in the following statement by Yuri Vdovin, the Tokyo correspondent of *Pravda*: "The Soviet Union has in fact repeatedly demonstrated its preparedness to develop and deepen its relations with Japan. *A good basis* for this could become a treaty of good-neighborliness and cooperation... The conclusion of such a treaty would *elevate the relations* between the two countries *to a new level* and *open the perspectives for the further development* of broad relations in various fields."[81] (emphasis added) The Kremlin unilaterally and quite arbitrarily announced the drafting of a treaty in the spring of 1977,[82] just as Tokyo had finally decided to sign a peace treaty with Peking. This was well-timed from Moscow's point of view, for it gave the Soviets a tactical advantage: the Japanese were completely free to do with the Chinese whatever they wanted, but the Soviets would demand similar treatment on the grounds that the Japanese ought to treat their two neighbors with equal fairness. When Tokyo simply ignored the draft treaty proposed by the Soviets, the Kremlin was greatly disappointed and even infuriated. Expressing such feelings, an *Izvestiia* commentator, V. Kudriavtsev, wrote: "While clearing the way for a treaty with Peking, the Japanese ruling circles did not regard it necessary to discuss the draft of good-neighborliness and cooperation, recently proposed by the Soviet Union, even though the latter proposal would be much better in stabilizing Soviet-Japan relations and the basis of peace and security in the Far East."[83]

In contrast, the ultimate objective of Tokyo's policy toward Moscow can be summarized as aiming to improve Japanese-Soviet bilateral relations in a comprehensive way,[84] so that all issues would be covered and linked together. This basic policy orientation stems from a realization by Tokyo that it could not otherwise effectively counter the customary Soviet strategy of circumventing or even completely excluding some important issues in Soviet-Japanese relations, such as the territorial question, and arbitrarily linking together or cutting apart one issue from other. Tokyo is particularly careful not to play into the Soviet ploy of "picking a raisin out of the cake," by prematurely agreeing to start to negotiate with the Soviets relatively easy matters, with little hope of major long-term results. Tokyo's concerns can easily be understood and even justified by the nature of its past experiences. For instance, the Japanese government under Premier Ichiro Hotoyama agreed to normalize relations with the USSR under First Secretary Khrushchev in 1956 with the signing of a Soviet-Japanese joint declaration, which stipulates in Article 9 that "the USSR agrees to transfer to Japan the Habomai Islands and the island of Shikotan" upon conclusion of a formal peace treaty between the two countries.[85] A few years later in 1960, however, Tokyo discovered that the Soviet Union under the same leadership had negated the passage in the joint declaration concerning Soviet promises on the return of the two islands to Japan, unilaterally adding a new condition to the declaration that all U.S. troops depart from Japanese soil

---

81. *Pravda*, 19 IX, 1977.

82. *Izvestiia*, 23 II, 1978; *Pravda*, 24 II, 1978.

83. *Izvestiia*, 25 VI, 1978.

84. Of course, verbally the Soviets have also been saying that "the Soviet Union is making an effort toward the development of *all-round* [*vsestronnye*] mutually-beneficial relations with Japan." (emphasis added) A. Gromyko, "Programma mira v deistvii," *Kommunist* 14 (September 1975): 16.

85. Swearingen, 225; John J. Stephan, *The Kuril Islands: Russo-Japanese Frontier in the Pacific* (Oxford: Claredon Press, 1974), 247; Johō-bunka-kyoku, Gaimusho, *Warera-no Hoppo-ryōdo (Our Northern Territories)* (Tokyo: Gaimushō, March 1981), 46.

before the islands would be returned.[86] Later, without even mentioning the return of the two islands to Japan, the Soviet government under Brezhnev simply set the territorial question aside by bluntly saying that "the Soviet Union was no longer bound by its promise to return to Japan the two islands off Hokkaido as written into the 1956 Joint Declaration."[87] This Soviet announcement naturally led the Japanese to wonder how a unilateral statement by one party could retroactively make a certain portion of a legal document invalid.

The Tokyo government had a similar experience in the mid-1970s. Japanese Prime Minister Kakuei Tanaka signed a Japanese-Soviet joint communiqué in 1973 which stated: "Both sides confirm that the settlement of outstanding questions left over since World War II and the conclusion of a peace treaty would contribute to the establishment of good-neighborly relations."[88] Understanding that the northern territorial issue constituted nothing other than an "outstanding question left over since World War II," Tanaka agreed to exchange this for a clause in which the Japanese government pledged to extend a huge amount of Japanese bank credit and other forms of economic cooperation for the development of Siberia and the Far Eastern region of the USSR. Once again the Japanese were disappointed by the Soviets' subsequent actions. While not hesitating to accept Japanese support for its Siberian development project, the Soviets failed to show any interest whatsoever in discussing the territorial question with Japan, saying that the territorial issue is not regarded as one of "the outstanding questions left over since World War II." Writing in the major party organ, *Kommunist*, Soviet Foreign Minister Andrei A. Gromyko asserted in 1975 that the "Japanese demand for the so-called 'northern territories' is 'unfounded'."[89] What further amazed the Japanese is that the Soviets made another proposal of a similar kind. Immediately after unilaterally reinterpreting the above-cited portion of the Tanaka-Brezhnev joint communiqué in 1973, Nikolai Tikhonov, the Soviet prime minister, still had the nerve to make the following proposal:

> [For Japan] to assert that the Soviet Union has admitted the existence of a "territorial question" [in the 1973 Joint Communiqué] is to deliberately distort our position and mislead the Japanese public. In connection with the question of the treaty basis of Soviet-Japanese relations, I would like to recall our proposal to conclude a treaty of good-neighborliness and cooperation. This proposal remains on the table to this day.[90]

At last Japan seems to have learned that a "step-by-step" approach or, in Soviet terms, "let's do what we can first" approach for improving bilateral relations does not necessarily work for Japan, but on the contrary only benefits the Soviets, who are interested in picking up quick gains and ultimately not keeping their word. As a result, Tokyo appears to have decided, somewhat belatedly, that its best policy stance toward the Kremlin is a firm "all-or-nothing" position. As long as Moscow shows no interest in a comprehensive improvement of relations with Tokyo, Japan should not conclude even a minor agreement with the USSR. More specifically, so long as any Soviet proposal falls short of settling the northern islands question, the Japanese government has no incentive to come to terms on other subjects. If,

---

86. *Warera-no Hoppo-ryōdo*, 46.
87. *FBIS(SOV)*, 24 October 1979, c3.
88. *Pravda*, 10 X, 1973.
89. Gromyko, 16.
90. *Pravda* and *Izvestiia*, 17 II, 1982.

unfortunately, these conditions are not met by the Kremlin, the Tokyo government has decided that it should be content with maintaining the *status quo*. In the face of Soviet pressures for Japan to make a greater effort to improve the bilateral relationship, Tokyo seems ready to answer that "regrettably, this is normal for now and the foreseeable future."[91] Given the fact that it is now the USSR which needs improved relations more, Japan's readiness to open talks with the Soviet Union seems to have become its most important bargaining chip vis-à-vis the USSR. Thus, if Tokyo were to respond to the Soviet proposal, let alone take the initiative, it would almost automatically lose this bargaining leverage.[92] Acknowledging that "up until now Japanese diplomacy has made many mistakes in this regard," Ambassador Takashima explained to the Japanese public what he considers to be the best policy to pursue toward the Soviet Union: "If our side moves closer to the Soviets, then clearly from the outset the game will be lost for us. Therefore, wait until the Soviet Union comes to consider Japan important enough. In my opinion, this would be the best posture to assume." [93]

CBMs Agreement as a Political Instrument

Nearly all arms control or disarmament overtures combine a serious effort to reach some sort of an agreement with a propagandistic appeal to impress the public at home and abroad with its peace-oriented intentions.[94] In the case of Japan and the Soviet Union, CBMs are designed to function as a political instrument of diplomatic change directed at breaking a major impasse in relations. Moscow would benefit greatly from CBMs with Japan, both in symbolic terms and in a concrete political and economic sense. In this regard, the Soviet CBM proposal ought to be viewed as just another in a series of proposals which has included the Asian collective security system and the treaty of good-neighborliness.

CBMs in the Far East were first proposed by Leonid I. Brezhnev in his speech on 23 February 1981 at the 26th Party Congress, when the general secretary made it clear that "the Soviet Union would be prepared to conduct concrete talks on CBMs in the Far East with all interested countries."[95] Despite the fact that "Peking hastened to call our proposals propaganda," Konstantin U. Chernenko, Brezhnev's longtime protegé and once a prime candidate to succeed him, expressed the USSR's determination to stick to the proposal one month later — at the 111th anniversary celebration of Lenin's birth. In his initial overtures, Brezhnev clearly gave the impression that the USSR was interested in having a CBM arrangement in Asia on a collective basis. He invited "all interested countries" to discuss the proposal, particularly mentioning "the USSR, China, Japan" and even the United States, which has, in Brezhnev's words, "a military basis there."[97] It is, of course, hard to determine whether this was a reflection of Brezhnev's real intentions, simply rhetoric, or a sort of *ballon d'essai*, as was the

---

91. Swearingen, 89.

92. Drifte, 25.

93. *Nihon Keizai Shimbun,* 9 December 1982.

94. For an argument that almost all disarmament proposals and negotiations have propagandistic elements as an integral feature, see Joseph L. Nogee, "Propaganda and Negotiation: The Case of the Ten-Nation Disarmament Committee," *The Journal of Conflict Resolution* 7 (September 1963): 510-511; and John W. Spanier and Joseph L. Nogee, *The Politics of Disarmament: A Study in Soviet-American Gamemanship* (New York: Praeger, 1962), 32-36.

95. *XXVI s'ezd,* Vol. I, 46.

96. *Pravda* and *Izvestiia,* 23 IV, 1981.

97. *XXIV s'ezd,* Vol. I, 46.

case of his earlier Asian collective security proposal, which was first proposed on a multilateral basis but later recast in bilateral terms. In any event, Brezhnev's position shifted very rapidly on the application of his CBMs proposal from a collective to a bilateral scheme. This transition was signaled in the communiqué issued after the meeting in the Crimea in August 1981 between Brezhnev and the Mongolian party leader, Yumjaagiyn Tsedenbal, which stated: "The application of these [confidence-building] measures is possible on a collective basis, with the participation of all the interested sides." The document added that "It is also possible on a bilateral basis."[98] As expected, it soon became clear that, while the Soviets continue to claim that they are advocating an application of CBMs in the Far East on a collective basis, what they are really envisioning is obviously a conclusion of an agreement on CBMs on a bilateral basis, particularly with the PRC or Japan. The well-known Tashkent speech of 24 March 1982, in which Brezhnev made diplomatic overtures to Tokyo and Peking, evidently marked a clear step in that direction. Emphasizing that the proposed CBMs in the Far East did not necessarily imply the immediate collective involvement of all countries in the region, the CPSU general secretary stated that "progress along that path could also provide a good basis for a new bilateral start, for example, between the USSR and Japan,"[99] thus calling upon Japan to weigh the proposal more seriously. Vsevolod Ovchinnikov, a political commentator for *Pravda*, stated more articulately a month later, at the third Japan-USSR roundtable conference at Tokyo on April 20-22, that "the Soviets do not think that the establishment of CBMs will immediately have a collective character."[100] The fact that Moscow desperately needs CBMs or an appropriate substitute is sufficiently obvious from these repeated overtures, the most notable

of which was Brezhnev's reply letter to the group of Japanese writers protesting against nuclear weapons, which read: "We see no obstacle to beginning an exchange of opinions with Japan either within the framework of the proposal . . . on CBMs in the Far East or *in any other form (v liubykh drugikh formakh)* acceptable to both sides."[101] (emphasis added) As was stated at the very outset of this essay, Andropov has renewed proposals made by his predecessor with regard to CBMs, saying in general that all "peace proposals since the 26th Party Congress are still valid," and particularly mentioning the CBM proposal to Japan.[102]

Despite strenuous Soviet efforts, the Japanese reaction has been cold and decidedly negative. The Japanese government under Prime Minister Suzuki considered the proposal unacceptable, and so has the present government under Prime Minister Nakasone. On 29 April 1981 Japanese Ambassador to the Soviet Union Tōkichiro Uomoteo conveyed to Soviet Foreign Minister Gromyko a formal message, in which Suzuki noted that unless certain conditions were met by the Soviets, Japan could not discuss these proposals. This served as an official reply to the Soviet proposal advanced by Soviet Ambassador Dimitrii Polianskii to Japanese Foreign Minister Masayoshi Ito[103] on March 15 of the same

---

98. *Sovetskaia programma mira dlia 80-kh godov v deistvii: Materialy i dokumenty* (Moscow: Politizdat, 1982), 108.

99. *Pravda*, 25 III, 1982.

100. Ovchinnikov, "Sonichi-kyōryōku wa kyokutōni okeru heiwa no tame ni (The Soviet-Japanese Cooperation for Peace in the Far East," *Jiyū* 279 (July 1982): 59.

101. *Izvestiia*, 1 III, 1982; *Pravda*, 2 III, 1982. See also Nikolaev and Pavlov, 33.

102. *FBIS(SOV)*, 17 March 1981, c1.

103. For the Soviet message conveyed by Polianskii to Ito, see *FBIS(SOV)*, 17 March 1981, c1.

year. When Brezhnev repeated the Soviet proposal a year later at Tashkent, Suzuki, clearly enunciating the conditions to be met by the Soviet Union prior to any serious discussion, stated in the Diet on 26 March 1982: "We welcome in part the overtures made by General Secretary Brezhnev at Tashkent, for example, the part dealing with confidence-building in the Far East. Yet the Soviet Union needs to prove such intentions with its own deeds. That is to say, it must withdraw its nuclear weapons such as the SS-20s from the Far East, return the northern islands to Japan, and stop its military build-up of the islands. We cannot take the Soviet words literally, inasmuch as they are solely appealing verbally to us."[104]

Given the essentially modest goals of CBMs with respect to the exchange of information about the military activity of neighboring adversaries, the preconditions that Suzuki attached to the Soviet CBM proposal appear too demanding. However, it must be recalled that, although implementation of arms control and disarmament agreements are military in character, the negotiation and signing of them cannot completely escape political realities. The same reasoning should be applied to CBMs. After all, CBM talks, like any other arms control and disarmament talks, do not take place in a political vacuum.[105] They are conducted in the midst of an international political environment with specific historical elements. Each participating state pursues a variety of interests by mobilizing a variety of available means. It is thus natural to assume that CBM negotiations, like other arms control and disarmament talks, are used to pursue objectives other than those for which they were originally convened.[106] In short, CBMs should be viewed as an integral part of overall Soviet foreign policy.

Tokyo's negative response to the Soviet proposal on CBMs can probably only be understood in the historical context of the bilateral efforts by Japan and the Soviet Union to negotiate a treaty. Whatever arguments or excuses the Japanese government may be making, what really concerns Tokyo is nothing more than its suspicions that once it agreed to the Soviet proposal, it would lose any chance it may have had to press the Soviets to come to terms with the Japanese treaty proposal. Japan and the Soviet Union have each been promoting their respective treaties. Based on what was written into the two previously signed documents, including the Soviet-Japanese Joint Declaration of 1956 and the Japan-Soviet Joint Communiqué of 1973, Tokyo merely wants to extend previous lines of negotiations toward a peace treaty settling the territorial question. Moscow argues that the joint communiqué and declaration are important documents, while conveniently ignoring those parts of the documents which are unfavorable to the Soviet Union. Moscow further argues that since Japan and the USSR have been deadlocked in the peace treaty negotiations, the time has come for them to seriously discuss another type of arrangement. What the Soviets have been proposing is, as noted above, an Asian collective security treaty with Japan on a bilateral basis, or a Soviet-Japanese treaty of good-neighborliness and cooperation, or any other kind of legal document. Based on such an interim document, Moscow insists a peace treaty will be reached sometime in the future between the two countries. In 1967 Soviet Prime Minister Alexei N. Kosygin hinted to Japanese

---

104. *Nihon Keizai Shimbun*, 27 March 1982.
105. John Garnett, "Disarmament and Arms Control Since 1945," in Laurence Martin, ed., *Strategic Thought in the Nuclear Age* (Baltimore: The Johns Hopkins University Press, 1979), 216.
106. *Ibid.*

101

Foreign Minister Takeo Miki during the latter's visit to Moscow that "an interim document" between Moscow and Tokyo might be concluded on the grounds that neither side is currently willing to sign a peace treaty on terms acceptable to the other. In an interview with Shōryū Hata, the editor-in-chief of the *Ashai Shimbun* on 6 June 1977, Brezhnev stressed: "After all, the point is not the name but the content of the treaty...the important thing is to promote a bilateral relationship serving the objective of establishing genuinely good relations between our two countries."[107] Judging from past Soviet behavior, Tokyo knows well that should any one of the Soviet-proposed interim accords be agreed to, it will be the final one, thus precluding any chance to return to the right track. More specifically, what Tokyo fears is that once Moscow establishes the rapport it wants with Tokyo through CBMs, the need for a formal peace treaty will lose its urgency for the Soviet Union. This seems the real reason why Tokyo is so hesitant to discuss the Soviet proposal on CBMs.

Conclusion

The one thing that has become clear in the aforementioned discussion is that the "northern territories" form the crux of the problem around which nearly all questions in Soviet-Japanese relations revolve. It may not be an exaggeration to say that the future course of the bilateral relationship depends largely upon whether these two neighboring countries will find a way of settling this territorial issue. Serious discussion of this question would constitute the subject of another paper, and hence we must limit our treatment to a single aspect of the problem. We must attempt to answer the following basic question: Why are both the Japanese and Soviets so adamant in holding to their positions concerning a group of small islands at the expense of the overall relationship?

There are several explanations for Japan's insistent adherence to its position on the territorial issue. One reason is an irrational feeling of national pride and prestige. A majority of the Japanese public and hence all political parties support Japan's claim to the northern islands, on the self-righteous ground that the islands are nothing but "inherent" Japanese territories, which, as such, must be immediately returned to Japan. Another reason is that the Japanese are well aware of the fact that, by pressing its territorial demands vis-à-vis the Soviets, Japan does not lose much in practical terms. In other words, even if Japan surrendered its claim to the islands, from the Japanese perspective, it would not necessarily bring substantial benefits either. For instance, it is true that Japanese business is attracted to the idea of expanding trade and other economic intercourse with Soviet Union, particularly in light of the present economic slump. However, unlike in West Germany, where relatively small enterprises are engaging in trade with the USSR, in Japan it is comparatively large corporations that trade with the Soviet Union. This difference enables most of the Japanese economy to get by without having corporate relations with the Soviet Union. In addition, since the joint economic development of Siberia and the far eastern part of the USSR requires a huge amount of investment capital, Japanese business cannot go ahead without the relatively cheap credit provided by the Japan Export-Import Bank. These special circumstances help businessmen in Japan refrain, however reluctantly, from doing much

---

107. *Pravda*, 7 VI, 1977.

business with the USSR when they are persuaded that it would be against the national interest of Japan to do so. From a security perspective, it is also doubtful that Japan would benefit greatly by surrendering the islands once and for all to the Soviet Union. Some Japanese are even afraid that security might in fact be undermined by such a move. As the famous German legal philosopher, Rudolph von Jhering, warned in his book *The Struggle for Right:* "From the nation which allowed itself to be deprived of one square mile of territory by its neighbor, unpunished, the rest also would be taken, until nothing remained to it to call its own, and it had ceased to exist as a state; and such a nation would deserve no better fate."[108]

The intransigent Soviet attitude on the territorial issue with Japan is also often described as "one of the most puzzling facets of Soviet foreign policy, very imaginative, if not stupid."[109] Why is this then the case? The main reason seems to be that Moscow has not yet ascertained what benefits it could obtain from Tokyo in exchange for a return of the disputed islands. Should these islands be given back to Japan, Japanese national feeling toward the Soviet Union would surely improve, and yet nobody can predict for sure to what extent it would improve. Soviet political leaders are thus reluctant to take the chance. Soviet disinclination to take a risk for such an intangible and unreliable thing as Japanese national sentiment can in part be justified in the light of past Japanese behavior. The reversion of Okinawa was greatly appreciated by the Japanese but not to the extent that had been expected by some Americans. The Japanese appeared to take the U.S. action somewhat for granted. The great "China euphoria" and "Deng Xiaoping fever" following the signing of the Sino-Japanese Peace Treaty in 1978 turned out to be a very

short-lived phenomenon. Can economic benefits serve as an incentive for the Kremlin to give the islands to Japan? There is no doubt that at present the USSR under Andropov badly needs the Japanese credit and technology, as recently illustrated by the enthusiastic welcome given to the Japanese economic mission headed by Shigeo Nagano during its February 1983 Moscow visit. Thus, from an exclusively economic vantage point, it would not be impossible to predict, as some Western specialists on Soviet foreign policy including Seweryn Bialer[110] have done, that the new Soviet leadership will take a more flexible policy on the territorial issue. However, what these otherwise very shrewd observers of the Soviet conduct of foreign affairs and domestic politics neglect when it comes to Soviet behavior in the Far East is that economics is not the sole determinant of Soviet foreign policy.

Another important determinant is the military-strategic factor, which appears to be even more important than economic elements in the case of the issue of the northern islands. Historically, the geopolitical value of the four islands has been deemed quite large. Located north of Hokkaido, the islands could potentially affect the access of Soviet ships to the Pacific Ocean. Their strategic importance has been publicly affirmed by

---

108. Rudolf von Jhering, *Der Kampf um's Recht* (Berlin: Philo-Verlag and Buchhandlung, 1925), 29. For an English translation, see *The Struggle of Law,* translated by John J. Lalor (Chicago: Callaghan and Company, 1915), 27.

109. "An Air of Expectancy in Moscow," an interview with Seweryn Bialer, *Newsweek,* 11 October 1982, 60.

110. *Ibid.; The Christian Science Monitor,* 8 November 1982. For another optimistic view, see Jerry Hough, *Soviet Leadership in Transition* (Washington, D.C.: Brookings Institution, 1980), 67.

Joseph Stalin and Nikita S. Khrushchev.[111] Furthermore, the military-strategic significance of the Sea of Okhotsk has recently increased, largely due to the Soviet deployment of SLBMs which are capable of reaching the United States. In addition, external factors such as Soviet-American relations and Sino-Soviet relations play a great role in Soviet policy concerning the islands. Concessions to Japan might open a Pandora's box of claims by other countries on the USSR.

Thus, the question is whether the reversion of the northern islands to Japan will be worth the cost to the Soviet Union. Even if the answer to this question is positive, such a balance sheet of pros and cons does not automatically point to a policy decision for the Kremlin, since neither Soviet political leaders nor the Soviet public can be counted on to make political decisions based on rational calculations. Like their Japanese counterparts, they also have a strong sense of national pride and find it difficult to overcome the inertia of past policies. Therefore, unlike some Western observers, the author would be surprised to see the new Soviet leadership under Andropov improve relations with Japan by returning the northern islands in the foreseeable future. Recent remarks by top Soviet foreign policymakers seem only to reinforce this prediction. General Secretary Andropov reportedly said to Hans-Jochen Vogel, the West German Social Democratic leader, on 12 January 1983, that the Soviet government is now considering redeploying SS-20 medium-range missiles that exceed an agreed-upon quota for the European zone in Siberia, "in order to counter a new military base at Misawa in Japan."[112] What is relevant in the context of this article is the follow-up statement by Soviet Foreign Minister Gromyko made on 17 January to his West German counterpart, Hans-Dietrich Genscher. The Soviet minister said that his government would redeploy these missiles in Siberia, partly because "there exists no *agreement* and no negotiations on arms control are currently underway in that region."[113] (emphasis added) These statements by Soviet leaders indicate, among other things, a strong determination to pursue the objective of a treaty agreement with Japan, not through the process of negotiating all problems between the two countries—especially the territorial question—but rather through blackmail and intimidation. In this regard, one can safely conclude that the new Soviet leadership's Japan policy has so far been nothing but a continuation of Brezhnev's policy, as the Soviets themselves have publicly asserted.

---

111. See I.V. Stalin, *Sochineniia*, vol. 2 (1941-1945), by Robert H. McNeal (Stanford: The Hoover Institution on War, Revolution, and Peace, 1967), 213-215. For statements by Khrushchev, see *Pravda* and *Izvestia*, 20 IX, 1964; *Hokkaido Shimbun.* (evening edition) and *Asahi Shimbun* (evening edition), 15 July 1964. For similar remarks by First Deputy Premier Anastas Mikoyan during his visit to Japan in May 1964, see *Hokkaido Shimbun* (27 May 1964) and Young C. Kim, *Japanese-Soviet Relations: Interaction of Politics, Economics and National Security* (Beverly Hills: SAGE Publications, 1974), 46. A Soviet specialist on Soviet-Japanese relations also emphasizes the strategic importance of the region. L.N. Kurakov, *Vneshnaia politika i diplomatiia Iaponiia* (Moscow: Izdatel'stvo mezhdunarodnye otnosheniia, 1964), 298.

112. *Die Welt*, 17 January 1983; *Mainichi Shimbun* and *Yomiuri Shimbun* (evening edition), 18 January 1983; *The Washington Post*, 18 and 19 January 1983; *The Times*, 19 January 1983; *The Christian Science Monitor*, 21 January 1983.

113. *Die Welt*, 19 January 1983; *Mainichi Shimbun* and *Yomiuri Shimbun*, 19 January 1983.

Timothy J. Curran

THE POLITICS OF TRADE LIBERALIZATION IN JAPAN

On December 15, 1982 the United States House of Representatives passed by a wide margin a bill that would require automobiles sold in the United States to include a large percentage of American-made parts. This "local content" legislation, which the Senate did not have time to vote on, was one of the more visible signs of growing protectionism in the United States. Earlier the Congress had considered several "reciprocity" bills which would empower the president to retaliate against countries which did not open their markets to American products. To a great extent the recent upsurge in protectionist sentiment in Congress is a reaction to deteriorating U.S. trade relations with Japan. The U.S. trade deficit with Japan has been spiralling out of control in recent years, threatening to exceed $20 billion in 1982. In specific sectors, such as automobiles, semiconductors, and machine tools, Japanese imports into the United States have caused considerable distress among politically important constituencies. Perhaps more importantly, there is a widespread perception that the bilateral trade imbalance is largely caused by import barriers in Japan. American officials have specific complaints about Japanese trade barriers in agriculture, tobacco, financial services, and other areas, but they are uncertain about how to compel Japan to remove these remaining impediments to trade. According to one newspaper, American officials are becoming "exasperated" at the slow pace of talks aimed at opening the Japanese market.

It should be noted at the outset that the Japanese government has moved actively in recent years to open Japan's market. Senior politicians and administrative officials have demonstrated a new attitude toward foreign commerce and a new commitment to the principles of free trade and open markets. There is no doubt that there are areas of Japan's market that remain relatively closed. These areas are holdovers from Japan's previous protectionist policy, or more likely, the result of Japan's economic and bureaucratic history. Japan's remaining barriers to trade must be removed through negotiations, and the Japanese government has indicated it will approach such negotiations in a forthright and cooperative manner. The following essay is about the politics of trade liberalization in Japan; that is, about the obstacles the Japanese government has faced in opening its markets and the ways in which it has gone about overcoming those obstacles.

Obstacles to Free Trade in Japan

Some analysts have found the roots of Japan's reluctant approach to free trade in the nation's unique cultural traditions or historical experience. Specifically, Japan's apparent tendency toward "groupism" and its expansive system of hierarchical interpersonal relationships are thought to "place certain limits or restraints on the outward projection of relationships."[1] As a result

---

1. Robert Scalapino, "Perspectives on Modern Japanese Foreign Policy" in Scalapino, ed., *The Foreign Policy of Modern Japan* (Berkeley: University of California Press, 1977), 393.

of its difficulty in relating effectively with the outside world, Japan is seen as having remained somewhat isolated from the international community, reluctant or unable to open its markets to free intercourse with other nations.

Historical factors are also seen as impeding Japan's development of an open economy. In particular, some observers believe that Japan's experience as a "late developer," striving to catch up with the West and avoiding foreign domination, has made the theories of free trade and comparative advantage inappropriate for Japan's needs.[2] And although the circumstances of Japan's economy have changed drastically in the postwar years, the thinking of many Japanese policy-makers has not. As a result, many Japanese have continued to be hesitant about advocating completely free and open trade, even after the economy matured. As Hisao Kanamori suggests, "the power of protectionism in Japan may be said to be a result not only of economic factors but also the underdevelopment of social consciousness concerning the virtues of free competition in general."[3]

The historical development of Japan's economy has also produced institutions and systems which can impede trade. For example, a recent report prepared by the Office of the United States Trade Representative cited Japan's distribution system and pattern of industrial groupings as barriers to trade.[4] The distribution system, which relies on primary, secondary, and tertiary distributors, is difficult for foreigners to penetrate and adds considerably to the retail cost of imported products. Of course the system was not designed with this object in mind; indeed, many Japanese manufacturers have similar difficulties. One reason Sony has placed so much emphasis on foreign sales is that Matsushita, its chief rival in the electronics industry, dominates the domestic network of electronics distributors and retail outlets.[5] Similarly, the Japanese pattern of industrial groupings, or *keiretsu,* was not originated with the object of excluding foreigners from the market, although this is often the result.[6]

In its May 28, 1982 package of trade liberalization measures the Japanese government offered to take certain steps to improve foreign access to the distribution system and to monitor practices by Japanese industries that restrict competition. There are undoubtedly further actions that Japan could take, such as speeding the authorization of large-scale retail stores which facilitate the distribution of foreign products. However, because the distribution system and patterns of industrial organizations are deeply embedded in Japanese society, there is not much the Japanese government can do to change them in the short-run.

A second approach to the study of Japan's foreign economic policy focuses on interest group pluralism. According to this approach, Japanese trade policy does not so much reflect unique cultural or historical characteristics as the divergent pressures imposed on the Japanese government by various domestic interest groups. This approach has been used widely to explain

---

2. See Calleo and Rowland, *America and the World Political Economy* (Bloomington: Indiana University Press, 1973), 204-98.

3. Cited in Robert Ozaki, *The Control of Imports and Foreign Capital in Japan* (New York: Praeger Publishers, 1972), 59-60.

4. Office of the United States Trade Representative, *Japanese Barriers to U.S. Trade and Recent Japanese Government Trade Initiatives* (Washington: Government Printing Office, November 1982).

5. See *The Economist,* 20 February 1982.

6. See Edward Lincoln, *"Keiretsu,"* United States-Japan Trade Council, *Council Report,* No. 41, 31 October 1980.

the foreign trade policies of other countries as well, particularly those of the United States. Beginning with Schattschneider's famous study, for example, observers have seen U.S. foreign economic policy primarily as the handiwork of powerful interest groups such as manufacturers and farmers.[7] These groups are believed to have been able to pressure the U.S. federal government into taking actions favorable to their specific group and contrary to the interests of the nation as a whole. The reason, as Schattschneider and others have pointed out, is that interest groups vary in their ability to influence the government with small, well-organized groups often prevailing over larger, more diffuse organizations. As a result, narrow interest groups such as trade associations or specific farm groups are often able to gain protection for their industry even though they damage the interests of citizens at large and are opposed by large consumer movements.

Powerful interest groups have exerted a strong influence on Japan's postwar trade policy. In the early postwar years, when the Japanese government pursued a clearly protectionist policy of vigorously pushing exports and severely limiting imports, the influence of Japan's business community could be clearly seen. Major industrial sectors such as automobiles, steel, petrochemicals, and electronics pressured the Japanese government to restrict imports. For a variety of reasons the government was willing to acquiesce; the ruling Liberal Democratic Party (LDP), because it was heavily dependent on big business for financial support, and the Japanese bureaucracy, because protection was part of its overall plan for industrial development. As a well-known Japanese economist noted in a recent book, the attitude of the Japanese government towards trade policy during much of the postwar period was that "liberaliza-

tion should not be authorized until genuine international competitiveness had been achieved."[8]

In the late 1960s many Japanese economists and foreign observers began to call for accelerated trade liberalization. Despite the improvement in the economy, however, the Japanese government remained slow to open its markets. A major reason for the hesitancy with regard to free trade was that the Japanese government, particularly the LDP, was vulnerable to pressure from a wide variety of interest groups. As one analyst notes, "The conservative party's many constituencies were sprawled across the country's economic and social landscape, their interests invariably different from one another."[9] Thus, when pressure mounted from domestic and international sources in the late 1960s for greater liberalization, "there was somebody to object to every action: this industry was not competitive, the state of the balance of payments was still in doubt, the giant multinationals threatened to swallow up Japan's industries."[10]

By the late 1960s and early 1970s the international competitive position of Japan's major industries had strengthened considerably, and as a result the business community relaxed its attitude toward trade liberalization. Indeed, by the early 1970s big business as a whole

---

7. See E. E. Schattschneider, *Politics, Pressures and the Tariff* (Englewood Cliffs: Prentice-Hall, 1935) and Robert Pastor, *Congress and the Politics of U.S. Foreign Economic Policy* (Berkeley: University of California Press, 1980).

8. Takafusa Nakamura, *The Postwar Japanese Economy* (Tokyo: University of Tokyo Press, 1982), 21.

9. Philip Trezise, "Politics, Government and Economic Growth" in Hugh Patrick and Henry Rosovsky, eds., *Asia's New Giant* (Washington: Brookings Institution, 1976), 776.

10. Philip Trezise, "Japan" in Wilfred Kohl, ed., *Foreign Economic Policies of Industrial States* (Lexington, Mass.: D. C. Heath Co., 1976), 155.

became a strong supporter of free trade. Writing in 1972, an American economist noted an "emerging consensus in favor of liberal trade policies" among Japanese business executives.[11] As business attitudes changed, Japanese tariffs and other trade barriers began to decline. For example, in 1961 Japan's tariff council endorsed a policy which would result in new tariffs for raw materials and products which did not compete with Japanese goods, and high tariffs for manufactured goods. Beginning in the mid-1960s, however, tariff protection in Japan was significantly reduced. During the Kennedy Round (1963-67) Japan reduced tariffs on 2,147 products.[12] In 1971 the tariff council recommended broad tariff liberalization and in 1972 the Japanese government unilaterally cut tariffs by 20 percent on an across-the-board basis. This process was accelerated during the Tokyo Round (1973-79). As a result Japan will have the lowest tariff structure of any industrial nation by the end of the phase-in period. The same pattern of broad liberalization can be seen in the area of quotas. In 1962 Japan applied import quotas to 473 items, covering a broad variety of industrial and agricultural imports. By 1971 the number of restricted items had been reduced to 40, and in 1975 the number was further lowered to 27, including 5 industrial items (especially leather goods) and 22 agricultural items.[13]

Despite Japan's progress in reducing industrial tariffs and quotas, agriculture remains a heavily protected sector of the economy. The government's desire to protect agriculture derives in part from policy concerns, such as the goal of increasing national food self-sufficiency. However, it is largely because of pressure from Japan's farmers that the government has been unable and unwilling to completely liberalize Japanese agriculture.

The political power and influence of Japan's agricultural sector is derived from a number of factors, two of which are of major importance. First, the ruling Liberal Democratic Party is heavily dependent on the rural vote for staying in power. The second reason for agriculture's political clout is the fact that Japanese farmers are extremely well organized in a system of agricultural cooperatives through which they are able to bring enormous pressure to bear on the Japanese government to resist expanding agricultural imports.

The LDP's reliance on the farm vote has changed in recent years. In the early years after the party's formation in 1955, the LDP was solidly a rural party. In 1960, for example, 68 percent of the party's support came from farmers and the self-employed (43 percent from the farmers and 25 percent from merchants and self-employed), while only 28 percent of its support came from white- and blue-collar workers. In 1980, however, white- and blue-collar workers made up 52 percent of the party's support while farmers accounted for only 19 percent and the self-employed for 24 percent. Thus, as one recent study of the LDP concluded, "the LDP has been able to shift its base of support away from the rural electorate (which still gives it overwhelming support but accounts for a smaller portion of the electorate than in the 1950s) and to the new urban electorate."[14]

---

11. Gary Saxonhouse, "A Review of Recent U.S.-Japan Economic Relations," *Asian Survey*, September 1972, 741.

12. For background see Timothy Curran, "Japanese Foreign Economic Policymaking: A Case Study of Japan in the Kennedy Round," East Asian Institute Certificate essay, Columbia University, 1977.

13. See Japan Economic Institute, *Japan Import Barriers: An Analysis of Divergent Bilateral Views,* Washington, 1982.

14. Gerald Curtis, "Japanese Security Policies," *Foreign Affairs* 59 (Spring 1981): 869.

Nevertheless, despite this shift in its support base, the LDP is still heavily dependent on the countryside. One reason is that seats in the national Diet were not reapportioned during the 1960s and early 1970s even though there was a massive shift of population out of the rural areas. The result was that the dwindling rural population continued to elect the same number of representatives, thus increasing the electoral power of each individual rural voter. Since the rural areas remain strongly behind the LDP, this malapportionment was a boon to the conservatives. Through this system, the LDP has been able to capture more seats in the national Diet than their share of the total vote warrants. For example, in 1972 the LDP gained control of 55.2 percent of the seats in the lower house with 46.8 percent of the votes. And in 1976, even though the LDP's percentage of total votes declined to 41.8 percent, it still managed to capture 48.7 percent of the seats.[15]

Another reason the conservative party depends on rural areas is that many LDP Dietmen still hail from rural and semi-urban election districts. In 1972, for example, with a total LDP strength of 271 seats in the lower house of the Diet, 174 of the successful LDP candidates (64 percent of the party's total) were elected from rural or semiurban districts. In 1976, when the party's strength in the Diet declined to 249 members, 62 percent were elected from these rural or semiurban districts. Thus in recent years, well over half of the LDP members of the lower house of the Diet had sizable numbers of farmers in their districts.

A third reason why the farmers of Japan are able to exercise considerable influence over the LDP despite their declining share of total party support is that the farmers are effectively organized by Nōkyō, the Agricultural Cooperative Association.[16] Nōkyō is important in political terms because it represents virtually every farmer in Japan. More importantly, however, the agricultural cooperatives gain political clout because of the organizational support they provide to individual politicians.

It is well known that the LDP has a weak organizational base at the rural level.[17] As a result, individual LDP candidates cannot rely on the party organization to get out the vote. Instead, each candidate tries to develop his own local organization based on existing groups such as local merchants and professional associations. The agricultural cooperatives play an important role in this process; indeed, it is not uncommon to find the head of a rural cooperative association serving simultaneously in the campaign organization of an LDP candidate. During the course of a politician's career, intimate ties develop with local farmers and especially with Nōkyō officials. As a result, when the cooperative leaders pressure the LDP to resist agricultural liberalization, they confront the government not as faceless voters but as political intimates upon whom many in the LDP depend for survival.

Resistance to trade liberalization in Japan has also been found within the bureaucracy. There are both procedural and substantive aspects of bureaucratic

---

15. Michael Blaker, "Conservatives in Crisis" in Herbert Passin, ed., *A Season of Voting* (Washington: American Enterprise Institute, 1979), 34.

16. For background, see Suda Yuji, *Nōkyō* (Tokyo: Kyōikusha, 1978); and Haruhiro Fukui, "The Japanese Farmer and Politics" in Isaiah Frank, *The Japanese Economy in International Perspective* (Baltimore: Johns Hopkins University Press, 1975).

17. See Gerald Curtis, *Election Campaigning Japanese Style* (New York: Columbia University Press, 1971) and James Foster, "Ghost-Hunting: Local Party Organization in Japan," *Asian Survey*, September 1982.

resistance to trade liberalization. Japan's bureaucracy plays a more central role in national decision making, a function of Japan's parliamentary system of government, the relative weakness of the Japanese Diet, and the historical necessity of a strong executive voice in national policy-making. An important feature of bureaucratic policy-making in the postwar period has been the intense rivalry between the various ministries. On issues of trade and foreign economic policy during the 1960s and early 1970s, for example, the Ministries of Foreign Affairs and Finance often fought a pitched battle against the Ministry of International Trade and Industry (MITI). In more recent years, the position of the various ministries has changed. MITI is now a strong internationalist, for example, but the rivalry and intense sense of sectionalism which characterized inter-ministry relations remains the same.[18]

Decision making among the different ministries is based on the Japanese system of consensus, or what one Japanese scholar has labeled "the unanimity rule" — the need for complete consensus among all officials concerned with a problem before a decision can be made.[19] On broad trade issues, which usually cut across ministerial boundaries, the need for consensus permits a recalcitrant ministry to block any decision at all. During a series of trade negotiations with the United States in late 1977, for example, Japan's ability to implement broad trade liberalizing measures was hampered by the opposition of the Ministry of Agriculture. More recently, several of the trade liberalization packages which Japan decided upon during 1981 and 1982 were either delayed or significantly diluted because of opposition from one or another section of the bureaucracy.

In addition, Japan's ability to pursue a coherent strategy in a multilateral trade negotiation such as the Tokyo Round or to implement broad trade liberalization measures is hampered by the absence of a bureaucratic or political institution capable of overcoming the divisions among the different ministries. In the United States, the problems caused by bureaucratic conflict are sometimes solved through the coordinating role played by officials in the White House or the National Security Council.[20] In Japan, however, as one scholar has noted, "The absence of a single leadership center in the bureaucracy compounds the problem of decision making and often contributes to immobilism."[21]

There is also important substantive resistance to trade liberalization. As noted, MITI resisted all attempts by the Foreign Ministry for trade liberalization during the 1960s because of the Trade Ministry's fears about the weakness of Japanese industry. During the Kennedy Round of trade negotiations, MITI officials tenaciously defended Japan's high tariff structure and tried to make exceptions of a wide variety of products such as automobiles, petrochemicals, machines, and computers in order to exempt them from across-the-board tariff cuts. In addition to maintaining a high wall of tariff protection, MITI has tried to block foreign investment in Japan. In the late 1960s, for example, when American automobile companies expressed interest in investing in Japan,

---

18. See Chalmers Johnson, *MITI and the Japanese Miracle* (Stanford: Stanford University Press, 1982).

19. Haruhiro Fukui, "The GATT Tokyo Round: The Bureaucratic Politics of Multilateral Diplomacy" in Michael Blaker, ed., *The Politics of Trade* (New York: Columbia University's East Asian Institute, 1978), 147.

20. The view that the United States faces equally difficult problems of coordination is expressed in I.M. Destler, *Making Foreign Economic Policy* (Washington: Brookings Institution, 1980), especially Chapter 13.

21. Haruhiro Fukui, *The GATT Tokyo Round*, 142.

MITI "mobilized" its old-boy network throughout the auto industry to prevent Japanese companies from entering into joint ventures.[22] When Mitsubishi Motors defied MITI's guidance by hooking up with Chrysler in 1969, senior MITI officials were stunned.

The Mitsubishi-Chrysler deal was only one of several events at the turn of the decade which shocked MITI officials and caused a reevaluation of the ministry's policy. Other important spurs were the "Nixon shocks" of 1971 that led to a revaluation of the Japanese yen, the bitter negotiations over Japanese textile exports to the United States that lasted from 1969 to 1971, and the general increase in protectionist and anti-Japanese sentiments in the United States. In addition, by the turn of the decade, the industries which MITI had worked so hard to protect and nurture, such as automobiles, steel, and petrochemicals, had reached a high level of international competitiveness. The result was a gradual easing of MITI's attitude toward trade and capital liberalization. By the end of the 1970s, MITI had become one of the champions of free trade, in part to stem the tide of protectionism abroad.

Although MITI's attitude toward trade affairs has changed, other ministries and government agencies have emerged as obstacles to free trade in Japan. In part the emergence of these new ministries is the result of the shifting focus of international trade negotiations. With the success of the Kennedy Round in reducing industrial tariffs as a major impediment to international commerce, the attention of economic officials shifted to other, as yet untouched trade barriers. Especially during the Tokyo Round, quotas in the agricultural sector and other non-tariff barriers such as government procurement practices and standards and testing procedures became the focus of trade negotiations. As a result of this shift in focus, ministries and other government agencies in Japan which had not been involved in the trade liberalization debate became the center of controversy. The dispute over Japanese restrictions on beef and orange imports which occurred during 1977-78 (and again in 1982) centered on the Ministry of Agriculture. Negotiations on a government procurement code during the Tokyo Round turned attention on Nippon Telephone and Telegraph Company, a Japanese public corporation. Tension over Japan's customs valuation procedures and standard-setting processes brought the Ministry of Health and Welfare into the limelight.

Bureaucratic officials in these latter ministries have been more isolated from international affairs than their counterparts in MITI and the Ministry of Finance, who are thoroughly familiar with international economic institutions. For example, officials in the Ministry of Health were surprised when in 1981 and 1982, world attention focused on their practices in setting standards for pharmaceutical products. Even though Japan had signed a code of standards during the Tokyo Round, many in the Ministry of Health seem to have believed that the new standards setting procedures were the business of the Foreign Ministry, which had negotiated the code, and did not concern the Ministry of Health. In the case of the Ministry of Agriculture, officials see their duty as protecting Japan's uncompetitive farmers. In addition to the desire to protect uncompetitive sectors of the economy, more parochial interests sometimes motivate bureaucratic officials in trade negotiations. For example, during the negotiations over a government procurement code during the Tokyo Round, American officials pressed

---

22. Chalmers Johnson, 286.

for the opening of Japan's government-owned Nippon Telephone and Telegraph. Until then a small group of domestic suppliers, known as the "NTT family," had almost exclusive control over NTT's $3 billion in annual equipment procurements. NTT officials resisted opening these procurement contracts to foreign bidders, partly out of a desire to preserve post-retirement jobs. When NTT officials, who are government employees, retire at the relatively early age of fifty-five, many find good jobs in the "NTT family" of suppliers. NTT officials were also legitimately nervous about applying a rigid international code to the sensitive process of telecommunications equipment procurement.

In summary, Japan's progress toward trade liberalization has been hampered by cultural and historical factors, interest-group pressure, and bureaucratic inertia and resistance. These factors can explain Japan's slow approach to liberalization during the late 1960s and early 1970s, when many both inside and outside Japan thought the nation's economy was strong enough to implement considerable liberalizing reforms. During the Tokyo Round as well, Japan's participation sometimes was restricted by domestic problems, although in general Japan played a positive role in the multi-lateral negotiations. And even though Japan has carried out a series of unilateral trade liberalization measures in the early 1980s, full liberalization of the agriculture sector, standards and testing procedures, and tobacco distribution will be difficult to achieve.

And yet, despite these obstacles Japan has made major progress in the trade field over the last decade. As noted, tariffs have been reduced so much that they will soon be the lowest in the world. Quotas have been virtually eliminated and major Japanese government initiatives have significantly liberalized Japan's customs valuation procedures, banking regulations, foreign investment rules, and standard-setting practices. In carrying out these various measures over the past several years, the Japanese government has been subject to many of the difficulties cited above: strong pressure for protection by interest groups, intense disagreements among the bureaucracies, and a historically-rooted aversion to taking the lead in international affairs. Nevertheless, in spite of these problems, the government of Japan has been able to achieve a considerable degree of trade liberalization by calming the fears of interest groups, settling the squabbles of the bureaucrats, and overcoming its aversion to the international spotlight. The Japanese government has moved with difficulty in the area of trade liberalization, but in the end it has made major progress in opening its markets.

Overcoming Obstacles to Free Trade

Three sets of factors can help explain Japan's success in overcoming domestic opposition to trade liberalization. The first is international pressure, particularly American pressure for greater access to specific sectors of Japan's economy. Domestic political leadership has been another crucial factor enabling the Japanese government to cope with the varying opponents to trade liberalization. Finally, the effectiveness of issue networks linking the political leaders, the bureaucracy, and domestic interest groups has been an important factor determining the course of policy implementation and the outcome of trade negotiations.

---

23. See Timothy Curran, "Politics and High Technology: The Case of NTT" in I. M. Destler and Hideo Sato, eds., *Coping with U.S.-Japanese Economic Conflicts* (Lexington, Mass.: Lexington Books, 1982).

International pressure is an important factor in the policymaking processes of many countries. When opinion within a country is split on an important issue and significant bodies oppose a particular policy or action, it is often easier for the government to act in response to an external threat or pressure. In the United States a recent example of the usefulness of external pressure can be seen in the case of energy policy. Despite the clear imperative of fashioning an energy policy in the aftermath of the 1973 oil crisis, the government vacillated until forced into action by a new crisis in 1979.

International pressure has played a particularly important role in the policymaking process of Japan. Beginning with Commodore Perry's "Black Ships," which forced a reluctant Tokugawa government to open Japan to the West, foreign pressure has been useful in enabling the Japanese government to overcome domestic resistance to change. Resistance to change comes from many sources, including the previously mentioned cultural and historical inhibitions, interest-group pressure, and bureaucratic rivalries. Foreign pressure is often needed to overcome domestic inhibitions of this sort. As the authors of *Managing an Alliance* note, "The stress on consensus in Japan can result in inaction, in stalemate. But if an outside force brings a change in the situation that all Japanese must contend with, a new policy can sometimes be put across domestically as a means of coping with a new outside challenge."[24] An example of the effectiveness of outside pressure in forcing a difficult policy change in Japan was the first so-called Nixon shock—the suspension of U.S. dollar convertibility and the imposition of a 10 percent surcharge on all imports—which helped bring about the revaluation of the Japanese yen. This policy change had been resisted by the business community and parts of the bureaucracy until American pressure forced the Japanese government to act.[25]

Over the past decade international pressure for greater access to the Japanese market has increased substantially, particularly from the United States. During the late 1960s the United States pressed for greater access to Japan's automobile market. In the early 1970s the focus shifted to monetary affairs, as the United States urged Japan to revalue the yen. By the mid-70s the United States was pushing for greater access to Japan's high technology market, and during the latter stages of the Tokyo Round, American officials pushed for the liberalization of Japan's remaining agricultural quotas and government procurement contracts. During 1981 and 1982 attention continued to focus on agricultural problems and important non-tariff barriers. In addition, European countries and several of Japan's Asian neighbors, as well, have recently begun to demand greater trade liberalization.

Generally speaking, international pressure has succeeded in forcing Japan to adopt important trade liberalizing measures; at least it has contributed to the steady opening of the Japanese market as noted earlier. However, foreign pressure is often applied in the wrong way, thus achieving less than maximum liberalization or causing a counterproductive backlash in Japan. For example, American demands are often too vague— calling on Japan simply to do something to open its market and ease trade frictions. Recently a senior U.S.

---

24. I. M. Destler et al., *Managing an Alliance* (Washington: Brookings Institution, 1976), 140.

25. See Robert Angel, "U.S.-Japan Economic Relations: Lessons from the 1971 Yen Revaluation Crisis," paper presented to the University Seminar on Modern Japan, Columbia University, 14 April 1978.

trade official stated that the United States intended to get tough with Japan, but exactly what the Japanese should do remained unclear. "We are waiting for Japan to take broad, far-reaching measures that will ensure long-term open access to the Japanese market," the official stated, "but we have no specific price in mind for trade peace."[26] Vague and unspecified pressure of this kind is not useful because it places the Japanese government in the position of having to decide which domestic interest groups will suffer.

The problems created for the Japanese government by the lack of specificity in foreign demands were seen in the early stages of negotiations to open Japan's telephone monopoly, Nippon Telephone and Telegraph (NTT). The NTT negotiations began during the Tokyo Round as part of the attempt to devise a multi-lateral code on government procurement; that is, a set of rules to ensure that foreign firms could bid on GATT member governments' procurement contracts. Since NTT is a part of the Japanese government, the United States wanted the telephone monopoly's nearly $3 billion in annual procurements included under the new rules. However, in the early stages of the negotiations, lasting throughout 1978 until early 1979, the United States never specified that it wanted NTT under the code. Instead, it requested only that the amount of government contracts Japan placed under the code be proportionally equal to the amount the United States was willing to place under the code. Later in the talks, after NTT had been identified as the object of American interest, U.S. officials would not specify which NTT contracts should be opened. The lack of specific demands made it extremely difficult for Japanese government officials to persuade NTT's managers to open the monopoly's procurement system. Although NTT is a public corporation, it is relatively isolated from central government control. Without a direct request from the United States for NTT's inclusion under the code, the telephone company was able to resist attempts to include it.

Related to the problem of too little specificity in foreign pressure is the tendency of foreign governments to employ highly visible and overpowering pressure to force trade concessions from Japan. Frequently, these governments resort to more overt forms of pressure when initial requests for Japanese action are not met. For example, in late 1977, when U.S.-Japan economic relations deteriorated as a result of the swelling Japanese trade surplus with the United States, American officials sent a high-level mission to Tokyo requesting Japanese action to help reduce the bilateral imbalance. There were several actions the Japanese government could take, including lowering industrial tariffs, expanding agricultural quotas, and stimulating the domestic economy, but each of these measures was opposed by various domestic interest groups. As a result, Japan took no action in response to the American requests, and consequentially frustration and anger in the United States grew. Two months later, in November, the United States sent another high-level mission to Tokyo, but this time the demands were quite specific, especially concerning beef and citrus liberalization and demands for increased Japanese economic growth. A deadline was set: If Japanese action was not forthcoming by January serious consequences would follow. A furor ensued in Tokyo—and eventually Japanese concessions

---

26. *New York Times,* 17 January 1982.

were forthcoming—but at the expense of bitter feelings and a sense of outrage at American strong-arm tactics.[27]

If the only cost of highly visible pressure tactics was bruised feelings, they might be worth the ensuing gains in trade liberalization. Often, however, strong pressure tactics put Japanese leaders in an awkward political spot and limit the ability of the Japanese government to carry out liberalization policies. During the NTT negotiations the United States linked demands for access to NTT high technology contracts to an upcoming bilateral summit meeting between Prime Minister Masagoshi Ohira and President Jimmy Carter scheduled for May 1979: If the Japanese did not make the necessary concessions the summit meeting might collapse. This strategy backfired, however. Bilateral summit meetings are politically important events in Japan, and if Ohira had made painful concessions on the eve of the meeting it would have opened him to charges of capitulation. With his political career thus in danger Ohira refused the American demands. Fortunately, a last-minute withdrawal of U.S demands and a complex agreement to continue the talks following the bilateral meeting allowed the summit to proceed undisturbed.

The problem with U.S. pressure tactics in the NTT case is that the force of American pressure was targeted on the wrong people. Japan's prime minister would have suffered from a failed summit meeting, but this threat had little meaning for those forces actually opposing Japanese concessions, especially NTT itself and, more importantly, the domestic telecommunications firms which supplied NTT and which benefited from its closed procurement system. The agreement that was reached on the eve of the summit talks changed this calculus by making continued Japanese access to the U.S. government market for telecommunications dependent on greater American access to NTT. This gave Japaenese companies an incentive to cooperate, and in the eighteen months of talks which followed the pre-summit agreement a system was devised which allowed American companies to bid on virtually all of NTT's $3 billion in annual procurements. This low-key, well-targeted type of pressure took a good deal of time, but in the end it produced a settlement far better than that which might have been achieved by directly threatening the prime minister.

A second example of the effective use of pressure can be seen in the negotiations over access to Japan's beef and citrus market during 1978.[28] During the course of these year-long talks, the United States clearly specified what it wanted, and it avoided confrontational and inflammatory tactics designed to embarrass the Japanese. Indeed, American negotiators went out of their way to keep the talks on a low-key basis. After a series of negotiations in Washington between the chief American negotiator, Robert Strauss, and Japan's minister of agriculture, Ichiro Nakagawa, broke down in September 1978, for example, tensions rose and it appeared Nakagawa would be criticized upon his return to Japan. In order to set the stage for follow-up talks, Strauss visited Nakagawa just before the latter's departure. Strauss reiterated American demands for beef and citrus liberalization, but he also expressed his feeling that a

---

27.   See I.M. Destler, "United States-Japanese Relations and the American Trade Initiative of 1977: Was This Trip Necessary?" in William Barnds, ed., *Japan and the United States: Challenges and Opportunities* (New York: New York University Press, 1978).

28.   See Hideo Sato and Timothy Curran, "Agricultural Trade: The Case of Beef and Citrus" in Destler and Sato, eds., *Coping with U.S.-Japanese Economic Conflicts.*

settlement was near, and he thanked Nakagawa for his efforts. Strauss's attempt to avoid an awkward break-off of the negotiation process was appreciated by the Japanese, and it set a constructive tone for the talks to follow. As one Japanese official commented, Strauss's gesture "was very Oriental."[29]

Throughout the agricultural negotiations the United States made specific demands, avoided confrontational tactics, and allowed sufficient time for Japanese officials to build support for concessions among the nation's farmers and rural politicians. Although the American goal of total liberalization of beef and orange imports was not achieved, Japan offered a substantial enlargement of the import quotas for these items. The quota for high quality beef was raised from the 1977 level of 6,800 metric tons to 30,000 metric tons by 1983; the limit on fresh orange imports went from 15,000 metric tons in 1977 to 82,000 in 1983. Moreover, these concessions were obtained from Japan without damaging the electoral prospects of the conservative Japanese government.

Another example of steady, low-key pressure yielding substantial results can be found in the area of Japanese customs procedures. For years American exporters have complained about Japan's customs procedures, especially overzealous customs officials, excessive documentation requirements, lengthy delays, and the absence of an appeals mechanism.[30] During a series of discussions with their Japanese counterparts throughout 1980 and 1981, American trade officials explained in detail the problems faced by American exporters, and they urged Japanese action. In response, Japan announced in January 1982 a package of proposals to simplify Japanese customs procedures. According to a U.S. government report, the Japanese measures "removed the most serious problems" in the customs area.[31]

The second factor contributing to Japan's success with trade liberalization was governmental leadership, which consists of political leadership and bureaucratic support. Key questions concerning this factor involve the nature of effective leadership in Japan, the motives of a political leader in deciding to get involved in an issue, and the determinants of bureaucratic support.

Some analysts have doubted the importance of political leadership in Japan's policy-making process. Chalmers Johnson, for instance, writes that "policy of all kinds in Japan has been made almost exclusively by the bureaucracy."[32] However, it is clear that in certain cases the absence of political leadership has had a detrimental effect on Japan's ability to make and implement policy. In the textile negotiations, for example, despite enormous American pressures on Japan to restrain its textile exports and a serious deterioration of bilateral relations, Japan was unable to settle the issue. Although Prime Minister Sato personally favored some form of textile restraint, he took little action to facilitate a consensus in favor of such action among the bureaucracy or various domestic interest groups. "Sato's lack of decisive leadership," one analyst has written, "was among the most crucial factors making the textile wrangle of 1969-71 . . . an especially unhappy event."[33]

More recently, in the early stages of the Tokyo Round the absence of effective leadership prevented Japan

---

29. *Washington Post,* 9 September 1972.
30. See Japan Economic Institute, "Japan's Import Barriers," 11-13.
31. Office of the United States Trade Representative, "Japanese Barriers to U.S. Trade," 31.
32. Chalmers Johnson, "MITI and Japanese International Economic Policy" in Scalapino, ed., *The Foreign Policy of Modern Japan.* (Berkeley: University of California Press, 1977), 245.
33. Akio Watanabe, "Foreign Economic Policymaking, Japanese Style," *International Affairs,* January 1978, 85.

from playing a more active role in the trade negotiations, in spite of the fact that important elements of the bureaucracy favored increased liberalization. A Japanese scholar who studied this period concluded that "the lack of political leadership makes it inevitable that those issues too controversial for the bureaucrats to settle among themselves would be left to fester and complicate the decision process."[34] One of the things that made Japan's performance in the latter stages of the Tokyo Round different from both the earlier stages and the previous textile dispute was the exercise of effective leadership by the prime minister and several important cabinet ministers.

What constitutes effective political leadership in Japan? After comparing the policy-making processes in Japan and the United States, some analysts have decided that a more American style of leadership would be appropriate in Japan. For example, one scholar writes that Japanese leaders should "intervene more vigorously" in the policy-making process.[35] Another observer, who finds American leadership characterized by "aggressiveness" and "innovation," feels that these qualities could be usefully adapted to Japan.[36] In short, the Japanese leader should be more forceful by aggressively taking charge of an issue and by intervening in the bureaucracy to see that his decisions are carried out. The problem in adapting this American-type leadership to Japan is that the American pattern springs from a unique set of institutional factors. America's distinctive style is presented in a comparative study of the policy-making structures in the United States and five European countries by the political scientist James Sundquist:

> Because the institutional structure of policy-making in the United States is more complex and pluralized than those of the other industrial democracies in the Atlantic community, because the policy-making circle is broader and more amateur and less disciplined, public participation more intense, and points of potential veto of policy innovation more numerous, and because political parties are weaker integrating mechanisms, *a higher degree of national consensus and a more intense commitment of political leadership are necessary before new departures can be developed and approved* and a narrower range of innovation can be successfully attempted at any one time.[37]

Japan, with its emphasis on consensual decision-making, its efficient and politically insulated bureaucracy, and its disciplined political parties, requires a different style of leadership from that found in the United States. In the words of one analyst, "A Japanese leader must be able to put the right man in the right place and then let him have free play without destroying harmonious and efficient teamwork. In other words, he is expected to be an educator . . . and manager rather than a decision maker and ruler."[38] In the case of Japan's recent experience with trade liberalization, it has been the emphasis on good "management" rather than vigorous intervention that has characterized effective Japanese leadership.

Perhaps the most vivid recent example of effective "management" by a Japanese political leader occurred in late 1977, when Prime Minister Fukuda shuffled his cabinet in order to bring in ministers who could cope with the growing trade crisis. At that time, the major problems facing Japan were American demands for

---

34. Fukui, "The GATT Tokyo Round," 129.
35. Fukui, 139.
36. Taketsugu Tsurutani, "The Causes of Paralysis," *Foreign Policy,* Spring 1974, 127.
37. James Sundquist, "A Comparison of Policymaking Capacity in the United States and Five European Countries" in Michael Kraft and Mark Schneider, eds., *Population Policy Analysis* (Lexington, Mass.: D. C. Heath and Co., 1978), 79.
38. Watanabe, "Foreign Economic Policymaking," 84.

agricultural liberalization and the need for Japan to help conclude the lagging Tokyo Round. Fukuda knew that to deal with the agricultural problem he would need the help of a politician with a strong standing in the agricultural community, who at the same time was not overly vulnerable to pressure from farmers.

One of the reasons Fukuda selected Ichiro Nakagawa as minister of agriculture was that the new minister from Hokkaido was not overly exposed to pressure from citrus or beef producers. Fukuda was certain these commodities would have to be liberalized to a certain extent, and he wanted a man as agriculture minister who could carry out liberalization without committing political suicide. Fukuda's selection of Nakagawa with the specific problems of citrus and beef in mind was somewhat unusual. Japanese prime ministers traditionally select cabinet ministers in order to balance off competing factional interests within the party, rather than to address particular policy issues. The selection of Nakagawa thus reflected Fukuda's deep concern with the mounting trade friction between Japan and the United States and his determination to take measures to ease the tension.[39]

Fukuda's problem with regard to the Tokyo Round was more complex. Japan had been stymied in the negotiations until that time because of intense disagreements within the bureaucracy and a resulting inability to present a united front in the multilateral trade talks. In order to deal with this problem, Fukuda created a new cabinet post, minister of external economic relations, and appointed the career diplomat Nobuhiko Ushiba to fill it.

By appointing Ushiba, who was neither a member of parliament nor a party member, Fukuda denied a cabinet position to a member of his own party, since the number of cabinet seats is limited by law. The appointment of Ushiba thus exposed Fukuda to criticism from within the LDP. However, Fukuda was deeply concerned about the need for Japan to have a chief negotiator (like the USTR) and about the problems which could arise in the upcoming bilateral and multilateral negotiations as a result of bureaucratic rivalries in Japan. Fukuda selected Ushiba because he believed that the former ambassador to the United States could skillfully negotiate with the United States and other countries as well as coordinate the competing bureaucracies in Tokyo.

What motivates a Japanese politician to play a leadership role on issues of trade liberalization? For many Japanese politicians in the current leadership generation, the desire to promote trade liberalization and to stem global protectionism is rooted in vivid memories of the prewar years, when global protectionism contributed to the outbreak of war. For others there is a felt need to repay the United States for its past assistance. Masumi Esaki, a senior LDP politician who spearheaded an attempt to liberalize Japanese trade practices in early 1982, said recently, "Japan has to be grateful to the United States because it helped us to achieve our current prosperity. When the U.S. economy is faltering, it is our duty to pay them back."[40]

Bureaucratic support is another important element of governmental leadership in Japan. When that support is lacking, the decision process is short-circuited and policy implementation thwarted. For example,

---

39. See Timothy Curran, "The Politics of Trade Liberalization in Contemporary Japan: the Case of the Tokyo Round of Multilateral Trade Negotiations" (unpublished doctoral dissertation, Columbia University, 1982).

40. *Wall Street Journal,* 14 January 1983.

during 1980 Prime Minister Ohira tried to push his government into a leading role in international talks regarding a Pacific Basin Community. However, little was actually done in response to the prime minister's initiative because key bureaucratic elements were unenthusiastic in their support.[41] Thus, one of the basic tasks of Japan's political leaders is to define issues in such a way that they win bureaucratic support, or to gain control of the bureaucracy through internal personal shifts and the strategic placement of ministers.

International pressure and governmental leadership are often not enough to enforce trade liberalization measures in Japan. Unless the specific groups to be affected by the proposed opening of the market can be made to acquiesce in the decision to liberalize, the Japanese government will be reluctant to move. In short, a consensus between all the parties involved in a particular trade problem—the party, the bureaucracy, and private sector groups or firms—must be forged before decisions to liberalize can be made. The importance of achieving a domestic consensus in Japan was made painfully clear during the textile crisis of the early 1970s, when the Japanese government refused to limit textile exports despite intense pressure from the United States to take such action and broad agreement among party and bureaucratic leaders that some export restraint was inevitable. According to the authors of *Managing an Alliance*:

> Political leaders and senior bureaucrats were repeatedly deferring to their colleagues, to business leaders, to subordinates. They seemed unwilling to force a position on them, reluctant to move toward decisive action to settle issues until the other interested parties, including especially the textile leaders, were "on board." The premier, the MITI minister, senior officials, business leaders—all deferred strong moves time and again because a consensus had not jelled.[42]

Domestic consensus-building on questions of trade liberalization is especially important for the LDP because, as we noted earlier, "the conservative party's many constituencies are sprawled across the country's economic and social landscape."[43] A decision to liberalize inevitably damages one or another of the LDP's support groups, which are invariably organized and ready to defend their interests. Agricultural liberalization threatens the nation's farmers, while an opening of the distribution system would imperil thousands of small retailers. The recent decision to loosen standards for baseball bats brought forth an outcry and pitched resistance from the Japan Softball League.[44]

An important element in the Japanese government's attempts to forge a consensus on issues of trade liberalization is the existence of issue networks, or informal links between groups or individuals concerned with a similar issue or problem. In the case of Japanese agriculture, for example, an informal network connects agricultural specialists of the LDP, key officials of the Ministry of Agriculture, and the leadership of the most important agricultural interest group, the cooperatives. The existence of this policy network was essential to the central political leadership in its effort to generate a consensus in favor of limited agricultural liberalization. The agricultural network facilitated an easy flow of information between the LDP and the agricultural ministry and between the bureaucracy and the cooperatives. It provided the channel through which party leaders were

---

41. See James Morley, "The Pacific Basin Movement and Japan," paper presented to the University Seminar on Modern Japan, Columbia University, May 1981.
42. Destler et al., *Managing an Alliance*, 105.
43. See footnote 9.
44. *New York Times*, 25 October 1981.

able to develop a sense of trust among farmers and acceptance of the need for some liberalization. Thus when negotiations over beef and citrus quotas were concluded in December 1978 the Japanese government was able to agree to a substantial expansion of import quotas without a damaging backlash among the nation's farmers. The *absence* of an effective issue network in the case of Nippon Telephone and Telegraph is an important reason why negotiations to open Japan's telecommunications market were so difficult. Because the Japanese government did not have effective lines of communication to the public corporation, it was difficult to explain the content of the new procurement code and to build a consensus on the necessity of Japanese concessions.

Finally, an important element in the Japanese government's efforts to persuade domestic groups to accept trade concessions is its ability to offer financial compensation. For example, during the textile crisis MITI Minister Kakuei Tanaka was able to win the textile industry's acquiescence to export limitations only after promising a substantial loan program to assist damaged manufacturers. Similarly, during the agricultural negotiations in 1978, Prime Minister Fukuda's government won the agreement of domestic farm groups to its plan for limited liberalization after agreeing to substantially increase the budget allocations for certain farm programs. This method of winning domestic support will not be easy in the future because of the enormous budget deficits in Japan. Japanese officials will have to look for other reasons to justify greater liberalization.

Conclusion

How can the United States help Japan overcome the remaining obstacles to free trade? First of all, it is important to recognize that the Japanese policy-making process is not unified, nor is it dominated by a single bureaucratic or political center. Instead, as we have seen, different groups compete for influence, power, and protection. On trade and domestic issues, powerful groups often bring enormous pressure to bear on the government and individual political leaders to protect their interests. The bureaucracies are often divided, struggling to protect the interests of a particular client group or to promote parochial policy goals. Even the ruling party, often noted for its high degree of discipline in parliamentary voting, is split between backbench, locally-oriented politicians and the more nationally-oriented leaders. The result of these divisions within the party, bureaucracy, and interest groups is a policy-making system that moves slowly, finds it almost impossible to take initiatives, and reacts only haltingly to outside pressure.

But the system does move. As we have seen, foreign pressure *has* moved the Japanese government to open its markets. In pressuring Japan it is important to avoid impossible demands and to focus instead on trade areas in which the United States has a competitive advantage. For example, American interest in having Japan totally revamp its distribution system to make foreign penetration easier is virtually impossible for Japan to implement. Similarly, the focus on Japanese beef restrictions is largely misplaced because Australian beef, which is generally cheaper than American beef, is more competitive in Japan and would therefore reap most of the benefits of liberalization. As *The Economist* commented recently, it is more effective in dealing with Japan to "take a single issue, get agreement from all government agencies and companies concerned, make sure they are ready to exploit any [Japanese] concessions when offered, and then roar."[45]

It is also important to target pressure so that it gives those groups in Japan with an interest in a particular issue an incentive to cooperate. In other words, it is important to have a bite as well as a roar. Broadly directed pressure, such as threatening to disrupt a prime minister's visit to the United States, or somehow shake the foundations of the U.S.-Japan alliance, does little to influence specific firms. As we saw in the NTT negotiations, the possibility that Prime Minister Ohira's visit to the United States would be disrupted did not disturb the public corporation or its family of domestic suppliers. However, the possibility that these companies might be shut out of part of the U.S. market unless NTT opened its procurement system did indeed threaten the interests of these companies and gave them an incentive to press NTT to expand its bidding procedures. In short, it seems that negotiating approaches that draw attention to the specific costs of failure have a greater chance of success than more broadly based threats.

The importance of foreign pressure in encouraging Japan to eliminate trade barriers should not cloud the fact that it is individual politicians and bureaucrats who make the decisions to carry out liberalization. For example, Japan's concessions during the Tokyo Round in the areas of agriculture and government procurement were initiated in response to foreign pressure, but implementation required the cooperation of Prime Ministers Fukuda and Ohira and cabinet ministers Nakagawa and Ushiba. Low-key, targeted pressure of the kind noted above can give a Japanese prime minister the incentive to get involved in a trade issue without making it politically dangerous to cooperate. In 1979 American pressure on NTT was so visible and con-

frontational that the only politically safe course open to Prime Minister Ohira was to refuse any concessions. In contrast, recent American demands for a reform of Japan's customs procedures have been very specific, very low-key, and very productive.

The specificity of American demands also helps the Japanese government deal with interest groups. Even if a particular organization or industrial sector in Japan agrees with the general principle of liberal international trade, it naturally resists concessions that will damage its constituents. Ushiba noted during a serious trade dispute in late 1977, for example, that even though most businessmen agreed with the Japanese government's program to reduce Japan's trade surplus, each wanted the program carried out at someone else's expense. If the United States is not specific in its requests vis-à-vis Japan, it places the burden of deciding which domestic groups will suffer onto the Japanese government. Specific demands leave no doubt in the minds of particular Japanese interest groups that the reason their government presses them for trade concessions is because of specific American pressure.

Also important in this regard is the allowance of sufficient time to permit Japanese officials to build a consensus with the various groups involved with a problem on the need for concessions. During the agricultural negotiations Japanese officials consulted tirelessly with Japanese farm groups and farm-bloc politicians in order to keep them abreast of the negotiations. The result was a degree of trust between the government and farm community that allowed Japan to grant a substantial expansion of farm quotas.

In 1983, as trade tensions between the United States

---

45. *The Economist*, 15 January 1983.

121

and Japan rise, and frequent mention is made of forcing Japan to open its markets, a clearer understanding of the Japanese policy-making process and the role played by outside pressure may help to achieve the maximum result in terms of trade liberalization with a minimum of needless and destructive confrontation.

Susan C. Schwab

JAPAN AND THE U.S. CONGRESS:

Problems and Prospects*

To the average member of Congress, Japan is an economic superpower that does not play by the same rules as other industrialized nations. Japan has achieved its economic status by keeping its market closed to imports and by pumping exports into an open American market. Japan is at once admired and suspect.

To the average Japanese, the Congress of the United States represents a powerful, often unreasonable, group of politicians who do not understand Japan. The Congress uses Japan's hard-won economic achievements to make it a scapegoat for domestic economic problems arising from America's bout with "advanced-country disease." The Congress represents the worst side of the benevolent big brother who, through no fault of Japan's, has turned on a vulnerable and loyal sibling.

These stereotyped images are the products of mis-perceptions and self-righteous tendencies on both sides, as well as the propensity of each to read too much into the actions and rhetoric of the other. This paper explores the perceptions, motivations, and actions that underlie such images—from the politics and perspectives on Capitol Hill, to the nature and effectiveness of the Japanese response. In assessing prospects for the future, one finds that there is just enough truth to the perceptions on both sides to make mere explanations unsubstantiated by actions insufficient to ease the troubled relationship.

JAPAN: THE VIEW FROM CONGRESS

During the course of the Ninety-seventh Congress (1981-82) U.S.-Japan relations occupied a significant place in congressional activities and rhetoric—although the attention was not nearly as all-consuming as one would be led to believe by following the Japanese press.

Congressional concern about trade was particularly evident. Of over 330 trade bills and resolutions introduced in Congress, some 14 percent focused directly or indirectly on Japan. Removing routine tariff bills from the total, the Japanese share rises to over 19 percent. Not surprisingly, two-thirds of this total legislation dealt with automobile imports and reciprocal market access. Although only a small fraction of all legislation introduced in the Ninety-seventh Congress, Japan's 19 percent share in trade compares with slightly over 4 percent for Canada. America's largest trading partner, and with 15 percent for legislation pertaining to agricultural export embargoes—the only other major topic of trade legislation in that period.

There was decidedly less legislative attention to Japanese defense spending. Two bills were introduced in the House, along with a handful of resolutions and amendments in resolution form in both the House and the Senate. This apparent lack of action on defense has several explanations. As with foreign policy matters

---

* The views expressed are those of the author and do not necessarily reflect the views of any individual or institution with which she may be associated.

in general, there is limited constituent interest on the issue of defense burden-sharing. To the extent that domestic sentiment exists, it does so in the context of bilateral trade problems—where the United States is perceived as spending money for better tanks while Japan can spend it on better cars.

The congressional role in trade is far more pronounced than in defense. The Constitution of the United States places responsibility for trade into the hands of Congress, which in turn delegates to the executive branch a degree of negotiating authority and responsibility for implementing trade statutes. The fact remains that Congress can always choose to limit imports through legislation. Its control over defense is less clear, and there is not much Congress can do directly to affect decisions by a foreign government involving defense matters.

Finally, while there appears to be virtual unanimity among members of Congress on various aspects of U.S.-Japan trade relations, there is less of a consensus as to Japan's proper defense role. The view that Japan should do more for its own defense has widespread acceptance, but there is no clear focus on how much or for what purpose.

Emphasizing legislation alone would be misleading, since it ignores the innumerable amendments offered in committee or on the floor during the course of each legislative session. Individual sector-specific reciprocity and "Buy American" provisions were particularly popular in the Ninety-seventh Congress and appeared in appropriations bills, authorization bills, and legislation pertaining to every topic from deregulation of telecommunications to the Pentagon budget. Similarly, the numerous hearings on trade held in the Ninety-seventh Congress were both a source of information for members and a forum for airing grievances or getting press attention. Many focused on U.S.-Japan trade relations and were often held in committees without an active jurisdictional role in trade. In the Senate alone, hearings on U.S.-Japan trade relations were held in at least eight standing committees as well as the Joint Economic Committee.[1] Complaints about Japanese trade practices were also aired in floor debates and in statements placed in the *Congressional Record.*

Congressional attention to Japan, particularly in relation to trade, is nothing new. While much of the flurry in the Ninety-seventh Congress can be attributed to the recession, its growing intensity cannot be ignored. To appreciate the situation, one needs to understand the recent politicization of trade in America and the perspective and motivation of a member of Congress.

The Politicization of Trade

The politicization of international trade in the United States is a relatively new phenomenon. Since World War II, U.S. trade policy has been designed, negotiated, and understood by a small number of Washington players occupying positions within the executive branch, in Washington law offices, and in trade associations. Congressional participants were confined primarily to key members of the two committees with principal jurisdiction over U.S. trade—the Finance Committee in the Senate and the Committee on Ways and Means in the House.

---

1. The following standing committees held hearings on U.S.-Japan trade in the Ninety-seventh Congress: Agriculture, Nutrition, and Forestry; Banking, Housing, and Urban Affairs; Commerce, Science, and Transportation; Finance; Foreign Relations; Governmental Affairs; Judiciary; and Small Business.

The politics of trade was largely bipartisan, and differences were generally based on the divergent economic make-up of the members' constituencies. Congress, recognizing the political risks of having to make decisions on specific products, turned over day-to-day responsibility to the executive branch. To the extent possible, individual constituent trade problems were channeled into the network of trade procedures legislated by Congress and administered by the executive branch. One administration's trade policy was virtually indistinguishable from that of the next—firmly grounded in a traditional liberal trade philosophy.

However, trade has now become a Man-In-The-Street issue. There is a growing awareness of trade at the grassroots level, and it has already become an issue in the 1984 presidential campaign. The recent growth of imports—particularly in such visible consumer items as automobiles and consumer electronics—has made Americans much more aware of trade; while growing unemployment in many of the same industries has invited the conclusion that such imports may be responsible. When managers often cannot admit to having been short-sighted and union officials are unwilling to acknowledge that their successful negotiations have produced uncompetitive wage rates, it is not surprising that imports have become the focus of their frustrations. Meanwhile, as more businesses try to export, more foreign barriers are brought to light, further aggravating trade tensions. Since the Tokyo Round of Multilateral Trade Negotiations (MTN), non-tariff barriers are no longer accepted as inevitable.

The media has picked up on this concern with trade and has, in turn, fueled it. Prominent articles on international trade—particularly on U.S.-Japanese trade—have appeared in virtually all major newspapers and business magazines.[2] While the print media endeavors to explain complex trade problems and tends to voice a clear free-trade editorial position, the electronic media's approach is more likely to feed protectionist sentiment. Although this may not be intentional—merely a result of having to condense every issue into two- to three-minute segments—the effect is the same: frequent mention of imports during almost daily stories on unemployment and inevitable references to well-known examples of Japanese protectionism.

It is not surprising that the increased exposure of the American public to international trade has not resulted in understanding and appreciation of the complexities of the multilateral trading system that accrues from years of negotiations, consultations, and hearings. While the American educational system continues to preach the virtues of free trade, it cannot withstand the growing perception that the United States is the only country that practices what everyone preaches.

The credibility gap characterizing perceived American and foreign trade practices also extends to American laws dealing with trade problems. A number of particularly visible market access problems have remained unresolved for years. Procedures for obtaining import relief have become extremely expensive and complex. These problems, exacerbated by the virtual elimination of financial help from trade adjustment

---

2. Examples include Art Pine and Urban C. Lehner, "Trade Winds: Protectionist Feelings Against Japan Increase in the U.S. and Europe," *Wall Street Journal,* 14 January 1983; Christopher Byron, reported by S. Chang and Edwin M. Reingold, "How Japan Does It: The World's Toughest Competitor," *Time,* 30 March 1981; Murray Sayle, "Explaining Japan to America—and Vice Versa," *Harper's,* November 1982; and "High Technology Gateway: Foreigners Demand a Piece of NTT's $3 Billion Market," *Business Week,* 9 August 1982.

assistance programs, have encouraged most industries and labor groups to bypass formal procedures and come straight to the administration and the Congress to seek import restraints.

These factors have resulted in increased pressure on the Congress. Where there is strong constituent pressure, there is obviously a need to be responsive; for the first time, members of Congress with little experience or understanding of the fine points of trade policy must act. Since most members of the Finance and Ways and Means Committees have some appreciation for the international trading system, they would prefer not to act on many of the more blatantly protectionist proposals offered by their colleagues. Thus, it was no accident when legislation requiring domestic content in autos was drafted to fall under the jurisdiction of potentially more receptive committees—in this case, the Senate Commerce Committee and the House Energy and Commerce Committee.

Congressional Motivation

Members of Congress are motivated by various factors. Among the most important is service to the constituency they will eventually ask to return them to Congress.

Every constituency is made up of special interest groups who pay particular attention to issues that affect them. Most voters identify with at least one interest group—the elderly, farmers, women, steelworkers, and so on. The degree of organization and the intensity of each group's interest in specific legislation determine the level of pressure it exerts on its representatives. This explains why, for example, someone who represents thousands of organized autoworkers may well be found supporting auto import restrictions—in spite of

the fact that he also represents hundreds of thousands of consumers. Editorials criticizing that position may have some limited impact on his support at home, but in the final analysis, only the autoworkers are likely to vote solely on the basis of his trade position.

Regardless of appearances, most members who are concerned about the plight of an import-sensitive industry realize that imports are not the only, or even principal, consideration. However, there is nothing that a member can do about short-sighted business practices or uncompetitive wage settlements. Complaining about either is of no value and could be detrimental to a representative's political health. Neither suggestions that constituents lower their standard of living nor promises of future employment in the high technology or service sectors have much political appeal. Virtually any other remedial measures, such as special tax breaks, adjustment assistance, or other forms of financial aid, cost the government money. At a time when Congress is trying to reduce the federal deficit, such measures have a limited chance of being passed. Import restrictions, on the other hand, do not show up as a line-item in the congressional budget process: Protectionism is free.

All of these elements bear heavily on imports from Japan. Looking at the trade statistics for 1982,[3] a member notices that the United States imported almost $40 billion worth of goods from Japan—$19 billion more than Japan purchased from the United States. He knows that the bilateral trade deficit is likely to increase and that many of the imports are in precisely those sectors where his state or district is hurting the most. That textile, television, or footwear producers

---

3. Source: U.S. Department of Commerce.

in his district may have already gone out of business as import penetration soared compounds his concerns. Finally, comparing the relative rates of economic growth and unemployment, or the levels of defense spending between the United States and Japan, he may logically conclude that Japan is taking undue advantage of the American market.

This member of Congress probably knows that in theory an open trading system is in the best interest of the American economy. However, if he knows that the United States has a trade surplus with Europe comparable to the trade deficit with Japan, he is also probably aware that the Europeans rarely complain about access to the U.S. market.

Herein lies the biggest problem facing any member of Congress inclined to oppose protectionism, particularly as it relates to Japan. If the Japanese market is perceived to be closed to competitive American exports, it is very difficult to argue in favor of leaving the door open to Japanese products.[4] Similarly, when little or no political pressure exists to counter protectionist sentiments, there is little motivation to support free trade.

In this context, the declining strength of America's free-trade coalition—those groups that joined in the past to promote free trade—is extremely significant. Until a few years after the passage of the Trade Expansion Act of 1962, organized labor was part of that coalition. Some multinational corporations are still included in the group, but many major industries, such as the automobile and steel industries have dropped out. American agriculture remains the backbone of the coalition, but the depressed state of the farm economy, combined with a growing perception that farmers are not getting a fair shake in international trade (attributable primarily to European export subsidies), has clearly dampened their free-trade enthusiasm. The major business and civic groups that helped organize the coalition have become preoccupied with other problems or are struggling to counter the growing protectionist sentiments voiced by their own membership. Major consumer groups have never been members at all. In fact, the Consumer Federation of America came out in support of domestic content legislation in 1982, attributed by some to the close ties between labor unions and the consumer movement.[5]

Another factor in the decline of anti-protectionist sentiment in Congress is the growing unwillingness of those in the best position to speak out on behalf of Japan to do so. On issues as complex as international trade, legislators still look to their more knowledgeable colleagues and those in key committee leadership positions for guidance when it comes time to take a position. For example, certain members of the Ways and Means Trade Subcommittee are generally considered experts on U.S.-Japanese trade. Over a period of years, they have visited Japan and have filed comprehensive reports highlighting trade problems and offering recommendations to Japan in the area of market access and to the United States in terms of enhancing U.S. competitiveness.[6] Japan's slow and agonizing progress toward

---

4. It probably would surprise many Americans to know that by some estimates, 70 percent of Japanese exports to the United States are already subject to some form of "voluntary" restriction, "gentleman's agreement," or similar arrangement.

5. Robert L. Simison, "UAW vs. Japan," *Wall Street Journal,* 3 September 1982.

6. Subcommittee on Trade of the Committee on Ways and Means, "Task Force Report on United States-Japan Trade," 2 January 1979, Committee Report No. 95-110; "United States-Japan Trade Report," 5 September 1980, Committee Report No. 96-68; "Report on Trade Mission to Far East," 21 December 1981, Committee Report No. 97-27.

further opening of its market reflects on their credibility with their colleagues and, not surprisingly, lowers their enthusiasm for speaking out in support of Japanese interests.

Other members of Congress, or knowledgeable administration officials who might otherwise be in a position to defend Japan in a public forum, face similar constraints. United States Trade Representative Bill Brock best expressed this at a hearing on the domestic content bill when, in answer to a barrage of criticism of Japanese trade practices, he said, "Don't put me in the position where I have to defend the Japanese!"[7]

Perceptions and Realities

Although there is widespread admiration in the Congress for many Japanese practices, particularly those involving cooperation between government, business, and labor, members of Congress generally recognize that Japan has been uniquely successful in manipulating the tools of industrial planning and protectionism to achieve its economic goals. Given the previous framework, it is clear that the future of American protectionism vis-à-vis Japan rests to a significant degree on Japanese trade and business practices; that is, the perception of Japanese import barriers and export targeting, the existence of such barriers and practices, and efforts — perceived and real — to do away with them.

Of greatest significance is the issue of barriers to American exports. The widespread perception that the Japanese market is closed has its basis not only in specific, well-known import barriers, but in their implications for broader market access.[8] While few legislators believe that the total liberalization of, for example, residual Japanese agricultural quotas will turn the trade deficit around, anecdotal examples of Japanese trade

barriers are the stuff of speeches long remembered. The number of these "horror stories" only increases the perception that the Japanese market is protected by an infinite number of barriers. Moreover, no one could convince someone from a tobacco-producing state that the $10 billion Japanese market for cigarettes, protected by tariffs, highly discriminatory price differentials, and restricted access to marketing opportunities, is only of symbolic importance to his constituency.

Even more important than any specific barrier may be what it implies about the rest of Japan's import practices. The artificially high duty placed on a new brand of potato chip imports (until a domestically produced substitute became available) has broader implications concerning Japanese customs and valuation practices. Similarly, it does not take a member of Congress to wonder about the fairness of Japanese standards, testing, and certification procedures in view of the experience of American sporting goods manufacturers.

The bottom line remains the statistics behind the trade imbalance — particularly the inability of many American exports to garner a share of the Japanese market commensurate with their competitiveness and comparable to the penetration of Japanese products in the United States. The striking contrasts were illustrated

---

7. Hearing on the Fair Practices in Automotive Products Act before the Subcommittee on Trade, Ways and Means Committee, House of Representatives, 21 September 1982.

8. I do not intend to address the question of whether or not the Japanese market is "closed." There are a sufficient number of examples of Japanese import barriers, legal or illegal under the General Agreement on Tariffs and Trade (GATT), to argue persuasively that the perception is not groundless. Suffice it to say that the Japanese market is more open than most Americans believe, but that it is far more closed than most Japanese realize.

recently in a speech by Ambassador Mike Mansfield when he commented:

> In addition to Japan's nearly one-quarter share of the U.S. auto market, many other Japanese products now hold major shares of the U.S. market. To illustrate my point, last year's figures indicate that in steel Japan held a 10 to 15 percent share of the U.S. market; in TVs, 20 to 30 percent; in motorcycles, 90 percent; in radios, 50 to 60 percent; in cameras, over 30 percent; in recording equipment, over 50 percent; in watches, over 50 percent; and in machine tools, over 20 percent. By contrast, representative competitive U.S. products hold only the following limited share of the market in Japan: cigarettes, 1.3 percent in comparison to more than a 50 percent share of cigarette sales in Hong Kong, a market very similar to Japan's; communications equipment, 1.3 percent; fresh oranges, 3 percent; medical equipment, 6.3 percent; office automation equipment, 11.2 percent; beef, 7 percent; as well as unreasonably low market shares for such competitive products as analytical instruments, wood products, industrial chemicals and pharmaceuticals.[9]

While stereotyped images of "Japan, Inc." are exaggerated, any member who suspects the existence of a Japanese industrial strategy designed to protect uncompetitive domestic industries and to target competitive American industries can find confirming evidence. Documented examples of past practices in the machine tool or semiconductor industries reinforce this conclusion, but do not create it. The "spontaneous" decision of Japanese pork importers in late 1979 to voluntarily limit their purchases of foreign pork (reducing imports by around 20 percent) is enough to make anyone believe in the powers of "administrative guidance" and close cooperation between business and government.[10]

For many Americans and their elected officials these examples of unusual Japanese trade and business practices nurture the perception of a country that carefully orchestrates its economic machine to maximize the advantages, while minimizing the disadvantages of an open world trading system—with little regard for the impact on its trading partners.

THE JAPANESE RESPONSE TO CONGRESS

The government of Japan, the Japanese press, and a number of key Japanese corporations spend a great deal of time, effort, and money learning about and interpreting the American body politic. When it comes to following events in Washington, few countries pay more attention than Japan, and Congress is naturally an important focus of activity. The Japanese press, U.S.-based government and business representatives and their army of lawyers, lobbyists, and consultants, along with visiting researchers, Diet members, and officials from Japan, all play a part in the process of finding out what the Americans are up to, how it is likely to affect Japanese interests, and what to do about it.

Reading Congress

A significant amount of the information-gathering and interpreting is carried out by some fifty Japanese reporters based in Washington. Unfortunately, with very few exceptions, these reporters may be the least responsible in carrying the message back.

---

9. Address by Ambassador Mike Mansfield before the Yomiuri International Economic Society, Tokyo, 9 December 1982.

10. There are sharp contrasts between the United States and Japan on the role of law. The United States has a multiplicity of trade statutes, each dealing with different problems faced by industries seeking relief. Japan's trade laws are less formal, less transparent, and, until very recently, never used. It is not surprising, therefore, that an American could easily draw one of the following conclusions: that Japan has no import problems; that it has import problems, but sticks with free trade principles; or that it has import problems, but fixes them quietly without going through legal formalities.

Congressional activities involving Japan get far more press play in Japan than in the United States. The multitude of bills and press releases emanating from congressional offices, designed primarily for consumption back home, are devoured by the Japanese press, often without regard for whether the bill has any chance of passage or the statement is noticed—yet alone reported—by the media in the United States.

This misguided attention on the part of the Japanese media is not surprising in itself. What is disturbing is the sensationalized, often distorted picture that appears in Japan, particularly as it affects Japanese attitudes about the United States in view of the enormous readership of Japan's major dailies.[11]

Japanese press coverage of Washington has a highly nationalistic slant. Virtually every story characterizes minor differences as major bilateral conflicts. As one observer noted, the Japanese press tends to portray U.S.-Japanese relations as "a continuing encounter between a bully (the United States) and a victim (Japan). Like all bullies, this one is a weakling deep down; its real problem is it can't compete with the virtuous victim. When America urges Japan to open its market more to foreign products or to provide more for its own defenses, the Japanese press portrays the urgings . . . as 'the bellicose barkings of an irrational foreign power that's lazy and effete.'"[12] The perception among Japanese that Americans blame Japan and Japanese imports for all their troubles is largely, although not exclusively, a function of Japanese press coverage.[13]

The tendency to put a nationalistic slant on many stories not only distorts Japanese understanding of American politics, but it also allows the evasion of debate on issues in the context of Japan's own self-interest. Even editorial positions that advocate lowering Japanese trade barriers tend to justify their viewpoint in terms of appeasing the Americans. They do not acknowledge that Japan, as a major beneficiary of an open world trading system, has some responsibility for maintaining it.[14]

In addition to innumerable individuals who stream into Washington to make their own assessments of the American political scene, the government of Japan and many Japanese businesses rely heavily on an array of American lawyers, lobbyists, and consultants. The long list of American firms and individuals registered under

---

11. The *Asahi Shimbun*, for example, has a circulation of 7,430,000 in the morning alone, making it second in readership only to the *Yomiuri Shimbun* with 8,580,000. The *Asahi*'s circulation, therefore, is greater than that of the *Wall Street Journal*, the *New York Daily News*, the *Los Angeles Times*, the *New York Times*, the *Chicago Tribune*, and the *Washington Post* combined. Source: Urban C. Lehner, "Black and White: U.S. News is Big News in Japan, but the Angle Always Seems the Same," *Wall Street Journal*, 9 December 1982.

12. *Ibid.*

13. The most striking recent example of biased reporting by the Japanese press was its coverage of the indictments of Hitachi Ltd. and Mitsubishi Electric Corporation on charges that they conspired to steal secrets from the International Business Machines Corporation (IBM). A story that could have been portrayed as a simple criminal case involving defendants and claimants in two different countries came across in the Japanese media as a major conflict between the two countries—a conspiracy between the American government and business to shatter Japanese technological prowess, with the Japanese defendants consistently portrayed as innocent victims of entrapment.

14. An excellent case study of this problem can be found in "What Does Amaya Think He's Doing?" *Shūkan Bunshun*, 14 May 1981, regarding the Japanese decision to restrain auto exports to the United States and Naohiro Amaya's response "Rejecting Soap-Opera Nationalism" in *Bungei Shunjū*, July 1981, translated in *Economic Eye* (September 1981), Keizai Kōhō Center.

the Foreign Agents Registration Act (FARA), while admittedly incomplete, offers evidence of Japan's almost insatiable appetite for information. To this end Japan spent over $13.4 million in 1981 on over eighty registered foreign agents, making it the most highly represented foreign client in the United States. This compares to $5.6 million for Canada, with a much larger stake in the U.S. market, and $6.5 and $6.3 million respectively for the United Kingdom and Germany.[15]

Although much has been made in the U.S. press about Japan's high-powered "door-openers" and revolving door graduates, many of the more sinister characterizations seem to overlook the fact that the hiring of access and expertise is common practice in the nation's capital.[16] While the magnitude of Japanese expenditures and the tendency of some companies to engage many firms to cover the same topic make the effort highly conspicuous, much of the focus remains on the gathering and interpreting of information. Japan's Congress-watchers attend hearings, pore through volumes of the *Congressional Record,* call and meet with members and their aides, and join organizations that publish newsletters or host speakers to address the inordinate number of meals that characterize the exchange of information in Washington.

To the extent that there is "lobbying" on behalf of Japanese interests on the Hill, it is generally undertaken by the Japanese themselves. Several dozen Japanese corporations now have offices in the Washington area—an enormous jump from three or four in the late 1970s. The effort late last year to defeat the domestic content bill has been cited as the first time Japanese companies and their Washington representatives visited congressional offices to state their case directly.[17] While this may have been the case, their

most effective anti-content activities were probably those involving the mobilization of what is left of America's free-trade coalition, notably, the farm organizations and various groups of multinationals.

Interpreting Congress

In view of the massive amount of information collected by the Japanese about the United States and its Congress, one may wonder why Japan's relationship with Congress has not been more successful. The answer lies in the differences between information and understanding, and between understanding and agreement.

While the Japanese know more about the United States than Americans know about Japan, it is also clear that having such knowledge gives many Japanese the false sense that they *understand* the United States. Just as Americans often read too much into Japanese words and actions, Japanese policy-makers read too much into the words and actions of the Congress.

To some extent, this misreading of congressional intentions must be attributed to the wide range of views collected in Washington and the natural tendency to choose whichever version best justifies the pre-established position of the recipient. More important, however, are

---

15. Payments registered under the Foreign Agents Registration Act of 1938 (FARA), as amended. Source: David Burnham, *New York Times.* Note that amounts cited do not include payments related primarily to key tourist or press promotion activities. FARA statistics also do not include payments for legal representation in courts, employees of American subsidiaries of Japanese firms, and so forth.
16. See, for example, James Coates and George de Lama, "American Lobbyists Help Japan Make Big U.S. Profits," *Chicago Tribune,* 10 March 1982.
17. Christopher Madison, "Is Japan Trying to Buy Washington or Just Doing Business Capital Style?" *National Journal,* 9 October 1982.

certain assumptions that seem to underlie the beliefs of many Japanese decision makers. For example, one such assumption is that Japan's problems with Congress are primarily an election year phenomenon and that most problems will go away after November of each even-numbered year. This has some basis in truth, but it is less relevant if one takes into account that one election cycle begins almost as soon as the one before it ends.

More to the point, however, is the basic assumption that Americans do not agree with Japanese positions simply because they do not understand (*rikai*) Japan. This belief is evidenced by the continuous flow into Washington of Japanese visitors and publications clearly designed to educate an ignorant public. Their frequent references to the need to "further mutual understanding" begin to appear to mean "if we just explain it often enough, you Americans will finally understand." It is not surprising, then, that many bilateral problems for which no solution is readily available are labelled a "misunderstanding" by Japanese officials. The situation is further exacerbated by the assumption that once Americans understand the Japanese position, they are sure to agree with it. To an American comprehension and agreement are far from the same, and Japanese appeals for "understanding" often invite further misunderstandings.

Influencing Congress

The principal means employed by the Japanese to influence the United States Congress fall into two basic categories: (1) efforts designed to educate the Congress and the American public about Japan and (2) actions to defuse political pressure and influence the perceptions that created the political pressure in the first place. It is clear that some of these efforts have met with greater success than others.

Japanese attempts to futher mutual understanding take many forms, such as the dissemination of publications about Japan and U.S.-Japanese relations, efforts to educate the American press, and the dispatch of Japanese envoys who endeavor to explain the Japanese position. To a lesser extent the promotion of visits by American officials to Japan is used for much the same purpose.

In recent years, the number of Japanese publications being directed to key congressional offices has increased greatly. Many originate with organizations funded by the government and are designed to offer a Japanese perspective on cooperative endeavors or bilateral tensions. They come in formats ranging from slick magazines to brief newsletters, from pamphlets to newspaper reprints.[18] Rarely, if ever, do members of Congress actually see any of the information, and it is difficult to judge whether such publications are incorporated into

---

18. Over a two-month period, the following (incomplete) list of materials on Japan arrived in the Danforth Senate office: *The Liberal Star* (monthly publication of the LDP), *Japan Economic Journal, Look Japan, Fujitsu In Touch, Journal of Japanese Trade and Industry* (MITI), *Nissan Newsletter, Japan Reports* (Japanese Consulate General, New York), *Economic Eye* (Keizai Koho Center, affiliated with Keidanren), *NTT Telecommunications Bulletin* (Nippon Telegraph and Telephone Public Corporation), *Japan Echo, Japan Monitor* (Japanese press clips distributed by MITI), *Japan Economic Survey* (Japan Economic Institute funded by embassy), *News From Japan* (Japanese embassy), *JMEA Newsletter* (Japan Machinery Exporters' Association), *News from the Special Representative's Office* (MITI/New York), informational letters from the Japanese ambassador, a brochure issued by ZENCHU (Central Union of Agricultural Cooperatives) entitled "Zenchō Position on the Japan Farm Product Import Liberalization Issue."

the advice that key staffers offer to their respective employers.

There also seems to be a growing awareness by the Japanese of the role of the American media in forming public opinion. In recent years it appears that prominent Japanese officials, both in Japan and in the United States, are placing increasing emphasis on briefing the American press. It was certainly no coincidence that during his recent visit to the United States, Prime Minister Nakasone's first activity after an informal meeting with the secretary of state was breakfast with key individuals at the *Washington Post*. In Japan, where American correspondents are excluded from the tight cadre of Japanese reporters connected to each ministry, separate background briefings are being provided to offer them a perspective beyond the traditional reliance (for all but the most fluent in Japanese) on formal press conferences and information provided by the American Embassy.

It would be inaccurate to attribute the free-trade editorial policy of many American newspapers to Japanese briefings, since it predates many of Japan's recent initiatives and since the American press remains highly skeptical of statements not corroborated by facts or actions. However, the Japanese effort is undeniably an efficient allocation of resources—particularly in view of the wide audience commanded by the domestic media.

Japan also relies heavily on its high-level government and business officials to present Japan's views on a wide variety of bilateral issues directly to American leaders. Much of the responsibility for direct approaches to the Congress is left up to Japanese government officials, including high level representatives from various ministries, and, during slow sessions of the Diet, roving groups of Japanese parliamentarians.

To an American politician receiving one or more of these delegations, there is the unmistakable impression that the Japanese visitors, rather than engaging in dialogue, are actually following a pre-rehearsed script. Whether the subject is trade or defense, the arguments rarely differ from meeting to meeting. On market access for American farm products, there usually is a reference to Japan's role as America's best customer and various Japanese consumption statistics. Related points include American agricultural import restrictions and Japanese concern for the survival of its farmers. On market access for manufactured goods, the principal arguments are that the Japanese market is relatively open (with particular emphasis on comparative average tariff rates) and that as a resource-poor island, Japan must import raw materials and export manufactured goods to survive. Related arguments include the accusation that American exporters do not try hard enough, the lack of competitiveness of American products, high American interest rates and the over-valued dollar, and America's global current account surplus. With respect to defense spending, officials cite Japan's three non-nuclear principles, the Japanese constitution, and the large Japanese budget deficit.

While many of these arguments are indeed valid, the Japanese offering them appear to assume that having explained the situation, the American politician will understand Japan's situation and shift his stance. That members of Congress are almost always polite and appear receptive to visitors only compounds the communication problem.

In fact, many of the arguments on market access bear no relation to what members of Congress have heard from American businessmen who sell competitively abroad but are unable to sell their products in

Japan. Arguments based on current account balances disregard the role of income from foreign investment and the lack of comparative job opportunities between service and merchandise exports.[19] Explanations presented in terms of one politician sharing his political pressures with another may strike a responsive chord, but the social and political problems posed for a Japanese politician by, for example, the leather or agricultural import issues may find their equivalent in the quarter-million unemployed autoworkers that worry his American counterpart. As for defense, nothing a Japanese politician can say will answer the concern that America spends over six percent of its GNP on defense—including a substantial amount that directly serves Japan's interests— while Japan appears unable, if not unwilling, to bridge the one percent psychological barrier. This is particularly significant when few, if any, American politicians have ever advocated changing Japan's constitution, or forcing Japan to accept responsibilities beyond a reasonable definition of self-defense.

Actions and Reactions

In addition to efforts to correct perceived misunderstandings, Japan has taken actions to solve problems and neutralize American pressure. These have included broad bilateral agreements such as the Strauss-Ushiba Joint Statement in 1978, the Nippon Telephone and Telegraph Procurement Agreement in 1980, the Agreement on Technology Transfer in 1982, among others; the establishment of bilateral commissions and working groups such as the Trade Facilitation Committee, the Japan-United States Economic Relations or "Wisemen's Group," and the Trade Study Group; and more recently, unilateral packages of market-opening measures in January 1982, May 1982, and January 1983. Japan has taken extensive steps to restrain its exports of textiles, televisions, steel, and automobiles. There have also been specific market access agreements on products such as leather and manufactured tobacco.

While these measures have helped to defuse political pressure from Congress, they have only offered a temporary respite at best, mainly because of the way in which such measures are decided upon in Japan and then judged in the United States.

Just as the United States Congress can be accused of using Japan as a scapegoat and American negotiators can be accused of using congressional pressure to gain trade concessions, the Japanese use American political pressure for their own purposes. In fact, outside pressure is frequently used and occasionally invited by Japanese officials to move an otherwise unresponsive decision-making process and to further certain interests in inter-ministerial rivalries. Particularly in the trade area, achieving consensus among the variety of government and business players is an agonizing process and often results in a lowest-common-denominator decision. The system relies on outside pressure and a sense of crisis fueled by ministerial visits, for example, in order to function. Thus decisions to open the Japanese market are made almost exclusively when outside pressure reaches a feverish pitch. By that time they become crisis management tools rather than long-term solutions. Trade barriers are lowered more with a view to their impact on American perceptions than American exports. Many of the more complicated problems such as customs clearance procedures, standards, testing, and

---

19. Eleanor M. Hadley, "Is the U.S.-Japan Trade Imbalance a Problem? Economists Answer 'No', Politicians 'Yes,'" *Journal of Northeast Asian Studies* 1 (March 1982): 49.

certification requirements, and restraints on investment and acquisition remain largely unexplored, let alone resolved.

Reliance on outside pressure by Japanese officials can only be detrimental to a long-term bilateral relationship. As Senator John C. Danforth, chairman of the Senate Subcommittee on International Trade, described the problem to one Japanese audience:

> America's reaction to the lack of access to the Japanese market has been characterized by diatribe and threats. We have sent over repeated missions of Cabinet officials . . . to make the same speech I just made. Then, having listed their grievances, they have pleaded, urged, begged, argued and admonished Japan to change its ways . . .
>
> The approach has had only limited success in terms of fundamental changes in Japanese import practices, and even this incremental progress has occurred at the cost of constant strain in the overall relationship caused by well-publicized diatribe and rhetorical attacks.
>
> This is no way for two great nations to behave. The constant rhetoric is demeaning to both sides. The United States should not be in a position where it must plead for equity. And Japan, as a sovereign nation, should not have to be told by outsiders to change its economic practices, customs and traditions to placate another country.[20]

While the exploitation of American political pressure is evident in the international trade area, nowhere is it more self-serving than with respect to Japanese defense policies. In spite of the relatively muted nature of American pressure, it would appear to the casual observer that the Japanese debate on defense expenditures is solely the product of American insistence. Although the subject of Japan's role in political-military affairs is understandably sensitive, one still gets the impression that politicians with their own objectives for the military and industrialists, who see the export of arms as potentially big business, use the excuse of American pressure to avoid taking responsibility for controversial decisions.

Although the Japanese decision-making process will not change overnight, recent attempts to impose "top-down" leadership in Japan are noteworthy. In his recent visit to the United States, Prime Minister Nakasone demonstrated leadership characteristics more readily understood by American politicians. Similarly, the stated desire of the president of NTT to open the Japanese telecommunications market is in sharp contrast to those Japanese leaders who rely on vague generalities in observance of the preeminent power of Japanese bureaucrats. While these strong statements of intent make a favorable impression on Congress, the key question is how successful this new breed of Japanese leaders will be in delivering on their commitments. The furor evoked in Japan by a number of the new prime minister's decisions and public statements bodes ill for his ability to exercise "top-down" leadership in a traditionally "middle-up" society.

Columnist George Will once defined political leadership as the ability to inflict pain and get away with it. In this regard, it is particularly unfortunate that Japanese actions in the past have not had sufficient impact to enable American politicians to react enthusiastically to ongoing efforts by Japanese decision makers. The reliance on symbols over substance explains why much of the impact of their efforts seems to have fallen far short of their political mark. The lack of success of past actions that were supposed to resolve long-standing problems has left many legislators deeply skeptical of more recent initiatives.

---

20. Speech by Senator John C. Danforth, delivered to the Federation of Economic Organizations (Keidanren), Tokyo, 12 January 1982.

Congressional reserve should be of particular concern to the Japanese, since it depreciates Japan's credibility as an international actor. Those American politicians and negotiators who openly applauded Japan's apparent commitments—to expand leather imports, purchase $300 million in auto parts, engage in major procurement of American telecommunications equipment, accelerate defense expenditures, and most recently, to remove all barriers to sales of American baseball bats—now wonder whether they were deceived and indeed made to look foolish. With all of these "solutions" falling so far short of expectations, it is small wonder that such politicians are skeptical about Japanese intentions vis-à-vis the recent tobacco tariff cuts and implementation of the agreement on technology transfer. Japanese politicians and negotiators should not be surprised that the most encouraging statements coming out of Washington in response to positive Japanese decisions are invariably couched in terms of "a step in the right direction."

To most members of Congress, many of Japan's responses to bilateral problems are akin to picking weeds or peeling an onion. Each answer presents a new problem. Using a Japanese analogy, the situation can best be compared to the popular arcade game *mogura tataki*. No matter how many times a player clobbers one of the jumping creatures with the rubber mallet, another will invariably pop up nearby.

PROSPECTS AND CONCLUSIONS

Prospects for the peaceful coexistence of Japan and the United States Congress are uncertain. The long-term bilateral relationship need not fall victim to conflicting political imperatives, however, if explanations are not employed as substitutes for action.

The development of a more positive, mutually beneficial defense relationship demands honesty on the part of Japanese policy makers about Japan's own security interests and motivations. The United States will continue to have fundamental reasons for maintaining a military presence in the region, regardless of Japanese defense spending. To the extent that Congress focuses on the defense spending issue in the trade context, both sides must remember that they are independent problems. Resolving one will not settle the other.

In the case of bilateral trade problems, the rest of the decade promises to be as much of a strain as the recent past. While Japan may place too much emphasis on congressional rhetoric, the role of Congress ought to be taken seriously.

Many of the economic problems facing the United States do not have short-term solutions. Adverse long-term structural changes and the need to adjust to them have been exacerbated—not created—by the current recession. To the degree that these growing pains fuel protectionist pressures in the United States, the search for import restrictions and political rationale for avoiding them will intensify. The United States Congress has not passed any major pieces of protectionist legislation since the Smoot-Hawley tariffs in the 1930s. However, widespread support for the Mills Bill in the late 1960s, the Burke-Hartke Bill in the early 1970s, and various measures related to the auto industry in the early 1980s should give pause to optimists and cynics alike.

The record of the Ninety-seventh Congress may be the best indicator of the trend toward protectionism. Especially noteworthy were the Senate's passage of strict reciprocity language on telecommunications, the overwhelming vote to override the president's veto of legislation to forestall the removal of protection for

136

American printers (the manufacturer's copyright clause), the passage of "Buy American" provisions included in highway construction legislation, and the passage in the House of domestic content legislation.

The lesson of the domestic content bill itself deserves special notice. While its momentum was slowed in the closing weeks of the Congress, due in part to the public awakening to the dangers of dabbling in protectionism, the bill remains a portent of things to come. The success of the General Agreement on Tariffs and Trade (GATT) in lowering traditional barriers to trade such as tariffs and quotas has not only laid bare many of the more complex non-tariff barriers in Japan; it has also prompted the search by other nations for even more sophisticated means of closing their markets. Seen as the first clumsy attempt of many to employ "innovative" protectionism, legislation like the domestic content bill has resounding implications for the future.

More dangerous are the growing number of minor protectionist provisions that are tacked onto non-trade bills. Unlike a domestic content bill, these addenda are not highly visible and do not provide a clean target against which to mount opposition. They are likely to grow in popularity and impact.

Japan will remain particularly vulnerable to protectionist moves by the Congress in the foreseeable future. Beyond the obvious lack of leverage created by a massive trade surplus, the fact is that virtually nothing Americans buy from Japan actually needs to be imported. Consumer preferences notwithstanding, American industry could still supply all of the automobiles, consumer electronics, and high technology products currently supplied by Japan. Moreover, there remains a sense in Congress that regardless of action taken against imports from Japan, there is little likelihood of Japanese retalia-tion, given Japan's apparent willingness to restrict exports when necessary and its reliance on imports of raw materials and farm products. In fact, many of those manufactured goods and value-added agricultural commodities that Japan can produce itself are the very ones restricted by Japanese import barriers. The strong lobbying effort by American farm interests against the domestic content legislation could be most appropriately attributed to the fear that nations other than Japan—particularly those in Europe—might be prompted to use protectionist American legislation as an excuse to enact measures of their own against U.S. exports.

Options are nonetheless available on both sides to lessen the prospect of the Congress enacting, or pressuring the government to undertake, protectionist measures. For the United States, there is an obvious need to get our economic house in order. American business and the Congress must be more honest with themselves about the reasons underlying the rise of such severe competition from abroad. Similarly, American business does itself a disservice by focusing on the problems of foreign market access and industrial targeting when capital availability factors, high labor costs, poor product mix, exchange rates, or domestic anti-trust laws may represent greater barriers to competitiveness. Finally, Congress needs to take a rational look at American trade laws. To the extent that they are unworkable, they may have to be modified. To the extent that the statutes cannot cope with innovative protectionism or government intervention abroad, they need to be broadened. Laws designed to ease adjustment must be made to do just that, but in a manner that cushions an otherwise devastating social and political process.

Insofar as questions of market access in Japan are concerned, congressional pressure is likely to remain a fact of life until there are tangible results from further corrective measures undertaken by Japan. To the extent Japanese decision makers continue to rely on U.S. pressure, the crisis/response approach will only be prolonged.

Finally, as long as the United States continues to push for Japan to play a more active role among major industrialized nations, Americans must be prepared for the results. Fair challenges to America's industrial strength must be accepted and countered in a competitive marketplace. In the international political arena, American policy-makers must be ready to deal with a Japan that may not share all of their objectives.

For Japan the challenge of the coming decade will require the sacrifices that come with taking on the responsibilities, as well as the benefits, of a major industrial power. In both the trade and defense areas this will entail mature policy-making and less self-indulgence in externalizing responsibility for its decisions to the pressure of others.

Japan's reliance on the American market for the foreseeable future dictates the need for both short-run and long-term action. Over the long haul, this will require meaningful market-liberalizing measures resulting in more American exports to Japan, thereby creating an American constituency for open trading arrangements with Japan. Japanese investment in productive capacity in the United States and meaningful joint-venture arrangements will also serve to create a body of American workers who will come to share Japanese interests. Japanese businessmen engaged in these activities will have to learn how to mobilize their American constituency and rely less on the Japanese government to champion their interests.

Japanese efforts to further open their market to imports from the United States will continue to face short-run political imperatives, but these must also yield substantive results to avoid the loss of Japan's credibility as a partner to trade agreements. Congressman Jim Jones once remarked that Japan needs to put a heavier dose of politics into its economic policy and that the United States needs to put a heavier dose of economics into its politics. Japan is capable of an effective political response to the United States Congress, as it demonstrated during the agricultural portion of the Tokyo Round of Multilateral Trade Negotiations (MTN). When asked by U.S. negotiators to think of the list of American requests for reductions in barriers as a "political mosaic," the Japanese negotiators drew up a map of the United States, complete with labels for each state and its major farm exports. In this context the "symbolic" problems of beef, citrus, and tobacco take on a whole new meaning.

For the present, a better strategy for using face-to-face contacts between members of Congress and Japanese leaders in government and business also needs to be considered. While visits of high level Japanese to the Congress have met with something less than resounding success, visits of American politicians to Japan offer greater opportunities for enhancing understanding on both sides. Congressional visits to Japan engage wider Japanese audiences and are more inclined to result in real communication because the American participants are away from jangling telephones and roll call votes. However, all of these moves will only postpone negative reactions by Congress in the absence of long-term solutions to market access problems. Such measures are unlikely to be undertaken in the rush of drawing up concessions to manage a crisis. Efforts to deal seriously with generic barriers to trade which can improve access for a broad range of U.S. exports will

138

result in fewer "horror stories" that reinforce Japan's image as a closed market.

In the final analysis, Japanese policy-makers must anticipate tomorrow's trade problems and act to alleviate them today, before the only option left is damage control. Had the Japanese market for automobiles been open in the early 1960s, the automobile trade situation might look quite different today. Japanese industrial policy involving products higher up the technological ladder should heed the lesson of automobiles. If competitive American industries in the high technology and service sectors are unable to meet increasingly competitive Japanese counterparts in their home market now, it is questionable how long American leaders, concerned with the future health of their own industrial base, will allow traffic to run only in the direction of the American market. There are many options available to Japanese policy-makers, but the notable lack of success of the first two years of operation of the Nippon Telephone and Telegraph Procurement Agreement offers little promise of meaningful results. The extent to which Japanese government officials and industrialists see meaningful market-liberalizing actions as being in their own interest will determine the final success or failure of such measures. Japanese and American supporters of a liberal trading relationship can only defend themselves against unreasonable demands by credible performances.

The stakes are high in the uneasy relationship between Japan and the United States Congress. The problems are not insurmountable, but understanding, measured responses, and less self-indulgence are required on both sides.

Akio Morita

BUSINESS AND JAPAN'S NEW WORLD ROLE:

As Seen Through Personal Experience

No one doubts the extreme severity of conditions in the world economy today. In Europe and the United States the rate of unemployment has surpassed 10 percent and national finances are plagued with serious deficits. This situation has led to a trend to reorganize or reform the present regime. Willy-nilly, we are faced with the critical task of finding a method to successfully emerge from this seriously unstable situation.

Japan is no exception to this world picture. The Japanese economy, which has been relatively stable in the past, is now confronted with a huge national deficit, internal recession, and increasing trade frictions. It seems that Japan is hemmed in on all sides. This is indeed an era of great difficulty for all of us businessmen.

However, when problems have arisen in the past, businessmen have often been the ones to come up with the solutions. Various problems must be overcome in order to achieve sustained growth.

In 1946, following World War II, when a small company that was later to become Sony was established, the Japanese economy was extremely unstable, and the business environment was far from favorable. At that time, I realized that our company would not grow if we depended solely on the Japanese market. We therefore decided to diminish our risks by expanding our operations into other countries. We thought that if we could spread our marketing channels throughout the world, we would be able to find customers willing to buy our products.

But we soon realized that selling our products would require more than just marketing channels. Unless a product can create demand among potential customers, it cannot be exported. For a while after the war, products labelled "made in Japan" were thought to be cheap and of poor quality. It was necessary for us to focus our efforts on producing products of superior quality in order to overcome the negative stigma of the term "made in Japan." This was easier said than done.

The fruits of our efforts were only felt much later. But in 1970, twenty-five years after the end of World War II, when Japan's international reputation had finally been clearly established, it was indeed a deeply moving experience.

In that year, Sony announced the building of a color television plant in the United States. This touched off a stream of letters from our American dealers asking whether Sony products made in the United States would have the same quality and reliability as those made in Japan. When I first visited the United States in 1950, Japanese products were considered cheap and shoddy. Now our image has improved so much that the quality of *American*-made products has been brought into question.

We had at last solved one of our major problems. But growth does not come merely by contemplating one's successes. We had to come to grips with the task of making sure that the quality of the products made in the United States would no longer be questioned.

The basic policy by which Sony decided on local production was simple yet fundamental: manufacturing a product in Japan for export to another country meant that we could not respond in a timely manner to the needs and desires of the customers of foreign countries. It is necessary to produce *within* major markets in order to serve their needs.

Many problems must of course be surmounted before local production becomes uniformly successful. To manufacture products of superior quality in a country having a different political, economic, and social environment, and moreover, to make the operation viable as a business, requires efforts in a variety of areas. Minute attention and care must be devoted to every aspect of the operation, from broad management strategies to the tiniest details in daily production.

For example, when the San Diego plant of the Sony Corporation of America started production, the workers on the line would stop work in the middle of an operation and go home as soon as the five o'clock bell rang. They probably thought that they had fulfilled their part of the contract with the company when they had worked the agreed number of hours. However, from the Japanese point of view, putting away the tools before completing a task impairs the following day's operations and generates various other problems. We therefore set aside a short period before quitting time for systematically putting away tools each day. It seemed like a simple solution, but it had a profound impact.

The lesson is that, of course, the Japanese style of management cannot and should not be forced upon Americans. Instead, a new style of management must be created. It is essential to remain flexible in responding to a variety of problems.

Local employment is important not only for reasons of quality control. Growing international trade friction has heightened the importance of local production. Over 80 percent of the Sony color televisions marketed in the United States are produced there. Nearly all of the Sony color televisions marketed in Europe are manufactured in the United Kingdom. The Sony Bridgend plant in Wales exports more than half of the color televisions it produces. This accounts for about one-third of all the color televisions exported from the United Kingdom. In 1980, Sony received the Queen's Award for Export Excellence in recognition of this achievement. Sony has a magnetic tape factory in Bayonne, France, which exports over 90 percent of its output. In this way, Sony endeavors to be a good business citizen of the host country by contributing to the national economy.

Of course Sony is not the only Japanese company that continues to exert its efforts in areas such as quality improvement and local production. Other Japanese companies are also engaged in this steady effort. Increasing trade frictions have heightened the importance of local production, and many Japanese firms have been surveying the possibilities. Some of them are already taking specific action. However, in spite of these widespread efforts, trade controversies continue unabated. This is of serious concern to businessmen.

In 1979, I was named to serve on the Japan-United States Economic Relations Group, the so-called Wisemen's Group,[1] where we considered and discussed

---

1. President Carter and the late Prime Minister Ohira, in their joint communiqué following the U. S.-Japan summit meeting in May 1979, announced that an eight-member group of private Americans and Japanese should be established. The purpose was to study the various factors influencing economic relations between the United States and Japan from a long-range viewpoint, and then to make recommendations to the prime minister and the president for strengthening relations.

142

various economic problems including trade friction. The group included a set of joint recommendations in the report submitted to President Jimmy Carter and Prime Minister Masayoshi Ohira. I believe that these were among the best recommendations made by the various groups and institutions dealing with trade friction. Especially worthy of note was the long-range perspective with which the issues were discussed. A total of eight members, headed by former Ambassador Robert Ingersoll and former Ambassador Nobuhiko Ushiba, spent a year and a half studying the various issues. They were successful in coming up with several effective recommendations. Rarely has there been a case in which views have been announced jointly by Americans and Japanese.

What is most important is to put into practice the various recommendations of not only the Japan-United States Economic Relations Group but also the various other important institutions, groups, associations, and commissions. An example of a recommendation being put into practice is the Office of the Trade Ombudsman (OTO).[2] Although it could not be established in exactly the same form as was recommended by the Wisemen's Group, due to domestic conditions in Japan, it was an important step towards the elimination of friction. The OTO assists in solving as quickly as possible problems of access to the Japanese market. Recently, to strengthen the OTO, an Advisory Council[3] has been established. These actions are in line with the spirit of the joint recommendations of the Wisemen's Group and are to be welcomed.

Steps have also been taken to follow up on the work of the Wisemen's Group in a systematic way. After the termination of the Wisemen's Group in 1981, Secretary of State Alexander Haig and Foreign Minister Sunao Sonoda agreed to continue the work of the group.

Consequently, three joint task forces[4] within the framework of the U.S.-Japan Businessmen's Conference[5] were organized. These three task forces are to be organized by the Japan-U.S. Economic Council and the Advisory Council on Japan-U.S. Economic Relations.[6] A report outlining joint recommendations is expected to be submitted to the heads of both governments in July of this year.

The reduction of trade frictions requires persistence and a great deal of patience. We hope that the necessary efforts will continue to be exerted in some form or another to prevent a crisis in the relationship.

If we now turn our attention to the global situation, we see that controversy over trade is on the rise in spite of concerted efforts to resolve the issue in various quarters. Trade problems between Japan and the United States, Japan and Europe, and the United States and Europe are looming large, posing the greatest threat to the international economy. Japan now finds itself in a predicament over trade imbalances with Europe and

---

2. This was established by decision of a cabinet conference on economic measures held on 30 January 1982. The headquarters was located in the Economic Planning Agency of Japan. The purpose of the OTO is to receive complaints about the Japanese market and to resolve them rapidly.

3. Established in January 1983, as an advisory group to the prime minister in order to enhance and strengthen the OTO. It is composed of private, working-level individuals.

4. The three task forces are in agriculture, in services, and in trade laws and practices.

5. The conference is held once a year, alternately in Japan and the United States, to discuss matters between the two countries. This year will mark the twentieth anniversary meeting.

6. Private bodies established to promote understanding between private individuals of the United States and Japan. The Japan-U.S. Economic Council is the Japanese body and the Advisory Council on Japan-U.S. Economic Relations is the American body.

the United States and the accusation that its markets remain closed. Of course I believe that Japan should open its markets further in order to promote a free global economic system. But I also believe that if some accusations are unreasonable, Japan should voice a firm rebuttal.

For example, the Europeans in their discussions of trade friction with Japan talk about a directed concentration of Japanese exports to Europe. They claim that Japan consciously targets a particular industrial sector for export, thereby damaging that industry in the European country. The fact is that Japan is producing merchandise that the European consumers demand. Japanese industry is not forcing anyone to buy its products. Europeans want them because they suit their needs and tastes.

But why have Japanese products become so attractive? How was the problem of low quality overcome after World War II? How could high-quality products be produced for such relatively low prices? The key to each of these questions is technology.

At the end of World War II, Japanese industrial technology was considerably behind that of other advanced nations. Japan therefore could not manufacture products of adequate quality to sell to consumers abroad. To catch up as rapidly as possible, the Japanese imported technology wholesale from the rest of the world. During a long period in which they were forced to pay high royalties, the Japanese adopted this technology and succeeded with surprising speed in incorporating it into their industries.

Today, the amount of royalties paid by Japanese industries to other countries remains far greater than the total royalties paid by industries abroad to Japan. In this area of payments, the balance between Japan and the United States is just the reverse of the merchandise balance of trade.

The Japanese have added their own knowledge and expertise to the technology they have imported and have used the combination to develop new and superior products. Aiming at expanding business on the basis of technolgy was a success. I continue to believe that technology is an essential element in management strategy and one that will continue to gain in importance.

At one time, when high growth rates had tapered down, some individuals began to give currency to the notion of the "post-industrial society." They claimed that innovation and technical developments had reached a plateau and that technology could no longer be the driving force of advancement. The industrial age, they said, was becoming a thing of the past and a new age was dawning.

I believe that this is an illusion. I am convinced that technology is the most important tool available to us for survival in this unstable world. The shortage of food, the growth of populations, the depletion of resources, and numerous other problems have plunged the peoples of the world into a state of serious uncertainty. But we must not allow such problems to make us pessimistic. We must not forget to continue striving for progress through the use of technology.

When considering technology in the context of business, another very important factor becomes apparent. The question is how the technology now at hand can be translated into a profitable business. As mentioned before, much of Japan's basic technology was imported from abroad. This technology was then further developed and expanded so as to be successfully applied to business uses.

On the other hand, the European nations and the

United States possessed a rich fund of superior basic technology which they had cultivated over a long period of time. However, the process of translating this technology into business applications did not always go well, and in many cases valuable technology remained idle. The fact that Japanese products have often met with greater international success than those of Europe and the United States is due to a capacity for incorporating technology into business. In recent years, the gap between Japan and the countries of Europe and America has become especially pronounced, indirectly leading to a worsening of trade problems.

In considering possible roles for Japan in the business world, the following scenario nalturally comes into view. Japan could make available to the industries of the world its engineering know-how, its production technology for manufacturing high-quality products, and its management system that makes the execution of these tasks possible. Such a role might contribute to a reduction of economic tensions.

Fortunately, some movement in this direction has started, though progress is slow. In October 1982, executives of the Japanese electronics industry travelled to Brussels to meet with their European counterparts. Discussions were conducted on the future of the electronics industry in Europe and Japan. This roundtable discussion between Japan and the EEC was a first on this subject in international relations. Given the current level of tensions in the area of trade between Japan and Europe, the fact that such a meeting of top executives could even be convened represents somewhat of an accomplishment. The purpose of the conference was to discuss future prospects in a serious way. Amidst the turbulence of technological change in the electronics industry, such gatherings may prove to have profound significance.

Of course there are many other matters besides management philosophy which Japan could make available. I imagine that other Japanese businessmen might point out much more important contributions that Japan could make. I have merely tried to suggest certain activities that would clearly have a positive effect on the world, with little danger of negative side-effects. In any case, Japanese businessmen must realize that now we are being called upon to take the initiative in assuming a significant role in world progress.

Reinhard Drifte

THE EUROPEAN COMMUNITY AND JAPAN:
Beyond The Economic Dimension

Europe discovered Japan in 1543 when shipwrecked Portuguese landed on the southern island of Tanegashima. More than three hundred years later, however, the United States was able to start a relationship with Japan which eventually overtook the Euro-Japanese relationship not only in its intensity but also in its comprehensive character. Today mutual interests beyond trade and a common concern for the management of a strife-torn world prompt political leaders in Europe and Japan to look beyond the economic dimension of their relationship. However, the latter remains the overriding concern. Much has already been written on Euro-Japanese and American-Japanese trade relations. This article is therefore less a reassessment of trade issues than an examination of the political and security dimensions of Euro-Japanese relations, which have recently come to the fore.

In the postwar period Europe and Japan have not matched the relationships which have developed either between Europe and the United States or Japan and the United States. It is important to explain why a greater degree of interaction has not developed. Japan, like Europe, suffered greatly during the war. Their economies lay in shambles, their political stability was shaky, and both depended to a large extent on American aid. These similarities did not give rise to close links, due to several factors apart from their geography and history. For seven years Japan was occupied by the United States and separated from the outside world. This experience could not help but have a decisive influence on Japan's postwar orientation. Japan's former allies — Great Britain, and later Germany and Italy — were seriously weakened and thus could not offer an alternative to American influence in Asia. Instead, the European countries concentrated on economic rehabilitation and efforts to save their colonial empires.

As a result Japan turned to the United States, which was then the dominant power in Asia, if not the world. Japan concentrated in the early postwar period on developing a comprehensive relationship with this superpower, while gradually turning to Southeast Asia for new markets, thereby replacing the European colonial powers. Western Europe, on the other hand, emphasized the Atlantic partnership with North America and moved toward the historic task of European integration. For these reasons, alliance with the United States did not imply any link between Europe and Japan. In turn, the United States viewed Europe and Japan as two distinct entities.

Of Transistor Salesmen and Whiskey Merchants
In the 1950s and 1960s resentment in Western Europe against Japan as a result of the past war experiences was still very deep-rooted. Europe had also not forgotten the aggressive Japanese trade practices of the prewar era and still feared inexpensive Japanese goods, trademark and patent piracy, and dumping

147

practices.[1] Geographical separation assured that outdated images of Japan would persist in Europe.[2] This situation was in contrast to the American attitude before the 1969-71 textile crisis when the United States, with few exceptions, had favored the entry of Japanese products into the world market. The United States promoted Japanese exports to Southeast Asia in the hope of stemming the tide of communism. It also sought to draw Japan away from its traditional market in China. The United States strongly supported Japan's application to the General Agreement on Tariffs and Trade (GATT) in 1952. The West Europeans finally accepted Japan in 1955, but still invoked Article 35, which provided that the agreement would not be applied under certain circumstances.[3] This was comparable with Japan's membership application to the Organization for Economic Cooperation and Development (OECD), to which Japan was finally admitted in 1963.

Faced with this history of European resentment, Japan became worried when the West Europeans created the European Community (EC) in 1957. It feared that integration would bolster Europe's competitive edge and exclude Japan from third country markets. In 1959 Japanese exports to Western Europe amounted to 10.6 percent of Japan's total exports.

Japan reacted by embarking on a diplomatic offensive, sending an unending stream of politicians and business leaders to European capitals. Their goal was to have Japan admitted to international economic organizations, gain most-favored nation treatment (MFN), and end the invocation of GATT Article 35. In return, Japan offered only minor steps toward liberalization. It was on the occasion of such a visit by Japanese Prime Minister Ikeda to Paris that President de Gaulle of France referred to him as a "transistor salesman." In 1963

France became the last EC nation to put commercial relations with Japan on an MFN basis. However, most West European countries had a safeguard clause in the bilateral commercial treaties with Japan which replaced Article 35.

By the end of the 1960s the impact of Japan's economy began to be felt in Europe and could no longer be ignored. In terms of GNP, Japan overtook Italy in 1966, Britain in 1967, France in 1968, and finally West Germany in 1969. After 1968 the EC no longer enjoyed a trade surplus with Japan. In 1970 the first book on the Japanese challenge was published in Europe.[4] Between 1968 and 1977, Japanese exports to the nine member states increased at an average compound rate of 25.9 percent. Japanese imports from the EC increased by 18.1 percent during the same period, whereas the share of imports from Japan to the EC remained at only 2 percent. However, Japanese exports were limited to a range of products with which they could achieve outstanding results.[5]

In the early 1960s, these exports consisted mainly of ships and textiles. Later other industries such as ball-bearings, steel, electronics, and automobiles became

---

1. Masamichi Hanabusa, *Trade Problems between Japan and Western Europe* (Westmead : Saxon House Teakfield, 1979), 5.
2. Endymion Wilkinson, *Misunderstanding, Europe vs. Japan*, (Tokyo: Chuokoronsha, 1981), 13.
3. "This Agreement . . . shall not apply as between any contracting party and any other contracting party: (a) if two contracting parties have not entered into tariff negotiations with each other, and (b) either of the contracting parties, at the time either becomes a contracting party, does not consent to such application."
4. Hakan Hedberg, *Die japanische Herausforderung* (Hamburg: Hoffmann und Campe, 1970).
5. Hanabusa, 51.

the object of heated disputes. During the 1960s Europe protected itself against Japanese textiles to such an extent that by the beginning of the 1970s the EC had actually become a net *exporter* of high-quality textiles. Then, as today, protection was sought through voluntary self-restraint agreements. In 1982 such agreements covered automobiles, color televisions, and some machine tools. In 1983 the EC is looking for restraints on video tape recorders, small trucks, and motorcycles.[6]

The rapid penetration by Japan of sectors such as optics, electronics, and the automobile industry plunged many Community companies into a crisis or simply drove them out of business, as has been witnessed in Britain's motorcycle or West Germany's camera industry. Japan's export boom, which accelerated after the first oil crisis in order to offset recession, affected Europe's most important and vocal industries.

Since 1973, the trade deficit with Japan has grown steadily worse, reaching almost $13 billion in 1980 and $14 billion in 1982. In contrast to these EC figures, Japanese statistics indicate deficits of $10.3 billion in 1981 and $9.51 billion for 1982. Japanese statistics are based on *fob* (free-on-board) exports and *cit* (cost, insurance, transit) imports, which tend to underestimate export value and overestimate imports, by an average of about 20 percent. Under these conditions, lack of accessibility to the Japanese market came increasingly under fire. In 1974 the Europeans started to attack Japan's non-tariff barriers (NTBs). French President Giscard d'Estaing, for one, did not consider it below his dignity to urge Japanese Prime Minister Ohira to lower the tariff on cognac on the occasion of his visit to Japan. Prime Minister Thatcher, on a similar occasion in 1982, expressed her concern over the equally prohibitive tariff on whiskey.

Japan's trade surplus, the difficulty of foreign access to the Japanese market, and the consequences of the depreciated yen are also well-known conflict areas in Japanese-American trade relations. Yet Japan's economic disputes with the EC "linger on like the prolonged drizzle that characterizes Japan's rainy season," whereas disputes with the United States are reminiscent of a showdown between pistol-drawing cowboys.[7] In order to understand differences in styles of conflict management we have to look at the organizational structure by which the EC deals with its external trade relations.

European Integration and the Trade Conflict With Japan

Article 113 of the Treaty of Rome, the charter of the EC, provides for a common commercial policy within the Community and toward non-member countries. It is the task of the EC Commission to propose initiatives on commercial policies and to negotiate trade agreements according to a mandate of the Council of Ministers (CM). As a result, the process of European integration has decisively affected the way in which the Euro-Japanese economic relationship has been managed.[8]

The EC Commission tried to assume a key role in the Euro-Japanese trade relationship by sending the first EC commissioner, Jean Rey, to Japan in

---

6. *Agence Europe,* 10-11 January 1983.
7. Shinichi Hakoshima, "Mutual Ignorance and Misunderstanding—Causes of Japan-EC Economic Disputes," *Japan Quarterly* 26 (1979): 481.
8. Albrecht Rothacher, *Economic Diplomacy between the European Community and Japan 1959-1981* (Aldershot: Gower Publishing Company, 1983), 17.

December 1961. His hosts paid their respects to the EC by granting him audiences with the emperor and the prime minister. Regular informational meetings between Tokyo and Brussels were agreed upon. It soon became apparent that Japan had overrated the role of the Commission; the six member states could not even agree to accept the institution of these consultations.

Since then, the Commission has tried to present a unified EC front to Japan. In 1963 it proposed a common safeguard clause and a common list of sensitive products. However, the Europeans and the Japanese were both afraid of losing advantages they had gained through previous bilateral agreements. Furthermore, Japan was opposed to institutionalizing the safeguard clause. After the member states finally gave the Commission a negotiating mandate for a common trade agreement in 1970, the negotiations broke down several years later because the Japanese resisted the EC's insistence on a safeguard clause. For this reason there is still no Euro-Japanese trade agreement.

Instead, the Commission has continued to pursue partial agreements with Japan, each facing a long struggle to obtain the support of the Council of Ministers. A 1969 cotton agreement constituted the first genuine common EC policy enacted towards Japan. The level of the Commission's role was raised in June 1973 with the advent of regular high-level talks between the Commission and the Japanese government, taking place every six months alternately in Brussels and Tokyo. These consultations are similar to those taking place between Japan and the United States. They cover bilateral issues as well as multilateral problems, such as GATT negotiations or the impending United Nations Conference on Trade and Development (UNCTAD), in Belgrade.

In February 1972 a high Commission official announced that the EC would open an office in Tokyo at the end of the year. It took two more years, however, for France to agree to such a step. In October 1975 the EC office in Tokyo was finally officially opened, seventeen months after Tokyo had granted it diplomatic status. Embassy officials of EC member states were not very enthusiastic about their new competitors in the narrow field of Euro-Japanese relations.[9] Finally, in 1976, a Japanese mission to the European Commission was opened in Brussels.

It is basically the absence of a common industrial policy in the EC which prevents a united trade policy towards Japan from emerging. This is partly due to a lack of trust between the member states. Appeals for solidarity have been belied by the persistence of purely national and bilateral approaches to Japan.[10] In addition, differences in economic philosophies hinder the development of a unified industrial policy. A recent example is the planned merger between the private German company, Grundig, and the nationalized French company, Thomson. Although electronics is an area where only a strong European competitor could hold off the Japanese, differences in cartel law in the two countries have proven a severe impediment to cooperation.

As a result, initiatives by the Commission are often rebuffed by a coalition of member states which do not want the Commission to encroach on their national

---

9. Rothacher, 160, 181, 199.
10. Economic and Social Committee of the European Communities, *The EC's External Relations— Stocktaking and Consistency of Action* (Brussels: Economic and Social Committee of the European Communities, January 1982), 33.

prerogatives and those who say that industrial policy should be left to the industrialists. Since the Commission depends on a *de facto* consensus in the Council of Ministers, its policies have been watered down to the "lowest common denominator."

In search of a comprehensive solution to the worsening trade conflict with Japan, the Commission proposed a package deal by which both sides would revoke their national restrictions simultaneously—a sort of tariff zero option—while strengthening industrial and scientific cooperation.[11] Later the Commission invoked GATT Article 23 § 1 provisions against Japan.[12] The Commission could not gain acceptance to this three-sided approach. Italy and France initially were opposed to the Article 23 procedures, arguing that they would take too much time, while others were afraid of bringing the trade conflict too much into the open. Some states vehemently opposed the lifting of national restrictions on trade with Japan, even as part of a package deal. So far, the Commission has never been allowed to offer even symbolic concessions outside of the framework of the GATT negotiations.[13] France argued that industrial cooperation would only give Japan the technology of those few sectors where the Community still maintains the advantage.[14]

On 22 March 1982 the Council of Foreign Ministers finally decided to "explore the possibilities of scientific and technological cooperation" and to initiate the procedures of Article 23 § 1 against Japan.[15] Since then, representatives from the EC and Japan met three times—in May, July, and October of 1982—in Geneva, at the headquarters of the GATT secretariat. The EC argued that Japan's low imports of manufactured goods, non-tariff barriers, and special features of the Japanese economy including a small number of extremely large business groupings, industrial oligopolies, a closed distribution system, and the low international profile of the Japanese currency were responsible for the failure of the two sides to achieve the GATT objective of "reciprocal and mutually advantageous arrangements."[16] Japan responded, not without good reason, that these arguments were beyond the scope of GATT.

Not surprisingly these negotiations produced no concrete results. However, they increased the pressure on Japan to reduce its tariffs and abolish NTBs. Japanese moves on these two issues in January and May of 1982 and again in January 1983 must be viewed against this background. In December 1982 the Council of Ministers authorized the Commission to initiate proceedings under Article 23 § 2, demanding the creation of the

---

11. Commission des Communautés Européennes, *Réexamen de la politique commerciale de la Communauté à l'égard du Japon* (Brussels, 15 July 1980), COM (80) 444 final.

12. Article 23 § 1: "If any contracting party should consider that any benefit accruing to it directly or indirectly under this Agreement is being nullified or impaired or that the attainment of any objective of the Agreement is being impeded as the result of (a) the failure of another contracting party to carry out its obligations under this Agreement, or (b) the application by another contracting party of any measure, whether or not it conflicts with the provisions of this Agreement, or (c) the existence of any other situation, the contracting party may, with a view to satisfactory adjustment of the matter, make written representations or proposals to the other contracting party or parties which it considers to be concerned. Any contracting party thus approached shall give sympathetic consideration to the representations or proposals made to it."

13. Rothacher, 329.

14. *Agence Europe*, 22 and 23 February 1982; 4 March 1982.

15. The European Commission and the Japanese government organized a symposium for this purpose in November 1981 in Tokyo and another one in January 1983 in Brussels.

16. *Le Monde*, 23 April 1982; *Neue Zürcher Zeitung*, 8 April 1982.

international panel.[17] The most important negotiations, however, will concern self-restraint agreements on ten different items and the continuation of other agreements such as the one concerning automobiles.[18]

The Commission is under conflicting pressures from its member states. France and Great Britain are threatening to take independent action, while the Netherlands and Germany are still reticent about formal agreements which would contradict their public stance against protectionism. Through its notoriously slow import clearance of video tape recorders in Poitiers—although there is no French VTR production to be protected—France has shown its determination to act alone and institute petty NTBs.

Lacking a common industrial and trade policy, the role of the European Commission is sometimes viewed rather critically. For example, it is charged that the Commission is only looking to appear active in order to justify its own existence.[19] It is clear that the lack of consensus among the member states has sometimes tempted the Commission to pay more attention to the effects of its policies on its own position than to the long-term consequences for Euro-Japanese relations. One such case involved prolonged negotiations of an EC-Japan trade agreement which had no chance of being signed. This only had a negative effect on relations with Japan. Of course, this kind of criticism tends to overlook the clear mandate given to the Commission by the Treaty of Rome in the field of external trade. Instead, the Commission has merely been considered by most member states as a welcome, although often unwieldy, additional lever against the Japanese, particularly in industry-specific negotiations, such as those concerning Japanese acceptance of European medical tests and industrial standards. However, it is precisely the interaction of the Commission with Japanese bureaucracies which prevented an explosion of the lingering trade conflict which Hokushima.

The Commission's attention to the calendar of the meetings of the Council of Foreign Ministers proved to be misplaced, resulting in considerable restraint on the part of the Japanese. The Commission's demands were often pressed too rapidly, leaving Japan with insufficient time to reply.

The Commission itself in many ways reflects the member states' dissent over self-restraint agreements. The Directorate General IV advocates free competition and has therefore been basically opposed to such agreements, as is not the case with other divisions of the Commission. This sort of internal bureaucratic disunity is also prevalent between the Japanese Foreign Ministry and MITI, the former proving often more ready for compromise than the latter. Recently, both of these ministries have come together on international trade issues and are calling for the abolition of agricultural tariffs against the vehement opposition of the Ministry of Agriculture. The Finance Ministry is opposed to tariff cuts which would mean reduced revenue in a period of budget constraints.

Politicization of the Political Dimension

The Euro-Japanese relationship had reached a critical juncture when a *Keidanren* delegation led by Toshio Doko visited the EC in October 1976. Chihiro Hosoya argues that structural changes in the interna-

---

17. *Agence Europe*, 15 December 1982.
18. *International Herald Tribune*, 28 January 1983.
19. Hakoshima, 485.

tional system since 1971, differences between European and Japanese perceptions of the character of the bilateral trade conflict, and European pressure tactics aimed at extracting concessions from the Japanese led to what he calls a politicization of Euro-Japanese relations.[20] Such perceptions were strengthened by other circumstances, including the 1976 federal election campaign in West Germany, during which attacks on Japanese imports became political instruments, and bickering in Japan between Doko and MITI Minister Komoto. Albrecht Rothacher, however, does not consider the term "politicization" appropriate. In his opinion, politicization means intervention by the political establishment in a way which changes "the hitherto pursued direction or quality of relations."[21] Yet, although the economic recession in Europe and a trade deficit of over $3 billion with Japan had lowered the threshold for political intervention, it did not permit a clear breakthrough in the Europeans' approach to solving the stalemate in their trade relations with Japan. Euro-Japanese relations continued to be bogged down in bureaucratic politics. A trade deficit which had grown to $14 billion, twelve million people out of work, and the British prime minister herself asking for a decrease of the whiskey tariff could not improve the situation.

However, it is not so important whether a term like politicization is used as a tactical ploy to impress the Japanese or as an accurate characterization of a certain level of conflict. What matters in the end is how far the political dimension of the Euro-Japanese relationship is being understood by both sides. This is not only central to a smooth resolution of the trade conflict but also to the protection of other mutual non-trade interests. Europe has increasingly come to the understanding that Japan represents a great deal more than just trade.

In a constantly changing world, Japan is an important element of stability.[22]

In spite of the relative decline in American power and leadership in the world, heightened conflicts demand a concerted approach by the West. North-South issues provide a major source of instability. There is a pressing need to assist the debt-ridden South through this period of crisis and recession. Western influence in international forums such as the United Nations has diminshed. In attempting to project its views, Europe now depends on Japan's support as the second-largest contributor to the UN general account. As a rising economic force in the world and a leader in Asia, Japan finds itself in a better position than Europe to cope with issues regarding Third World development.

Since the Iranian hostage crisis and the recent increase in East-West tensions, there have been several areas in which European approaches were more similar to those of the Japanese than to those of the Americans. One of these concerns the view of military force as a factor in international relations. Another is the difference in attitudes concerning the Palestinian issue, where the Japanese have begun to voice their position with greater confidence.

Europe and Japan also share a desire to preserve their political independence vis-à-vis the United States, although both maintain strong commitments to this power. Growing self-confidence as an economic super-

---

20. Chihiro Hosoya, "Relations between the European Community and Japan," *Journal of Common Market Studies* 18 (December 1979): 160.
21. Rothacher, 298.
22. Michael Hardy, "The European Community and Japan: Agenda for Adjustment," *The World Today* (November 1980): 432.

power has made Japan ever more conscious of its need for independence.

Europeans are becoming increasingly aware of the current movement toward integration in the Asia-Pacific region. This is the area with the greatest growth potential in the world and with most of the raw materials needed by highly industrialized societies. The United States already conducts more trade with the Asia-Pacific region than with Western Europe. Whereas Europe fears being left out, Japan by itself is incapable of developing the region and offering adequate markets for the local products. The French government is particularly sensitive to this issue, as demonstrated through a major ambassadorial conference in Paris last year.[23]

In July 1978 Prime Minister Fukuda declared that "the days are past when Japan and Europe could be content with an indirect relationship through the United States as an intermediary."[24] The Ōhira cabinet paid particular attention to the political dimensions of the Euro-Japanese relationship, as was demonstrated by the participation of the Japanese foreign minister in a 1980 Council of Foreign Ministers meeting in Luxembourg at the height of the Iranian hostage crisis. This was the first time that a non-member state had been represented at such a meeting. Since that time, Japan has often stressed that it is a part of the West, with which it shares basic political and economic values and with which its security and stability are closely related.[25]

Yet despite these common interests and declarations, Euro-Japanese political cooperation has so far been rather sparse.[26] In order to understand the difficulties facing this growing cooperation, it is necessary to understand the problems in moving from an awareness of common political interests to actual cooperation.

One major stumbling block in Europe is political pressure resulting from the soaring rate of unemployment, which is often linked to the Japanese export offensive. The twelve million people out of work in Europe demand immediate help from their political leadership. This thorny problem can only be resolved if both Europe and Japan recognize the overriding importance of their common interests and are willing to make some compromises. For the Europeans, this means restructuring industry, not only in order to become competitive with the Japanese, but also to create markets for the products of the Third World. For the Japanese, this means departing from past and current patterns of market control. Japan should open its domestic market further and agree to temporary voluntary restraints on the export of sensitive goods.

Another impediment to Euro-Japanese political cooperation is Japan's sense that it is not considered a full member of the Western camp. For example, Japan felt humiliated when it was excluded from the Guadeloupe meeting in December 1978 at the instigation of European participants.[27] On the occasion of Prime Minister Ōhira's funeral in July 1980, it was widely noted that Chinese Prime Minister Hua and President Carter were present to represent their countries, whereas the Euro-

---

23. For a critical appraisal of the Asian policy of the new French government, see François Joyaux, "Une nouvelle politique française en Extrême-Orient?" *Politique Internationale* 17 (Fall 1982).

24. *International Herald Tribune*, 20 July 1978.

25. Ministry of Foreign Affairs, *Diplomatic Bluebook 1981 Edition* (Tokyo: Foreign Press Center, 1981), 25.

26. Rothacher, 299.

27. Department of State, *Executive Seminar in National and International Affairs, 22nd Session,* April 1980; Robert Immermann, *European Attitudes Towards Japan: Trilateralism's Weakest Link, A Case Study,* 11.

pean countries sent representatives of lower rank.[28] The 1979 internal report of the European Commission, which referred to the Japanese as "workaholics living in rabbit hutches," also did little to endear Europe to the Japanese.

There are various factors accounting for this dismal situation. Europeans consider Japan as completely different culturally, politically, and economically. The Japanese only encourage these perceptions by maintaining their own obsession with considering themselves unique [Nihonjinron]. Many European leaders find it therefore difficult to accept Japan's repeated assertion that it shares common basic values with Europe. Knowledge of Japan remains rather limited in Europe. Exhibitions like the 1982 London display on the Edo period are not necessarily the answer, despite the high degree of effort expended for such cultural events. Europeans still tend to think that Japan is run by MITI. They have failed to develop a proper understanding of the ferocious competition prevalent among Japanese companies. Japan is often dismissed as a political dwarf who does nothing but take orders from the Americans. Gaullists in particular have trouble accepting a country which relies so much on a superpower for its own security.

Nor are Japanese ideas about Europe always correct, as Endymion Wilkinson has so aptly demonstrated in his book *Misunderstanding*. Whereas Japan's failure to shoulder its share of international responsibility in the past has cast doubts on its value as a dependable ally of Europe, Japanese are obsessed with their impression that Europeans turn to them only when in need of help.[29] Foreign Minister Shintaro Abe said during his visit to Europe in January 1983 that a system must be found whereby Japan's intentions can be reflected in joint actions, as opposed to present practice, whereby the United States and Europe agree to something and then attempt to persuade Japan to act accordingly.[30]

Recently Europeans have been startled by Japan's growing self-confidence. The Japanese now talk of the British or even German disease! They have even begun to refer to European countries as former developed countries (FDC). This kind of perception is clearly not conducive to an atmosphere of political cooperation.

A further obstacle is the absence of a coherent European foreign policy, one of the consequences of imperfect European integration. In the 1970s the Community instituted "European Political Cooperation." Political leaders of the member states have started to meet regularly to discuss a common approach to issues such as the Middle East conflict and East-West relations. Of course, this has not yet resulted in a common foreign policy. Japan would nonetheless like to participate with the Europeans in areas of shared views, such as the Middle East.

A final impediment to greater Euro-Japanese cooperation is the lack of an institutional framework for negotiations. The current organization of the EC does not provide an adequate mechanism. Still, the list of issues to be resolved through regular high-level consultations between EC and Japanese representatives run the gamut from trade issues to relations with the Third World, technological cooperation, the environment, and energy. In May 1980 German Foreign Minister Hans

---

28. Rothacher, 271.
29. Yukio Satō, "Opportunities for Broader Cooperation," in Loukas Tsoukalis and Maureen White, eds., *Japan and Western Europe* (London: Frances Pinter, 1982), 189.
30. *Asahi Evening News*, 5 January 1983.

Dietrich Genscher proposed the creation of a special EC-Japan consultative forum, but there has thus far been no action taken toward implementing his suggestion.[31] During his January 1983 visit to Europe, Shintaro Abe proposed ministerial-level meetings between Tokyo and Brussels as already practiced between Brussels and Washington. The foreign ministers of the EC agreed at their March 1 Council of Ministers meeting to consult regularly every six months.[32]

On the trilateral level, Japan has participated in annual economic summit conferences since 1975 and has been a member of the private Trilateral Commission since 1971. Occasionally public and private institutions organize Euro-Japanese conferences as did the Council of Europe in June 1982. Meetings alone, however, will not lead to political cooperation if the above-mentioned impediments are not properly taken into consideration. In addition, Europeans and Japanese have different styles of communication; the chances for misunderstandings are great, especially at high-level meetings. The lack of foreign language capabilities is also still a serious obstacle. Nothing expresses better the frustration of many European political leaders with their Japanese counterparts than French Foreign Minister Claude Cheysson's comment on former Prime Minister Zenko Suzuki at the Ottawa meeting in 1981: "It is not enough to smile in a language which nobody understands."[33]

The Security Dimension: From Portuguese Arquebuses to the French Mirage

The relative decline of American power and subsequent demands for more sharing of burdens between the members of the Western Alliance against the background of increased worldwide tensions could not fail to impress upon West European and Japanese leaders the existence not only of common political interests but also security or military-related interests. West Germany was the first European country to signal to the Japanese that the two nations had similar interests in the defense area, when Helmut Schmidt, then defense minister, visited Japan in 1971. Only in 1978 did the director of the Japanese Self-Defense Agency repay this visit. Since then exchanges of high-ranking defense officials from Europe and Japan have taken place regularly. When Foreign Minister Shintaro Abe visited Europe in January 1983, his talks included security-related issues such as disarmament, NATO, East-West relations, and Sino-Soviet relations.

In the final analysis, the absence of a security treaty between Europe and Japan is the most important difference between the Japanese-American and European-American relationships. But there have been recent developments which show that there can be consultation and cooperation between Europe and Japan on security-related matters without the existence of a security treaty. In time this may increase the comprehensiveness of the Euro-Japanese relationship.

The most prominent issue in the security area is probably the East-West relationship. This has been accentuated by the Soviet military build-up in the Far East and invasion of Afghanistan. Subsequent events have clarified differences in the ways in which East-West relations are perceived by Europe and Japan. First of all, there are differences concerning the nature

---

31. *Japan Times*, 4 May 1980; *News and Views from Japan*, 24 March 1983.
32. *Agence Europe*, 5 January 1983.
33. *The Daily Yomiuri*, 19 July 1981.

of the perceived Soviet threat. One reason for this is the feeling of complete security which had been nurtured by American military superiority in East Asia until very recently. This in turn has led to widespread pacifism, indifference, and non-military approaches to security. In addition, Japan is more concerned with China than Western Europe, which pays more attention to the Soviet Union. Another reason is that the concentration of Soviet troops on the Japanese-claimed northern islands is of an entirely different nature from the situation in Eastern Europe. These Soviet-occupied islands no longer have a resident Japanese population, whereas the Federal Republic of Germany must always take into account possible Soviet retaliatory measures against East Germans in cases of policies which might displease the Soviet Union.

These differences of circumstances and perceptions make Japan less interested in pursuing détente policies independently. Japan has not enjoyed the benefits of détente directly as Germany has, and it does not perceive a trade-off between détente and military confrontation in its own bilateral relations with the Soviet Union. For these reasons, Japan was more forthcoming in supporting the United States on the issue of economic sanctions and other retaliatory measures against the Soviet Union after the invasion of Afghanistan.[34] The difficulty of trilateral cooperation on this issue was dramatically demonstrated by the British participation in the Moscow Olympics (under a Tory government) and Japan's loss of substantial Soviet commercial orders to European countries.

The closely related issue of arms control has come into focus since 1980 in connection with the modernization of theater nuclear forces (TNF). At that time, Robert Immermann was still being told by West Ger-

man negotiators that the Japanese were hesitant to engage in any meaningful dialogue on this subject.[35] The reason for this reticence is the sensitivity of all security and military-related issues in Japan. One should also mention that the Japanese have a tendency to only consider the military equation between the United States and the Soviet Union, leaving no place for regional arms control. In addition, mutual and negotiated limitations and restrictions similar to those pursued through the Helsinki process still seem to the Japanese to be an alien approach.[36] On the contrary, West European acceptance of the territorial status quo on the Soviet western borders through West Germany's treaties with the Soviet Union and Poland, as well as the Helsinki Conference of 1975, led to Japanese dissatisfaction with Western Europe. Tokyo became concerned about the possible influence of these agreements on *its* territorial claims vis-à-vis the Soviet Union.

However, the possible redeployment of European-based SS-20s to the Far East as the result of Euro-American talks with the Soviet Union has heightened Japanese interest in the modernization of theater nuclear forces. Until 1981 the Japanese government had left any protest about the installation of SS-20s in the Far East to its American alliance partner. Changes in public opinion towards defense in Japan, the current

---

34. Shimoda Conference, *The Present State of U.S.-Japan Relations : An Overview by the Steering Committee*, The Fifth Shimoda Conference, 2-4 September 1981, 10.

35. Immermann, 7.

36. For a detailed analysis of Japan's arms control and disarmament policies see J.W.M. Chapman, R. Drifte, I.T.M. Gow, eds., *Japan's Quest for Comprehensive Security, Defense-Diplomacy-Dependence* (London: Frances Pinter, 1983).

presence of 108 SS-20s with 324 warheads in the Far East, and particularly, the likelihood of redeployment of even more missiles to the Far East have led to increased Japanese participation in discussion of this issue.[37] During his January 1983 visit to Europe, Shintaro Abe stressed the importance of the global balance, expressing his support for the zero option in Europe as well as in the Far East.[38] The strong demand for the zero option by Japan has significantly complicated the Geneva negotiations on TNF.

The modernization of theater nuclear forces remains on the agenda of Euro-Japanese consultations. Chances for cooperation are still questionable, though, since West European and American leaders may be tempted to sacrifice Japanese interests under the pressure of domestic public opinion. The Japanese position is handicapped by the primacy of the three non-nuclear principles, which make it impossible for the government to explain to the public that the principal danger posed by the SS-20s would be to disconnect Japan from the United States in a regional nuclear conflict. For the same reasons, the Japanese government is not only opposed to the deployment of American nuclear weapons in Japan but even on ships of the U.S. Pacific Fleet. In addition, Soviet SS-20s are directed not only against Japan but also against China, which does not wish to be party to the U.S.-Soviet negotiations.

Common interests on arms control go beyond the single issue of TNF. Western Europe is actively engaged in promoting various approaches to arms control, including confidence-building measures and a convention on chemical weapons. Japanese support and interest can only strengthen these projects' chances for success. Thus far Japan has been rather reluctant. In the case of the non-proliferation treaty, Japanese and German interests in safeguards were very close, but in 1969 both sides agreed not to coordinate their policies since they had different ideas of how to use the issue in bargaining with the United States.[39] Today, West European and Japanese interests on the issue of nonproliferation are again very close, particularly in view of the changes in American policy.

The Middle East

The impact of the Afghanistan invasion was amplified by simultaneous events in the Middle East. The Iranian revolution and the Iran-Iraq war constituted a common threat to vital oil supplies for both Europe and Japan. In contrast to the oil crisis of 1973-74, there was now a clear security threat involved. Sea traffic in the Middle East is composed largely of Japanese vessels. In addition, the forceful American approach (e.g., the aborted hostage rescue mission in Iran) was quite unpopular in Japan and pushed Japan closer to the EC. Japan was also attracted by the EC's conciliatory attitude on the Palestinian question. In both cases Euro-Japanese cooperation prevented Japan from becoming isolated and strengthened the European position.

The Middle East will continue to be important for Euro-Japanese relations. Yukio Satō has correctly pointed out that the Persian Gulf is the only geographical region where Europe and Japan seem to share common interests to a similar degree.[40] Yet cooperation is limited by the existence of NATO and the Japanese-American security treaty. The EC has

---

37. *Le Monde,* 19 February 1983.
38. *Neue Zürcher Zeitung,* 6 January 1983.
39. *Frankfurter Allgemeine Zeitung,* 23 May 1969.
40. Tsoukalis, 191.

had difficulties in coordinating its position on the Middle East. Another problem concerns the actual forms that cooperation might take. France and Great Britain sent some naval forces to the area on their own, without any coordinated action by the EC or NATO. Japan's constitution and public opinion do not allow for collective defense and the dispatch of military personnel abroad; it is also debatable whether this is even desirable. The Japanese point out that they currently support the American military forces stationed in Japan with $1 billion annually. Some of these forces are also deployed in the Indian Ocean for the security of the Persian Gulf region. In addition, Japanese financial assistance to Egypt for the improvement of the Suez canal has made it possible for large aircraft carriers belonging to the U.S. Sixth Fleet to pass through the canal.[41] In early 1983, the Japanese government also indicated that it might be willing to provide financial support for the multinational peacekeeping troops in Beirut.[42]

Concern over the Middle East is also closely related to a new policy of giving aid to so-called "strategic countries" or "countries bordering on areas of conflict," which is part of the Comprehensive National Security Concept developed since 1980. Turkey, Egypt, and Sudan are among this group of privileged aid recipients. Euro-Japanese cooperation plays a role in the case of Turkey. The original aid program for Turkey was determined at the Guadeloupe summit meeting of 1978, from which Japan was excluded. However, Japan was later asked to participate in this aid program. Other "strategic countries" include Thailand, Pakistan, Kenya, and Jamaica.

Europe and Japan share a common approach towards the Third World. Both support the idea that many threats to security come from underdevelopment, whereas the United States sometimes seems to focus on the purely military aspect, as is demonstrated in its policy toward Central America. Thus far, Japan's contribution to the Third World has been high in absolute figures, but very low as a percentage of GNP. With the United States drastically decreasing its aid and the European countries also facing economic problems which prevent them from expanding their aid programs, Japan has finally embarked on an aid-doubling scheme.

As with the political dimension of the Euro-Japanese relationship, the security dimension suffers from the lack of an institutional framework. The United States has been an important promoter of Euro-Japanese security cooperation. With its global outlook, the United States wants to encourage a linking of its two major security alliances—NATO and the Japanese-American security alliance.[43] However, it is doubtful whether this would constitute a contribution to international security. Moreover, it would jeopardize one major motivation for Euro-Japanese cooperation: the will to establish a political identity in a form perceived as independent from the United States.

The visit of a North Atlantic Assembly delegation to Tokyo in May 1980 has stimulated an institutional rapprochement between Japan and Western Europe. Since June 1980 Japanese parliamentarians have been invited to observe the functioning of this NATO-linked institu-

---

41. Motoharu Arima, speech to North Atlantic Assembly Session, London, 18 November 1982.
42. *International Herald Tribune*, 31 January 1983.
43. U. Alexis Johnson and George R. Packard, eds., *The Common Security Interests of Japan, the United States and NATO* (Cambridge: Ballinger Publishing Company, 1981); *Asahi Evening News*, 1 February 1983.

tion. Members of the Japanese Diet come from the ruling Liberal Democratic Party, the New Liberal Club, the Democratic Socialist Party, the Komeitō (Clean Government Party), and the United Social Democratic Party. In May 1982, a Trilateral Security League of Dietmen was also established.[44]

Direct contact between the Self-Defense Agency and NATO headquarters in Brussels now takes place regularly. The Japanese government has openly declared its appreciation of NATO; this would have been unthinkable some years ago. The Japanese consider such contacts extremely valuable for gathering information on the security situation in Europe. The members of the Japanese armed forces and of the Self-Defense Agency also appreciate the gain in status which goes with these contacts. On a bilateral basis, joint military exercises have been held with Great Britain in September 1980 and with France in February 1983.[45]

However, with the exception of the British and Germans, most European members of NATO seem not to be very sanguine about signs of NATO involvement with Japan. Recently it was reported that France had refused a Japanese demand for an association with NATO. Japan had apparently tried to become more closely linked since many measures concerning relations with the Soviet Union and the East European countries (sanctions, technology exchange limits, etc.) are discussed within NATO. Although Japan is always asked to join these Western measures, it does not feel properly consulted because of its absence from NATO.[46] Apart from the aforementioned reasons there is also a basic competition between Europe and Japan for American attention. Each side has at one time or another been fearful that in time of crisis the United States might be too busy elsewhere to respond to its needs effectively.[47]

The above discussion shows the delicate nature of the security dimension in the Euro-Japanese relationship. In addition to the problems of finding a proper institutional framework beyond bilateral contacts, there also exist differences of interest. When the British requested Japanese support in the Falkland crisis, Japan supported the UN Security Council Resolution 502 but did not join the EC ban of imports from Argentina, since it wanted to maintain friendly relations with Latin America. A similarly cautious approach by Japan could be imagined if Great Britian asks for support of its position on Hong Kong. The Japanese will certainly not be willing to risk their improved relations with Peking, but a strong Japanese government could perhaps act as a mediator.

Discussion of the security dimension in the Euro-Japanese relationship would be incomplete without mention of two important dead ends. One is the European demand for more Japanese defense efforts with the hidden intention of hindering Japan's economic competitive edge. It is true that Japan's defense expenditures are much lower than those of European countries and that Japan has so far enjoyed what could be called a "free ride on peace" [*heiwa tada nori*]. Demands for increased Japanese defense efforts should always take into account the impact a military build-up would have on the Far East and on Japanese society itself. In this respect Japan cannot be compared to West Germany, which is firmly integrated into NATO and the

---

44. *Japan Times*, 3 September 1980; *Süddeutsche Zeitung*, 8 February 1983.

45. *Japan Times*, 14 April 1982.

46. Immermann, 9; *Le Monde*, 11 March 1983; *International Herald Tribune*, 4 April 1983.

47. Johnson, 212.

EC. A military force of half a million troops in Japan would mean more to other countries than the same force level in West Germany.[48] Demands for more sharing of burdens should not solely focus on military contributions.

Demands for Japanese imports of European arms can be equally self-defeating in the long run.[49] Such demands are often based on the European trade deficit. Arms purchases from Europe, however, could eventually lead to the abolition of Japanese restraints on arms exports. It would be better not to test Japanese competitiveness in this area. When the Portuguese presented their Japanese rescuers with some arquebuses after their shipwreck in 1543, Japanese craftsmen learned very quickly how to build them. Very soon they played a decisive role in Japan's civil war—and in Hideyoshi's invasion of the continent.

Prospects

The most pressing issue in the Euro-Japanese relationship is still the trade problem, or more precisely, the damage to major European industrial branches, which has contributed to the high unemployment rate. A serious approach to this problem is not only in the Euro-Japanese interest but is also crucial for the survival of the European Community and the continued growth of world trade. EC protectionist measures directed towards the outside imply mounting protectionism within the Community itself. The solution is more complicated than merely proclaiming that Japan is the most open market in the world, as Foreign Minister Sakurauchi did in his speech at the last ministerial GATT meeting in November 1982. Nor should the European countries follow the example of Italy, which recorded a trade surplus with Japan of $77 million, due to its long-standing quotas

on Japanese products—most notably, an import limit of only 2,000 automobiles per year.[50]

Increasing common political and security interests will not lead to more than noncommittal communiqués if Europe's serious concern over unemployment is not properly addressed. Placing the blame on one or the other side for past actions or non-actions does not help. Aggravation of the trade issue will only do harm to the remaining common interests and lead to a "politicization" of the conflict and self-defeating demands in the security area.

However, both sides will need patience. Real solutions, such as Japanese investment in Europe and industrial cooperation, take time. The export promotion scheme of the European Commission, consisting of twenty-two annual scholarships for young European businessmen to learn the Japanese language and followed by an internship in a Japanese company, will improve conditions only in the long term. On the other hand, the Japanese government is limited in its capacity to share burdens by the high national budget deficit. In fiscal year 1983, 16.2 percent of all expenses went toward servicing the national debt. Future Japanese governments will therefore have to take into account the impact of their policies for conflict resolution on the stability of the political system.

---

48. Yukio Satō, "The Evolution of Japanese Security Policy," *Adelphi Papers* 187 (Autumn 1982): 38; *Western Security*, a report prepared by the directors of Forschungsinstitut der Deutschen Gesellschaft für Auswärtige Politik, Council on Foreign Relations, Institut Français des Relations Internationales, Royal Institute of International Affairs, February 1981, 14.

49. *Asahi Evening News*, 31 May 1982.

50. *Financial Times*, 21 January 1983.

R. B. Byers and Stanley C. M. Ing

SHARING THE BURDEN ON THE FAR SIDE OF THE ALLIANCE:

Japanese Security in the 1980s

In the current international climate the future role and position of Japan in world security affairs has assumed increased importance and significance. Economically—as reflected by participation in the Seven Nation Summit, by gross national product, by trade—Japan is a superpower second only to the United States. From the political and military perspectives, however, Japan has remained an important, yet, in many respects, limited power.

Potentially, of course, Japan has the attributes to be a major world power in both political and military terms. But will this potential be translated into reality? While oversimplified, there are at least two interpretations of Japan's possible security roles in the 1980s. On the one hand, it can be argued that Japan's unique postwar experience will continue to be the dominant factor to shape Japan's foreign and defense policies for the rest of the decade. This scenario acknowledges that Japan will expand as an economic superpower, but continue to be limited in terms of political and military influence and importance.

On the other hand, an increasing number of observers argue that the status quo is unrealistic and not in the interests of Japan or the West. This view holds that both external and domestic considerations and pressures are such that Japan will assume more active political and military roles. In effect, by the end of the 1980s Japan will have emerged as a more important and active participant in the global system, and this includes the security arena.

If the latter scenario is correct, even in part, then the implications for the international system both globally and regionally are of considerable significance. For the West, especially the United States, the role of Japan in security is obviously an issue of major concern. Can and will Japan make a meaningful contribution to Western security? If so, what does this mean in terms of the formulation and implementation of Japanese foreign policy? Would a politically and militarily resurgent Japan pose serious threats and challenges to the Soviet Union's aspirations? For the regional states of Asia, would Japan be perceived as a direct military threat?

There are no definitive answers to these questions. Nevertheless, it is essential to address the trends which have emerged as of 1982 in order to offer an assessment of Japan's possible security interest and objectives later in the decade. This being the case, there are four major areas which should be addressed: firstly, the current pressures for change in Japan's security role; secondly, perceptions of security threats; thirdly, the range of future security roles; and fourthly, the political and military constraints limiting change.

Pressures for Change

Pressures to modify Japan's security situation stem from a variety of domestic and external sources. From a domestic perspective the adoption of the American-imposed constitution, with its accompanying limitations on Japan's defense forces, in conjunction with the 1960 Mutual U.S.-Japan Security Treaty, has served as a powerful impediment to an expanded security role for the country. While these restrictions remain in place, they have come under increased scrutiny and criticism both from within Japan and from its allies, especially the United States.

With the deterioration of East-West relations in the late 1970s—especially after the Soviet invasion of Afghanistan, and the increasing debate over nuclear weapons given the inability of the superpowers to reach meaningful arms accords—the issue of Western military power has gained greater importance. Japan did not remain immune from a changed international environment, and with the election of President Reagan the issue of Japan's role and position vis-à-vis Western security assumed a higher profile.

Given the Reagan administration's predilection to respond to the Soviet Union primarily in military terms, it came as no surprise that the issue of Japanese defense spending, capabilities, and military roles and missions emerged as major items on the agenda for Washington. The perceived need to enhance Western military capabilities predated the Reagan era as indicated by NATO's 1978 decision to increase defense expenditures by 3 percent a year in real terms through 1984. Furthermore, the Carter administration had also adopted a policy of advocating increased Japanese military spending. In effect Japan found itself in a situation where its allocation to the Japanese Defense Agency (JDA) remained at 0.9 percent of gross national product at a time when, at least in theory, the remainder of the industrialized free world had committed itself to expanded military capabilities.

While the Reagan administration has avoided strident calls for Japan to resist armed intrusion by the Soviet Union or its surrogates, there have been dire warnings of possible Soviet coercion. However, in the process, the Reagan administration has tried to avoid recommending a specific defense budget for Japan. President Reagan realizes that such an exercise would be counterproductive as Japan cannot realistically meet the defense level desired by the Americans, and more importantly, it would raise strong protests within Japan. Nevertheless, as confusion and criticism grew over American pressure for increased Japanese military capabilities, the Reagan administration was forced to be more specific.

Washington thus chose to emphasize roles and missions which Japan could conceivably carry out by 1987. The primary role would require Japan to secure approaching sea lanes to Northeast Asia by acquiring the capacity to patrol a 1,000 nautical mile perimeter measured from Tokyo. In an effort to fulfill this mission, Japan has decided to acquire 138 F-15 fighters and 72 P-3C maritime patrol aircraft. But to the United States, this is still inadequate for the enormous scope of the sea lanes mission.

Japan's reluctance to respond more positively to American requests for increased Japanese support in regional defense has brought widespread criticism from both the Reagan administration and Congress. In the last two years numerous proposals urging Japan to increase its defense budget have been introduced in both the House and the Senate. These actions reflect Congress' growing frustration and disappointment with Japan and reinforce the perception that Japan is indeed getting a free ride on the backs of the American taxpayers.

To put matters into perspective, American pressure

164

on Japan to strengthen its defense capabilities did not begin with the inauguration of President Reagan. However, previous attempts to persuade Japan to shoulder a larger share of the defense burden were admittedly half-hearted and were not conveyed with any sense of urgency. This situation started to change after the humbling American experience in Vietnam. Even then, successive Japanese governments were able to rebuff American requests through promises of future defense increases or the initiation of ambitious arms acquisition plans such as the National Defense Program Outline of 1976.

In the current debate over Japanese defense a number of factors have emerged which not only distinguish it from previous discussions, but also make it more difficult for Mr. Nakasone's government to evade American pressure. Foremost is the preceived inability on the part of Washington to protect Western interests in the far corners of the world. This perception exists not because of any significant reduction of U.S. projection capabilities but because of an increasingly turbulent world. International conflicts and tensions have stretched U.S. resources, both diplomatic and military, to their very limits in an environment where Soviet military capabilities are deemed to be increasingly global in scope.

The widening gap between U.S. capabilities and missions has been made more apparent by the expansion of the Soviet naval presence in the Persian Gulf and its armed intervention in Afghanistan. Strategic developments in Asia offer further testimony to two increasingly disturbing factors: the ability of the Soviet Union to commit strong military forces in support of its interests and the American reluctance—some argue inability—to contain possible Soviet adventurism.

The inclusion of economic issues is the second feature which distinguishes the current debate from previous discussions of Japan's defense budget. The recession in the United States, highlighted by record unemployment, created a disillusioned and impatient American public eager to assign blame elsewhere for its own economic difficulties. With a $16 billion surplus in its trade with the United States in 1981, Japan was an obvious target for America's malcontent. But public anger could not be restricted to Japan's dominance of certain sectors of the U.S. market when the budget of the JDA was kept below 1 percent of the GNP and Washington was asked to pick up any deficiencies. This perceived imbalance of cost and benefits inevitably led to accusations that the Japanese enjoyed a free ride in the defense of their own country.

The current public linkage between economic and defense issues effectively broadens the scope and forum of the debate. Whereas the re-arming of the Self Defense Force (SDF) was previously a matter of concern primarily for the president, the State Department, and the Pentagon, Congress has now joined the debate. Similarly, where past discussions were confined to intergovernmental forums such as the U.S.-Japan Security Consultative Committee, congressional hearings and the news media have helped publicize the inequity of defense-sharing arrangements in Asia.

The effectiveness of participation by the Congress and the American public in the debate over Japanese military expenditures remains problematic, because such practices limit the degree of compromise which is required on both sides to achieve a satisfactory agreement. Issues of some sensitivity to either side, such as the introduction of American nuclear weapons in Japan, can no longer be easily deferred in order to facilitate an early resolution. Although the United States may welcome the linking of economic and defense issues as another means of exerting pressure on Japan to be more forthcoming in negotiations, it could produce the undesirable effect of fostering anti-American sentiments.

Domestic interference in defense relations is an infallible recipe for increased friction between two countries from which the only guaranteed result is protracted negotiations. Many members of Congress have already adopted a hard and unyielding position towards deficiencies in Japan's military preparedness. One short-term solution advocated by Senator John Glenn, among others, is to have Japan fulfill the first half of its National Defense Program Outline, which covers the 1980-84 period one year early.[1] An even more demanding position is taken by Congressman Stephen J. Solarz, who argued for a real annual defense increase of 10 percent by Japan instead of its present 6 percent. According to Mr. Solarz' calculation this would bring Japan's defense budget to just under 2 percent of its GNP.[2]

These relatively tough measures outlined by American legislators may appease domestic constituents, but are problematic in producing the desired results. Lecturing JDA officials before congressional committees is really preaching to the converted. Most senior Japanese government officials and members of the ruling Liberal Democratic party (LDP) are closer to the American position than they want to admit.[3] But in the absence of an overall societal consensus, any Japanese government must proceed cautiously in redirecting a larger share of the nation's resources to the defense sector.

It is therefore to the Japanese public that the United States must direct its warnings of a growing Soviet menace in Northeast Asia if it wishes Japan to accelerate the upgrading of the SDF. Attempting to convey perceptions of a Soviet threat raises, among others, the problem of credibility. To impress the Japanese public of the need to reinforce the capabilities of the SDF, the United States must make a reasonable assessment of the regional balance. Washington should thus begin by refraining from exaggerating the nature and immediacy of the Soviet threat if it hopes to develop a common perception with Japan of the strategic environment in Asia.

Divergent Perceptions of the Soviet Challenge

There seems to be an inverse relationship between increased Soviet military capabilities and the decreased ability of Japan and the United States to arrive at a common assessment of the Soviet challenge in Asia. To be more accurate, the apparent lack of a U.S.-Japanese consensus stems not from the Soviet military build-up itself, but rather from differing interpretations of how this will affect the strategic and political makeup of Asia.

The United States is more inclined than Japan to view Soviet capabilities as having a greater potential to influence and perhaps determine the course of future events in Asia. American policy-makers appear to have equated Soviet capabilities with intentions. The Soviet

---

1. John Glenn, "Defending the New Japan," *The Washington Quarterly* 5 (Winter 1982): 25-31.

2. Stephen J. Solarz, "America and Japan: A Search for Balance," *Foreign Policy* 49 (Winter 1982-83): 82.

3. Citing a January 1981 study by USCIA, Kamo Takehiko suggests that Japanese elites are more conscious of threats posed by global conflicts which in turn generates a sense of vulnerability. Unless these vulnerabilities are resolved they are likely to extend their economic nationalism into military nationalism. This could include the eventual acquisition of a nuclear capability. This is not to say that opinion leaders are in favor of such a policy, but "the constitutional barriers against nuclear weapons have already been lost." Kamo Takehiko, "The Risk of Nuclear War and Japanese Militarization," *Japan Quarterly* 29 (April-June 1982): 189-191.

build-up in itself has come to symbolize both Soviet interests in the region and, more importantly, a willingness to use coercion or armed intervention in the pursuit of those interests. In applying this equation to recent strategic developments in Asia, the United States necessarily emphasizes the emerging imbalance of capabilities and the urgency of redressing the situation. American strategic assessments tend to be dominated by developments in military hardware such as the threefold increase of Soviet ground forces in the Pacific, the establishment of a new military headquarters in Sakhalin, and the rapid improvement of Soviet weapons systems.[4] In addition to the stationing of thirty-one divisions in the Far East with fourteen divisions facing Japan, the Soviet Union has steadily improved its maritime and air capabilities.[5] The Soviet Union has replaced many of its old aircraft with high-performance fighters including 20 Backfire bombers, 220 MIG 23s, and 90 MIG 27s.[6] The Soviet Pacific fleet has 110 submarines of which 22 are nuclear-powered ballistic missile submarines (SSBNs) of the Yankee and Delta class. Its surface fleet has also been reinforced with the introduction of the Kiev class Minsk aircraft carrier. Recent access to Da Nang and Cam Rahn Bay in Vietnam should give the Soviet Union greater flexibility in its strategic planning.

In addition, the quiet military build-up by the Soviet Union's chief allies in Asia, particularly by North Korea, which has assembled the fifth largest ground army in the world, further convinces some Americans that Japan could not effectively resist Soviet diplomatic coercion.[7] The sudden reemergence of a simultaneous threat in the Persian Gulf and Asia calls into question U.S. reliance on its "swing" strategy to defend both regions in the event of a global war. Many Japanese have realistically concluded, and without much argument from the United States, that should conflicts arise in both areas, the two-carrier task forces of the U.S. Seventh Fleet would be dispatched to the Middle East and replaced by two aircraft carriers from the Third Fleet.[8] While this is less than a full commitment to the defense of Japan, Congress and the administration contend that an economically weakened United States could not provide more without some assistance from its allies.

Generally, Japan does not share the U.S. view regarding such scenarios which might result from the regional military imbalance, nor the immediacy of the Soviet threat. Although the Japanese Defense White Paper has described the Soviet Union as a "potential threat," Japan points to other strategic considerations which will limit the full impact of the Soviet military build-up. Japan is fairly confident that the unfavorable geostrategic position of the Soviet deployments reduces the latter's military advantage in Northeast Asia. The principal problem for the Soviet Pacific fleet is that operations at both of its ports at Vladivostok and Petropavilovsk are restricted by climatic conditions. Vessels based at Vladivostok must also pass through one of three strategic straits, the Tsushima in the south, the Tsugaru between Honshu and Hakkaido, and the Soya

---

4. Caspar W. Weinberger, *Annual Report to Congress, Fiscal Year 1983* (Washington, D.C.: U.S. Government Printing Office, 1982), 11-20.

5. International Institute for Strategic Studies, *The Military Balance 1982-1983* (London, 1982), 15.

6. Research Institute for Peace and Security, *Asian Security 1981* (Tokyo, 1981), 82.

7. Kenneth L. Adelman, "Japan's Security Dilemma: An American View," *Survival* 23 (March/April 1981): 77.

8. *Asian Security* 1981, 74.

Strait between Hokkaido and Sakhalin, if they are to break out from the Sea of Japan to the Pacific Ocean. The three straits could be blockaded or mined.

Of equal importance to Japan is the nature of the Soviet military build-up which is not deemed as menacing as the United States suggests. While the Soviet fleet has commissioned major surface vessels totalling 425,000 tons between 1964 and 1978, all of these are anti-submarine warfare (ASW) vessels assigned to protect the nucleus of its navy—the SSBNs and the nuclear attack submarines (SSN).[9] A review of other Soviet military capabilities appears to support the Japanese view that it would be difficult, as of 1982, for the Soviet Union to conduct sustained offensive operations. The ground forces of the Soviet Union and Japan are separated by stretches of water that are hard to bridge. The Soviet Pacific fleet's amphibious capabilities consist of only eleven landing ships and other smaller vessels capable of landing only 4,000 infantrymen.[10] Air transport of heavy equipment is lacking, as is sufficient air cover. Soviet ground attack fighters such as the SU-17 and SU-19 can barely reach Japanese air bases in Hokkaido given their combat radius of approximately 340 nautical miles. Soviet air-to-air fighters, the MIG-23 and MIG-27, which have longer ranges of 500 nautical miles and 450 nautical miles respectively, are still incapable of striking below northwest Honshu. The one exception which has shaken Japanese complacency is the deployment of approximately 70 SS-20 intermediate range ballistic missiles (IRBM). With a range of 5,000 km. the SS-20s are capable of reaching even the most southern point of Japan. The fear in Tokyo is that a successful conclusion to the intermediate nuclear force (INF) talks at Geneva could mean the release of more SS-20s for the Asian theater.[11]

The characteristics of Soviet forces in the Pacific have led some Japanese to argue that the military build-up is a defensive move designed to strengthen Soviet claims to the Kurile Islands. At the same time it is thought that the Soviet Union hopes to discourage Japan from improving its defense capabilities through military intimidation.[12] The underlying threat is that an enhanced Japanese capability would be matched by increased Soviet forces in the region.

U.S. concern that Soviet military power might be translated into political leverage is largely discounted by the Japanese. Despite its impressive military presence, the Soviet Union has been unable to restrain Japanese defense programs or to create major divisions with Japanese-American security relations. In fact, Soviet provocations have resulted in closer Japanese-American security collaboration as reflected by Japanese participation in the 1980 RIMPAC naval exercises and the U.S. deployment of two F-16 squadrons at Misawa. At the political level, growing Soviet military forces did not prevent the signing of the Japan-China Joint Communiqué and Peace Treaty of 1978. The inclusion of the anti-hegemony clause (Article 2) in the treaty is another graphic example of the failure of Soviet policies in the region. Yet growing frictions with the Soviet Union have not impeded Japanese efforts to join in the

---

9. *Asian Security* 1981, 76.
10. *Asian Security* 1981, 80.
11. Yukio Sato, *The Evolution of Japanese Security Policy*—Adelphi Paper 178 (London: International Institute for Strategic Studies, Autumn 1982), 8.
12. Makoto Momoi, "Strategic Thinking in Japan in the 1970s and 1980s," in *New Directions in Strategic Thinking*, eds. Robert O'Neill and D.M. Horner (London: George Allen and Unwin, 1981), 176.

exploitation of Siberian mineral resources. By 1976 trade with the Soviet Union reached $3 billion, much of which was concentrated in resource sectors such as lumber and oil.[13] As the oil crisis began to threaten Japan's energy supplies, Siberian oil projects acquired additional importance—a fact belied by the beginning of the Sakhalin oil project in 1972. The need to diversify its sources of raw materials has led Japan to moderate its perceptions of Soviet intentions. This view does not extend to the Soviet occupation of the Kurile Islands which Japan considers illegal. It acts as an irritant in what is already a historically antagonistic relationship. As a result, Japan has refused Soviet requests to enter into more comprehensive commercial relations.

Japan does not expect the United States to fully understand the politics of necessity, that is, the need to engage in commercial activities with an occupying power. However, Japan does expect some consistency and consultation in American policies, especially if it is to be made a reluctant partner to them. The sanctions imposed on the Soviet Union over the Afghan and the Polish crises suggested to Japan that neither could be expected. After having agreed to participate in the sanctions at great commercial cost to Japan, the United States unilaterally lifted the embargo. Worse, the United States had been unable to restrain West European countries from taking advantage of the vacuum left by the withdrawal of Japanese capital and technology. Frustrated, Japan could only watch as its trading position with the Soviet Union slipped after 1980 from second to fifth among the non-communist nations. Future American efforts to impose its perceptions of Soviet intentions and the consequent policy options on Japan will undoubtedly be measured by the latter's recent experiences with American policy reversals.

Roles for the 1980s

Japan's current view of national security issues is embodied in what has become known as the "comprehensive security concept."[14] This policy perspective was adopted by the government of Prime Minister Ohira and carried on by Prime Minister Suzuki. While somewhat vague in its articulation, the concept is based on at least two underlying principles. Firstly, Japan's security is not exclusively a function of augmented military capabilities. Secondly, foreign and domestic policies must be developed in a comprehensive and consistent manner. In 1981 Foreign Minister Ito identified four components which spelled out the policy in a more concrete manner: (1) continuation of the U.S.-Japan security relationship; (2) moderate but high-quality military capabilities to be used exclusively for self-defense; (3) international economic cooperation; and (4) international cooperation and collaboration in energy resources, science, and technology.

Given these principles and components several observations may be appropriate. Firstly, the concept of comprehensive security could be interpreted as a transitional stage from a Japan placing almost exclusive emphasis on its global economic role to a Japan gradually broadening the scope of its foreign interests, possibly including defenses. Secondly, the third and fourth components are related to economics, but in a manner which appears to recognize the increased importance of global

---

13. Hikaru Kerns, "Politics Hides the Riches of 'Treasure Island'," *Far Eastern Economic Review* 117 (23 July 1982): 48. For a review of Japanese involvement in Siberia and Japan's reaction to economic sanctions see Hikaru Kerns' article in the same issue: "An Outfall in the East," *Far Eastern Economic Review* 117 (23 July 1982): 43-47.

14. *Asian Security 1982,* 150-51.

economic interdependence. There is an implicit recognition that in the 1980s Japan cannot expect to pursue its economic policies without taking into account the interests of other economic powers. Thirdly, appreciation of the need to augment defense capabilities is growing, but in a cautious manner within the parameters of defense of the homeland. Fourthly, there exists an unstated awareness that both the continuation of the security arrangements with the United States and international economic cooperation will require a more active diplomatic and foreign policy role for Japan. If this latter observation is correct then it follows that the scope of comprehensive security will, in the future, be broadened so as to state the foreign policy premises in a more explicit manner.

If comprehensive security constitutes a transition to a more active international role for Japan, what is this role likely to be? From a global perspective it can be anticipated that Japan will slowly and cautiously become more diplomatically active, particularly in those areas which affect Japanese economic interests. It must be acknowledged, however, that lacking a history of active international involvement there is little experience to guide Japan in the formulation of more active foreign policy postures. Given the current scope of comprehensive security, it would be in the political and security interests of both Japan and the West to concentrate on the stabilization of mineral-rich Third World countries. This could take two forms: the strengthening of balanced trade relations and the extension of greater economic development aid. On this latter issue Japan has begun to target a larger portion of its aid budget to potentially unstable countries of the Middle East that require financial support. For example, in 1981 Tokyo extended $135 million in development aid to Egypt.

However, to have any long-term effect, Japan must increase its development aid to a more respectable level. Japan's foreign aid in 1981 was one of the lowest of the industrialized countries at only 0.24 percent of its GNP.[15] Furthermore, Japan would also serve Western interests by expanding its aid programs to politically important Third World countries.

While there are valid moral and political arguments for extending development aid, it should also be recognized that by itself it has limited utility as a foreign policy instrument. This inescapable reality, coupled with the fact that Japan has thus far been unable or unwilling to acquire a measure of political leverage in the international community, suggests that its considerable resources could be more effectively utilized at the regional level, particularly in support of the ASEAN states.

From a military perspective, a global role for Japan at this time is hampered by severe constraints. It is inconceivable that Japan could deploy the limited resources of the SDF in the defense of Western and Japanese interests outside of the Asian theater. An enhanced SDF capability would still not guarantee Japanese participation in the armed defense of the vital Persian Gulf given its domestic politics. Nevertheless, the agreement in principle with the United States that Japan will assume air and sea defense responsibilities out to 1,000 miles constitutes recognition of the requirement to assume more extensive security responsibilities. Again this could be interpreted as a transitional step vis-à-vis more active participation in Western security.

---

15. Adelman, 77.

This latter point raises the question of a "principal nation" role for Japan. The central tenet of this approach is that those nations which have the greatest military and economic stakes in resolving a particular problem should undertake a direct and leading role in its solution.[16] The principal nation concept has the advantage of being organizationally separated from NATO which will permit members of the West, including France and Japan, a degree of flexibility in confronting security problems outside of the European central front. Furthermore, as the urgency of a particular problem will demand a greater commitment of resources from those most affected, this can be hoped to reduce alliance frictions produced by accusations that some nations are enjoying a free ride. However, this concept would surely founder if nations lack the necessary capabilities to fulfill missions they themselves deem essential to their security.

The levelling off of the JDA budget may be of concern to some, but given the importance of the security of oil supplies for Japan and the West, it may be that appropriate political initiatives to further Western security are as important as defense capabilities. At a time when the ideological rigidities of the Reagan administration have led the United States to rely excessively on the East-West policy framework, Japan could use its position to moderate Washington's views.[17] In conjunction with major Western European countries, Japan needs to consult and persuade the United States to judge regional instabilities, for example in the Middle East and the Persian Gulf, on their intrinsic characteristics and not through the colored lenses of another "cold war".

The importance of this exercise lies as much in the need for a continuous dialogue among allies as in the need to moderate U.S. foreign policies. A constant exchange of views may oblige the United States to refrain from undertaking the sort of unilateral actions which have had such a damaging economic and political impact on Japan and Western Europe in the past. A repeat of the unilateral U.S. decision to impose economic sanctions and their subsequent cancellation without consultation could be catastrophic for the unity of the alliance. But more importantly for Japan, a dialogue with the Western nations ensures this nation a larger role in the defense of its security.

From this analysis flow two conclusions. Firstly, it is realistic to anticipate the emergence of Japan as a more active regional power. Secondly, however, it would be unrealistic for the United States and other NATO states to assume that the major thrust of such activities would be in the defense policy area.

Constraints on Japan

It would be wise for the United States and Western Europe to more fully appreciate the constraints on Japanese policy which will continue to limit policy options and military capabilities. The major constraint in assuming a regional responsibility continues to be Japan's militarist history. Nearly all Asian countries are concerned that the fine line between the need for self-defense and military imperialism may once more become blurred. The Soviet Union is of the view that Japan's weapons acquisition program has already crossed the boundary beyond which the Japanese SDF could be called defensive. The continuation of this trend, the

---

16. K. Kaiser, et al., *Western Security* (New York: Council on Foreign Relations, 1981).

17. Masashi Nishihara, "Promoting Partnership: Japan and Europe," *The Washington Quarterly* 6 (Winter 1983): 112.

Soviets warned, would seriously upset the regional balance.[18] If Japan intends to enhance substantially the Northern Army and Northern Air Defense Force, we could expect an increase in Soviet naval and air activity in the region.

However, any Soviet reaction must account for two factors. Japan remains a critical factor in American strategic policies in Asia and extreme Soviet provocations would only serve to further solidify an existing relationship. Furthermore, Japanese capital and technology are still required for the exploitation of Siberian mineral resources.

China is equally concerned that the Reagan administration's constant pressure on Japan to increase its defense capabilities could encourage a revitalization of Japanese militarism. China's fierce reaction to the revision of Japanese textbooks and the ensuing discussion during Prime Minister Suzuki's visit to Peking in September 1982 can be viewed as indicative of its serious concern.[19] China would have fewer reservations if it were certain that Japan's rearmament program would be directed solely at the Soviet Union.

Although attention has been focused primarily on Chinese and Soviet anxieties over Japan's possible military roles in the region, one suspects that the deepest concern and resistance would emanate from the ASEAN nations. These smaller nations have not totally adjusted to living under Japanese economic dominance and a powerful SDF would only add to the discomfiture. Their uneasiness is obviously attributable to the Japanese wartime occupation of the region. It can also be related to uncertainty regarding legitimate Japanese strategic concerns. This dilemma has led to some wavering on the part of ASEAN leaders. President Ferdinand Marcos of the Philippines is firmly convinced that Japanese rearmament would be the first step toward its political and military domination of Southeast Asia.[20] President Suharto is not fervently opposed to a stronger Japanese defense, but insists that Indonesian interests be taken into account in future U.S. arms transfers to Japan. Singapore's position best reflects the general feeling of the region in arguing that Japanese rearmament will not create frictions so long as its capabilities are confined to Northeast Asia and to the Western Pacific. South Korea accepts and encourages the enhancing of Japanese capabilities only because the security of the two countries is inextricably interwoven. Nevertheless, there is a lingering suspicion of Japanese motives which was once again heightened by the textbook incident.

The constraints on Japan's current and projected military capabilities must also be sufficiently appreciated.[21] As of the end of 1981, Japanese defense spending was $10.45 billion, constituting 4.8 percent of government spending and 0.9 per cent of GNP. The SDF totalled 245,000 troops allocated as follows: army, 155,000; navy, 45,000; air force, 45,000. In addition, there were 43,000 army reservists, 600 naval reservists, and paramilitary forces assigned to the coast guard. Land forces consist of one armored division, twelve infantry divisions, one airborne brigade, two composite brigades, one artillery brigade, two air defense brigades, one signals brigade, five engineer brigades, and eight surface-to-air missile (SAM) groups.

---

18. *Pravda*, 11 November 1982, 5, "Dangerous Step," *Current Digest of the Soviet Press* 34 (8 December 1982): 9.

19. Mike Tharp, "A Textbook Exercise," *Far Eastern Economic Review* 118 (8 October 1982): 12.

20. David Jenkins, "Measuring The Response," *Far Eastern Economic Review* 118 (22 October 1982): 25.

21. For data on capabilities see *The Military Balance 1982-1983*.

In terms of armor the SDF is equipped with over 550 main battle tanks and 530 armored personnel carriers. For anti-tank defense Japan currently possesses some 230 anti-tank guided weapons and 1600 recoilless launchers. The army has some 780 howitzers of 105 mm. or more, over 1300 mortars, and a number of surface-to-surface missiles and multiple rocket-launchers. The anti-aircraft systems consist of 300 guns and 54 HAWK SAMs. For air support the land forces have some 27 aircraft and 372 helicopters.

On the naval side Japan possess 14 submarines, 33 destroyers, 16 frigates, 31 coastal minesweepers and 29 other ships. The capabilities of the surface fleet vary from class to class, but most ships are equipped with ASROC and varying combinations of Sea Sparrow SAM, Standard SAM, and Harpoon SSM. In addition, three destroyers are equipped with anti-submarine warfare helicopters. The naval air arm has some 110 combat aircraft in the form of 7 maritime reconnaissance squadrons with 68 P-2Js, 28 S-2F-1, and 14 PS-1s, as well as six ASW helicopter squadrons with 54 HSS-2s. Finally, there are a number of training and search and rescue squadrons and flights.

The air force is composed of six combat air wings, one composite air division, and one reconnaissance squadron with a total of 314 combat aircraft. There are three fighter ground attack squadrons equipped with 60 F-1s and eleven interceptor squadrons. There are six squadrons made up of 130 F-4s, four with 90 F-104s, and one unit is converting to ten F-15s. In addition, there are three transport squadrons with 30 C-1s and 10 YS-11s. In terms of air-to-air missiles the air force has Sparrow, Falcon, and Sidewinder AAMs. For ground-to-air defense there are six SAM groups formed in 19 squadrons with 180 Nike-Js. A base defense ground

environment network exists with 28 control and warning units. There are also a number of search and rescue, test, weather, and training wings and groups.

With respect to future capabilities, Japan's land forces will continue to expand at a modest rate with the acquisition of additional main battle tanks, enhanced artillery capabilities, anti-tank systems, and SAMs. The maritime forces will be augmented with three submarines of the Yushio class, eight Hatsuyuki class destroyers, two frigates, fourteen P-3C Orion maritime patrol aircraft and air defense systems. The air force has ordered 38 F-15Js along with four training aircraft, seven F-1 fighters, four C-130 Hercule transports, seven E-2C AEW aircraft, a number of Sidewinder AAMs, as well as six Stinger and two Tan SAM launch systems.

On balance, therefore, the rearmament program is modest and does not promise to enable Japan to project military power on a regional level. With no viable sea and airlift capability, Japan poses no direct military threat to her neighbors. Thus a military role within the region appears to be out of the question unless it is undertaken in combination with American forces. If limitations on the Soviet ability to conduct sustained offensive operations in the region remain, it can be argued that no major reevaluation will be made of the type of Japanese capabilities being acquired.

Nevertheless, the key to military growth could well be future Soviet, and possibly Chinese, military capabilities. If the regional military balance shifts in such a manner that Japanese perceptions of outside threats coincide more closely with those currently held in Washington, then an accelerated rearmament program could emerge. This is particularly true if the Soviet Union continues to deploy additional SS-20s in the Asian theater. Similar concerns could arise over future Chinese nuclear capabilities. Finally, if either the Soviet Union or China is perceived to be acquiring a sustained offensive conventional capability which more directly threatens the Japanese homeland, changes in Japan's military capabilities would probably be more forthcoming.

On balance, efforts to enhance Japanese defense capabilties will face formidable challenges, a reality often underestimated by the United States. The most severe constraint is undoubtedly Article Nine of the Japanese constitution. In the past it has not only presented a legal barrier to rearmament, but has helped reinforce the pacificism of the Japanese people. When Japan "forever renounced war as a sovereign right of the nation and the threat or use of force as a means of settling international disputes," it was not done merely to satisfy American wishes. In defeat the Japanese nation genuinely sought a moral and peaceful base for securing its future.

However, Article Nine has proved not to be immune to global conflicts. Beginning with the Korean War, Japan started to rearm by establishing a Police Reserve Force, which in 1954 was elevated to the status of a Self Defense Force. This was followed by the signing of a revised U.S.-Japan Treaty of Mutual Cooperation and Security in 1960. Admittedly, general public support for enhanced defense capabilities has grown over the years.[22] Nevertheless, the government has also taken the lead in gradually improving the SDF despite strong opposition from certain sectors of the public and the press.[23] The fact that five opposition parties are in a constant state of disarray forecloses any credible challenges to LDP policies.[24] In recent years the main opposition parties, the Democratic Socialist party, Komeito, and even factions of the Japan Socialist party, have accepted the need for an independent SDF.

The high degree of maneuverability which the LDP previously enjoyed in the area of national security is now being curtailed by three relatively new developments. The most critical is the growing public reluctance to succumb to American pressure for increased defense spending. The general public does not view the Soviet build-up with any great alarm, but is apprehensive that once rearmament begins it will be difficult to contain. A 1981 survey revealed that only 37 percent of the public were concerned that Japanese security would somehow be affected by the U.S.-Soviet military balance. Closer to home, only 36 percent felt that the "disposition" of Soviet forces in Japan's northern islands gave cause for concern.[25] In the absence of any imminent threat the general consensus in Japan is that an increase in the size of the SDF cannot be justified. The same 1981 survey shows that only about 23 percent favor increasing Japanese military capabilities while about 51 percent were content with the present strength of the SDF.[26] This should not be confused with the overwhelming support for the maintenance of the SDF which reached 82 percent in 1981.

Financial problems, notably the small increases in the domestic budget and growing national debt, constitute a second obstacle which Prime Minister Nakasone

---

22. A public opinion poll by *Asahi Shimbun*, "Peace and Security in Statistics," *Japan Quarterly* 29 (April/June 1982): 197.

23. A review of the Japanese printed media's historical opposition to Japanese rearmament is available in Masushi Nishihara's paper, "The Media and the Image of Defense Policy," International Institute for Strategic Studies, 24th Annual Conference, (The Hague, September 1982).

24. Mike Tharp, "Their Own Worst Enemy," *Far Eastern Economic Review* 117 (3 September 1982): 26-29.

25. The Prime Minister's Office, *Public Opinion Survey on the Self Defense Force and Defense Problems,* translated by the Foreign Press Center (Tokyo, May 1982): 10.

26. Prime Minister's Office, Tokyo, 5.

174

must surmount if he wishes to attain his objective of building a credible independent defense. For fiscal year 1983 the Finance Ministry has drafted a budget calling for a total expenditure of $211 billion. This represents an increase of only 1.4 percent from the previous year and total tax revenue is expected to be about only $128 billion.[27] Given the austerity of the budget, financial increases were granted only to social security, energy, overseas aid, and the largest share to defense. The intensive struggle over the allocation of the 1983 budget indicates that future increases for the SDF would face stiff competition from less fortunate sectors such as education.

Finally, Mr. Nakasone's public image as a vigorous and decisive leader cannot disguise his weak political foundation within the ruling LDP. His rise to power was totally dependent on the still powerful support of former Prime Minister Kakuei Tanaka. The possibility of Mr. Tanaka being sent to prison for accepting bribes from the Lockheed Company could erode public confidence in Mr. Nakasone's leadership as well as his internal party support.[28] Should Mr. Tanaka retain control over his faction, either in or out of prison, Mr. Nakasone's freedom to initiate new policies would be no less restricted. To acquire an independent political base Mr. Nakasone needs to put some distance between himself and Mr. Tanaka, and somehow win over the latter's support. The forthcoming elections will give Mr. Nakasone such an opportunity, but even an electoral victory would not necessarily result in fundamental changes in Japan's posture or defense policies.

Conclusions

The appropriate security role for Japan in the 1980s remains to be clarified. Both the United States and other members of NATO would be well advised to proceed with caution before encouraging Japan to develop an independent military capability. If the United States advocates a rearmed Japan able to fulfill missions beyond the defense of its territory, Washington must be prepared to accept the consequences of introducing a new regional military power in Asia. Relations between the United States and ASEAN would be strained as a result. Furthermore, if Japan becomes the political and military leader of the region, it could develop interests which would conflict with those of the United States and Europe. Washington and other Western capitals would find that resolving differences with a regional power bent on the pursuit of more independent policies would be both arduous and perhaps humbling. In short, a rearmed Japan would be less likely to follow the American lead on many issues, including Asian security. The possibility of creating a more obstinate, independent Japan seems to be an issue largely neglected by American and other Western observers. It is one thing to argue that the United States does not want Japan to become a regional power; yet there must be a clear understanding of the implications of American policy vis-à-vis Japan.

This suggests that a more useful approach would include two basic elements. Firstly, encourage Japan to continue on its current path of modest increases in military expenditures in order to assume more responsibility for its own defense. Secondly, encourage Japan to assume a more active and responsible role, both economically and politically, within the global community—and more specifically, within Asia. Such an approach could, in the long run, make a meaningful contribution to Western security.

27. Geoffrey Murray, "Japan Struggles to Find More Money for Defense," *Christian Science Monitor* (27 December 1982): 4.
28. "Shogun's Mate," *The Economist* 285 (27 November 1982): 59.

THE ANDREW WELLINGTON CORDIER ESSAY

Tim Sears

CARROTS, STICKS, AND RICE:
Japan's Quest for Food Security

The Andrew Wellington Cordier Essay features the finest S.I.P.A. student work received by the Journal. This semi-annual competition memorializes Andrew W. Cordier, who served as Dean of the School of International Affairs (1962-72) and President of Columbia University (1968-70), in addition to having a distinguished diplomatic career.

California's medfly crisis of summer 1981 is sometimes said to have cost its governor, Edmund G. Brown Jr., a seat in the United States Senate. Yet the most important effect of the medfly crisis is widely overlooked — it also demonstrated the shocking degree to which the Japanese food supply is dependent on factors beyond Japan's control. Fear that imported medfly larvae would hatch and attack Japanese citrus orchards led the Japanese government to place an embargo on Californian produce which had not been fumigated. Sud-

denly there was a run on Japanese supermarkets and the price of lemons went sky high, when they were available at all. (Almost all Japanese lemons are imported from California.) Importers scoured the globe looking for supplies, and lemons soon began finding their way to Japan from Texas, Florida, and the Middle East.

While the lemon shortage had no lasting impact on Japan, it did underline the vulnerability of the lifelines which supply Japan with its food and fiber.

> An "original calorie" calculation will help put this situation in proper perspective, showing that Japan is far from being self-sufficient in its food supply. When one calculates self-sufficiency by means of calorie counts of all food items consumed by the Japanese, converting such items as meat, milk, and eggs into the original calories of foods and feeds, one finds that Japan is less than 50 percent self-sufficient, a level that is expected to continue through the 1980s.[1]

The lemon shortage can easily be dismissed as a temporary and vaguely comical inconvenience to the Japanese consumer. But it also points out a distinct Japanese foreign policy problem. Bad weather or a few unfavorable decisions by distant officials can directly affect what appears on Japanese dinner tables and Tokyo can do little by way of intercession.

This article is divided into two parts. The first part examines the nature and degree of Japan's dependence on imported food and the vulnerability of Japan's food sources and supply lines. The second part analyzes Japan's food security strategy, looking at efforts toward national self-sufficiency and importation strategies for securing adequate reliable supplies. Finally, it will conclude with a few suggestions on further meas-

---

1. The Comprehensive National Security Group, "Report on Comprehensive Security," 2 July 1980, 62.

ures which Japan might take to guarantee its food supply.

The Problem of Dependence

On the surface, Japan's food policy seems to be the product of paradoxical thinking. Japan is both heavily import-dependent and highly protectionist. The Japanese import an enormous quantity of grain while subsidizing exports of overpriced rice. Despite the great need for locally produced foods, 87 percent of Japan's farmers gain most of their livelihood from non-farm jobs.[2] All this in a country noted for efficient central strategic planning!

Fortunately, the *koan*-like logic of Japanese food policy can be subjected to more conventional forms of intellectual analysis. The traditional Japanese diet is based upon rice as its staple and chief source of carbohydrates, with seafood protein and vitamins from fruits and vegetables balancing the diet. Japanese farmers receive very high prices for their rice—and consumers pay very high prices for it—while much cheaper foreign rice is kept out. This enables Japan's farmers to fulfill the minimal requirements of the traditional diet. Certain other products are protected and subsidized in the same way, including a modern fishing fleet and seafood processing industry.

But the Japanese diet is rapidly changing to a protein-intensive mix, moving out of rice and into more meat, milk, noodles, and eggs. This demand for Western-style protein sources has spawned new egg, broiler, and feedlot industries, all of which require feed and protein supplements which the Japanese archipelago is unable to produce. Modern corn sugar and starch industries have also sprung up and are growing rapidly. Nearly all the inputs for these industries must be imported, mostly from the United States.

Because feed is bulky and expensive to transport for long distances, some of Japan's meat supply is now being directly imported. Chicken imports, for example, now play an important part in the Japanese diet, with per capita chicken consumption having risen 9.4 times since 1960.[3] American-style chicken has become very popular among the Japanese for Western dishes.

In the first eight months of 1981, Japan imported almost 68,000 tons of chicken. Nearly 41,000 tons came from the United States, an increase of 73 percent over the same period in record-setting 1980.

The greatest competitive advantage for U.S. chicken is price, which is half that of live chicken in Japan. Japanese producers must buy feed from the United States which raises the cost of the domestic product.[4]

Japan is also turning to Thailand and China as sources for the more traditional boneless chicken. Cheaper feed and labor costs and Japanese technical assistance have made Thailand and China important sources of poultry imports.

Seafood, Japan's traditional protein source, is also increasingly imported. The high cost of operating a worldwide fishing fleet and the assertion of 200-mile economic exploitation zones by countries all over the world have limited the size of Japan's annual catch while raising its price relative to animal protein.

Japan has become more dependent on imports of fishery products, reflecting a leveling off of its fish catch at 10-11 million tons annually since 1972.

Rising retail fish prices may lead consumers to shift further away from costly fish to meats, eggs, and dairy products. This

2. "Japanese Farmyard Follies," *The Economist*, 17 July 1982, 76.
3. Berman, Daniel K., "Japanese Develop A Taste for U.S. Chicken," *Foreign Agriculture* (December 1981): 9.
4. Ibid.

Table 1

U.S. Agricultural Exports to Japan, Calendar Years 1976-80

Item	1976 Quantity	1976 Value	1977 Quantity	1977 Value	1978 Quantity	1978 Value	1979 Quantity	1979 Value	1980 Quantity	1980 Value
	1,000 MT	$ Mil	1,000 MT	$ Mil	1,000 MT	$ Mil	1,000 MT	$ Mil	1,000 MT	$ Mil
Bulk commodities:										
Feedgrains:										
Corn	6,408	748	7,829	812	8,480	911	10,016	1,196	11,823	1,625
Grain sorghum	2,341	261	2,425	241	2,359	232	2,257	249	3,780	496
Total feedgrains	8,749	1,009	10,254	1,053	10,839	1,143	12,273	1,445	15,603	2,121
Soybeans	3,069	675	3,410	938	3,855	981	3,707	1,032	4,033	1,105
Wheat	3,311	522	3,315	374	3,276	432	3,351	537	3,331	596
Cotton	181	259	227	313	286	355	329	455	330	531
Tobacco	60	223	61	260	46	227	44	229	37	197
Hides & skins (1,000 pcs.)	10,279	187	9,458	194	9,620	243	8,399	315	8,743	260
Beef tallow	103	39	103	41	89	40	93	51	116	55
Soybean meal	120	21	270	55	267	58	205	49	246	65
Alfalfa meal & cubes	259	27	248	29	311	30	366	40	374	48
Others	*	102	*	217	*	256	*	327	*	318
Subtotal	*	3,064	*	3,474	*	3,765	*	4,480	*	5,296
Consumer Items:										
Citrus:										
Lemons	97	51	105	41	121	68	101	84	102	63
Grapefruit	144	31	149	36	132	36	142	47	129	46
Oranges	25	8	22	7	49	22	52	28	63	25
Total citrus	266	90	276	84	302	126	295	159	294	134
Beef	16	42	20	52	34	118	35	150	34	142
Pork	54	122	25	66	24	87	32	118	28	96
Poultry meat	24	26	33	37	39	50	38	49	43	54
Almonds	9	18	11	24	12	34	8	36	10	41
Peanuts	29	21	27	21	25	20	29	23	27	21
Raisins	22	16	7	10	16	22	9	16	15	25
Pulses	29	8	27	8	21	7	20	8	38	14
Canned peaches	8	4	12	6	20	11	11	7	13	10
Fruit cocktail	1	1	2	2	3	3	3	3	4	3
Prunes	1	1	1	1	2	3	3	3	3	4
Orange & grapefruit juice (1,000 lit.)	1,782	2	1,839	3	3,307	3	4,035	4	10,965	5
Others	*	148	*	69	*	106	*	199	*	266
Subtotal	*	499	*	383	*	670	*	775	*	815
Grand total	*	3,563	*	3,857	*	4,435	*	5,255	*	6,111

*Not applicable
Source: *Foreign Agriculture*, June 1981, 16.

could prompt increased imports of finished livestock products or expanded production, requiring larger imports of feedgrains and oilseeds.[5]

The alternative to importing more protein is to raise more domestically. Feedlot and broiler industries have rapidly developed in Japan to meet the new demand, but these industries depend heavily upon imported feed and oil seeds. Table One shows the discomfitingly rapid rise of feed and oilseed imports from the United States. The trends outlined in the chart have shown no sign of abating in the early 1980s. Indeed, as Dudley G. Williams, the U.S. agricultural counselor in Tokyo put it:

> Each year, Japan buys the harvest of 14 million acres in the United States—about equal to the area under crop production in Japan itself. These purchases are essential in meeting Japan's food and fiber requirements.[6]

The vast increases in imports of feed, oilseeds, chicken, and seafood are necessary because of a secular shift in demand by Japanese consumers. Japan's population has increased slowly in the last ten years, but real per capita income has increased quite rapidly. This income effect has been to decrease the amount of rice consumed by the average Japanese, but to increase his consumption of white bread, milk, eggs, and meat, all of which are either imported or based upon imported grain.

> Rice consumption per capita has been falling since the early 1960s. By 1970, Japanese were eating an average of 100 kilograms of rice per head annually. Today, they eat less than 80 kilograms a year.

> While rice consumption is down, the Japanese have been eating more of practically everything else. Over the past two decades, their calorie intake has risen 11 percent—to slightly over 2,500 calories per day (compared with around 3,100

calories in advanced Western countries). Consumption of oils, fats and sugars has climbed dramatically. The amount of meat eaten has quadrupled—up from a daily 17.5 grams in 1960 to 70 grams today.[7]

The Economist goes on to suggest a number of reasons why Japan is likely to continue shifting to a more import-dependent Western-style diet in the next twenty years. Increasing real income will give the Japanese more money to spend on Western-style food. The post-war generation has a taste for fast-food: McDonald's and Kentucky Fried Chicken are booming in Japan. The greater number of working wives means a trend toward fast, inexpensive dining out and towards the use of convenience foods at home. Also, the emergence of supermarkets has increased the selection available to the Japanese housewife, while education, foreign travel, and television have made her more open to Western tastes.[8] All of those trends point to an increasing Westernization of the Japanese diet and, with it, increasing food import dependence for Japan.

Japan's farmers have not risen to the challenge of producing food to satisfy Westernized tastes for three reasons. First, the Japanese farmer has a strong propensity for growing rice. It is what he knows how to do, and the Japanese government provides very high rice price supports, making it profitable for him to continue. Were the government to remove its domestic price supports and trade barriers for foreign rice, Japan would be importing enormous amounts of cheaper rice from America, Australia, and Southeast Asia virtually overnight.

---

5. Coyle, William T., "The Japanese Market: Where To Go From Here?," *Foreign Agriculture* (December 1981): 11.

6. *Foreign Agriculture* (June 1981): 16.

7. *The Economist*, 76.

8. Ibid., 77.

Because of high price supports and declining demand, the Japanese government maintains large stockpiles of expensive rice. The Ministry of Agriculture has offered considerable financial inducements to farmers willing to convert their paddy fields to import substituting crops. But this initiative has not caught on, since most Japanese farmers are only part-time farmers and rice is an ideal part-time crop.

> One reason why Japanese farmers stick by their traditional methods is that they are so easy. The paddy field is almost perfectly suited to part-time peasant-style farming. The rains wash away toxic residues from the previous crop, while introducing fresh nutrients in the silt they wash down into the fields. No fertilizer, crop rotation or even a fallow period is required. Little capital equipment is needed and, except in the planting out period, not much labor.[9]

The close relationship between Japan's farmers and the ruling Liberal Democratic party has also played a role in assuring that Japanese farmers continue to plant rice.

The second constraint on further Japanese food production is urbanization or, perhaps more to the point, post-industrial suburbanization. The excellent transportation and communications systems which come with industrialization allow service and high-technology industries to spread out from the major industrial centers in search of lower costs and a higher quality of life. This allows the population to disperse and assume a more land-extensive lifestyle, similar to America's sunbelt phenomenon.

> Regional development subsidies have combined with lower wages, lower land costs, and better environmental conditions to encourage Japan's most dynamic export sectors to open their new plants in rural areas. Kyūshū, home of much of Japan's beef and orange production, is now known as Silicon Island and produces 40 percent of Japan's integrated circuits in semi-rural surroundings. The rural Tōhoku region of the northeast produces another 20 per cent. Nagano Prefecture, long one of Japan's major fruit-growing areas, is now one of the largest manufacturers of video tape recorder components in Japan.[10]

The effect of population dispersal on Japanese agriculture is likely to be very serious. Since virtually every arable square meter of Japan is cultivated, nearly all of the land used for new houses, offices, factories, and shopping center parking lots will have to be land removed permanently from agricultural production. One estimate suggests that a 1 percent increase in self-sufficiency for feedgrains would require 150,000 square hectares and cost 0.9-1.3 trillion yen.[11] In order to keep this marginal land in production, Japan would have to raise price supports, domestic food prices, and import barriers—all politically difficult moves. Thus, because of increasing demand and domestic production constraints, we can confidently expect Japan's food import-dependence to increase significantly in the future.

Considering Japan's heavy dependence on imported food, it is surprising that the Japanese have not carefully outlined their points of vulnerability from the beginning. But the problem seems to have taken Japanese policy-makers by surprise, possibly because their traditional concerns have been focused on farm income and consumer prices. In any case, the 1973 soybean *shokku* had a wonderfully concentrating effect. Now the Japanese are well aware of their vulnerabilities and

---

9. Ibid., 76.
10. Calder, Kent E., "Opening Japan," *Foreign Policy* (Summer 1982): 91.
11. Comprehensive National Security Group, 69-70.

have developed strategies to reduce and diffuse their national risk.

Four types of contingencies threaten Japan's food lifelines: transport interdiction, long-term disequilibrium between supply and demand, poor world harvest, and politically motivated embargos. The first major threat, interdiction, comes in two distinct forms. The first problem, a point-security threat, might run as follows. Most of Japan's food imports from the United States must pass through certain vital chokepoints, such as the lower Mississippi River and the Panama Canal. Anything disrupting the flow of grain and oilseeds through these arteries—say, a dock strike or closure of the canal—would have an immediate impact on Japan's food supply. Such an interruption would result in short-term food shortages and rising food prices, while a longer cut-off could induce a significant shift back to rice in the Japanese diet.

> Fifteen million tons of such commodities as wheat, soy beans and corn are imported to Japan by way of the Panama Canal. Also bituminous coal from West Virginia is shipped to Japanese mills. This means that 40 percent of all ships passing through the Panama Canal are related in some way to the Japanese economy.[12]

The second interdiction threat to Japan's food lifelines consists of a regional security problem: the prospect of Soviet submarine attacks on Japan-bound ships in the event of a general U.S.-Soviet war. The anti-submarine and convoy capabilities needed to counter this type of attack are far beyond the current reach of Japan's Maritime Self-Defense Force. In addition, such a war would likely see much of the American Pacific fleet transferred to more urgent theaters of action—the Persian Gulf region, for example—making food ship-ments to Japan even more vulnerable than they appear in peacetime.

The second major threat to Japanese food security comes in the form of a long-term disequilibrium between world food supply and demand. Japan is certainly wealthy enough to endure a year or two of scarce food, but a secular increase in food prices similar to the oil price rise of the 1970s would present the Japanese with a serious drain on their balance of payments. At the moment, it seems very unlikely that Japan would be able to redress this imbalance through greatly increased exports of manufactured goods.

The Japanese do not seem to be worried about world overpopulation threatening their food supply. They assume (probably correctly) that the bulk of any population increase will come in the less-developed countries, and that the rich Japanese will always be at the head of the line to buy surplus food. This belief also applies to any food crisis induced by an energy shortage.

The prospect of a major long-term shift in the earth's climate seems much more threatening to Japan. An average temperature shift of only a few degrees per annum either way would have an extraordinarily disruptive effect on world agriculture, possibly eliminating the food surpluses upon which Japan increasingly depends.

> In the opinion of Junkichi Nemoto, a meteorologist, the earth has now already entered into a minor ice age. There is every likelihood that abnormal weather conditions, now prevailing worldwide, will, in the future, hit hardest in the wheat-producing areas of the Soviet Union, Scandanavia, Canada and the northern U.S., and northeastern and northern China.[13]

---

12. "The Second Panama Canal Project," *Japan Quarterly* (July-September 1980): 305.

13. Kaoru Murakami, "Comprehensive National Security in a Low Growth Era," *Japan Echo* (Spring 1977): 36.

A new ice age is not the only possible threat to Japan's food supply. Other scientists predict a long-term warming of the terrestial climate as a result of the celebrated "greenhouse effect." (Ironically, Japan's industrial pollution could play an important role in touching off either of these climate changes.) A major change in climate would be particularly devastating to Japan because of a time lag element in shifting agricultural productivity: a change in temperature and rainfall would affect productive regions immediately, but it would take years for nature to generate comparable soils in new regions.

> Rainfall and soil moisture patterns would also change as well— the predicted drying of the American Middle West, for example—so that a given pattern of agriculture could no longer be practiced even by moving poleward within a region.[14]

In light of this information, it is useful to once again stress Japan's heavy reliance upon the food surplus of a few distant regions: 56 percent of Japan's wheat, 80 percent of its corn, 50 percent of its barley, and 90 percent of Japan's soybean supply come from the United States,[15] most of it from only a few midwestern states!

Since so much of the world's food surplus comes from only a few key regions, it is likely that an occasional malevolent combination of events will conspire to limit the production in those areas. In this third vulnerability to the food supply, Japan would find itself in a bidding war with the rest of the world for the remaining exportable surplus. Exactly such a production drop occurred in 1973, when an unlucky combination of bad weather, economic mismanagement, plant disease, and pests caused worldwide food production to decline by about 3 percent. But the remarkable inelasticity of demand for food was demonstrated by a spectacular 300 percent increase in food-related commodities prices, causing hunger in the less-developed world and food shortages even in the United States.

Rapidly rising food prices and fear of shortages could lead an American government to impose export controls on vital foodstuffs. An example of this final vulnerability is what happened in 1973 when the United States cut off soybean exports to Japan.

> In the summer of 1973, just before the oil embargo, the United States government, fearful that heavy Soviet purchases of soybeans would create a shortage, suddenly declared an embargo on soybean exports to all countries, including Japan, even though it had long been America's chief export market for soybeans and these constituted a major source of protein for the Japanese diet. The embargo was soon lifted, and Japan was able to procure all of the soybeans it needed, but this third "Nixon shock" reminded the Japanese of their dependence on foreign sources for crucial supplies of food and showed them that even the United States could act in callous disregard of vital Japanese needs.[16]

The 1973 events represented a diplomatic fiasco for the Japanese. Few things could be less in Japan's interest than an embargo of a major source of protein by the United States. The embargo was soon rescinded as it applied to Japan but the damage had already been done: How could the Japanese ever feel secure about their food supply or their relationship with the United States after American allies had unthinkingly cut off one of their chief sources of protein?

---

14. Kellog, William W. and Schware, Robert, "Society, Science and Climate Change," *Foreign Affairs* (Summer 1982): 1091.
15. Ibid.
16. Reischauer, Edwin O., *The Japanese* (Cambridge, Mass.: The Belknap Press of Harvard University, 1978), 372.

Searching for a Strategy

Postwar Japanese food policy has generally focused on the twin objectives of high farm incomes and low consumer prices. The Japanese government has selected certain products for farmers to grow, guaranteed them a high price and has protected their markets from cheaper imports, making their consumer prices much higher than those paid by the rest of the world. In order to compensate Japanese consumers for their overpriced oranges and rice, Japan has encouraged the importation of feedgrains and oilseeds, which in turn has given consumers cheaper noodles, eggs, meat, and milk. Imported produce, much of which come from California, has greatly improved the consumer's selection of fruits and vegetables.

The food security problem calls for a partial reworking of postwar agricultural policy. The Japanese still use the same strategy as before—self-sufficiency and importation—but the new emphasis on security has occasioned the use of some new tactics.

Japan uses three policy tools to implement the first half of its self-sufficiency policy: selective protectionism, subsidized conversion of rice paddy land to other crops, and stockpiling. The policy of selective protection must be carefully examined because sometimes it represents clever strategic planning, while at other times the price mechanism is manipulated by special interest politics. Yet, the two motives sometimes work together serendipitously to line farmers' pocketbooks and to improve Japan's food security position.

Japan's agricultural protectionism serves only the interests of a particular group, partly because the ruling Liberal Democratic party is heavily based in rural areas although farm influence has been slowly declining.

In 1960 farmers comprised 43 percent of all LDP voters. By 1980 this proportion had fallen to 17.8 percent, with 44.5 percent of the LDP's total vote coming from urban and metropolitan constituencies. LDP leadership remains overwhelmingly rural because senority is a major factor in leadership recruitment, and the LDP was a largely rural party in the 1950s and 1960s. Its leadership will not become decisively urban until the 1990s.[17]

Politically motivated protection is slowly breaking down because of a coalition of consumers, industries based upon food imports, and trading companies. Pressure from foreign countries is also helping to remove the barriers. But strategic protection for a staple such as rice will go untouched. In fact, if anything Japan will produce less rice in the coming years as the Ministry of Agriculture tries to limit the soaring cost of rice stockpiles and export subsidies.

The Japanese government has also been trying to control overproduction through the conversion of rice paddies to dry field crops.

The government is trying to bully and bribe Japanese farmers into drying out paddy fields to grown wheat, barley, green vegetables, and fruit. Progress is slow. Despite being able to pick up about $2,200 for every hectare converted to growing wheat instead of rice, Japanese farmers are still producing as much rice as ever.[18]

Farmers stick to growing rice because it is easy and profitable for them to do so on a part-time basis. The Japanese are obviously satisfied with their rice security, since they are trying to persuade farmers to reduce production. Japan's rice mountain currently amounts

---

17. Calder, 91.
18. *The Economist*, 76.

to about 6 million tons, roughly half of the annual Japanese harvest.

Stockpiling is Japan's third major domestic self-help strategy. Large stockpiles are Japan's first line of defense in the event of a supply interruption. Stockpiles buy the time needed to reach a diplomatic accommodation or at least to search out an alternate source of supply. Unfortunately, stockpiles of imported agricultural products are still uncomfortably low.

> Stockpiling is at present the most important aspect of policies for temporary food shortages. At present, government funds are spent to keep approximately seven months of rice, three months of wheat, and one month of edible soybeans and feedgrains in reserve. The private sector dislikes to accumulate reserves because they increase the level of dead stock.[19]

Japan's stockpiles of feed and oilseeds will have to be larger if they are to buy the Japanese enough time for diplomatic or economic countermeasures to take effect in an emergency.

Even the most enlightened system of trade barriers and price supports would leave Japan far short of its grain and oilseed requirements. The Japanese realize that they will be heavily import-dependent in foodstuffs for the foreseeable future. How then can they make their foreign food sources more secure? Tokyo and the trading companies have taken three steps to reduce the risk of a supply interdiction.

The most important of these measures has been the dispersal of import sources. The Japanese understand the importance of not putting all their eggs (and milk and meat!) in one basket, so they try to buy feed and oilseeds from as many countries as possible. They also use a clever combination of foreign aid and generous

long-term contracts to encourage cultivation of corn for export in promising parts of Asia. This program has produced considerable results in Thailand, but has generally played to poor reviews elsewhere in Southeast Asia.

> Thailand had consistently supplied between 10 percent and 20 percent of Japan's corn needs since the late 1960s. Corn had been a focus of the Thai government's crop diversification efforts in the 1950s and 1960s, and Thailand had become the world's fourth leading corn exporter by the 1970s. Japanese trading companies had encouraged Thailand's development as a corn exporter by annually contracting through a trade association through the Board of Trade of the Thai government to buy a large share of Thailand's annual corn crop. Based on crop forecasts for the current year and on Japanese demand, the Board of Trade would assign quotas to Bangkok exporters for corn shipments to Japan.[20]

The Japanese sponsored several long-term projects to help develop the "corn belt" region of central Thailand. These efforts included the development of farmers' cooperatives to show Thai farmers how to grow corn and to establish the necessary credit and marketing institutions, the elimination of transport bottlenecks, storage facilities in Bangkok, and providing a steady favorable export price for Thai corn. Since Zen-Nō, Japan's National Federation of Agricultural Cooperative Associations, prefers to deal on a co-operative-to-cooperative basis, Zen-Nō took the initiative for setting up a national producers' cooperative in Thailand.

---

19. Comprehensive National Security Group, 68.
20. *Zen-Noh,* Harvard Business School Case (4-578-059), June 1978, 5.

Table 2

Total Production of Corn in Thailand, 1949-1973

(000 metric tons)

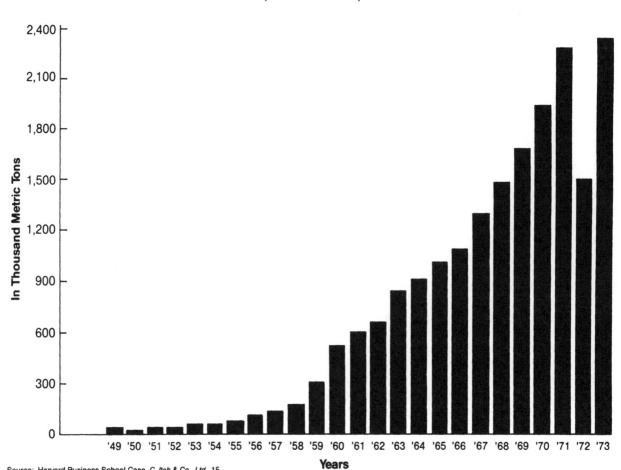

Source: Harvard Business School Case, *C. Itoh & Co., Ltd.*, 15.

All of this aid and the building of durable, institutions is expensive, but the Japanese are willing to make the effort, precisely because they realize that their rapidly rising demand is too narrowly based on American exports.

> Altogether, Mr. Ōnuma [the manager of Zen-Nō's Feedstuff Importing Section] was quite certain that Japan would require not less than 10 million metric tons of corn by 1985, and quite possibly 12 million.

> Mr. Ōnuma's experience in the Feedstuff Importing Department had made him sensitive to the vulnerability of Zen-Nō's supplies of corn and other grains. In the 1970s, shipments from its leading supplier [the United States] were curtailed on several occasions by a diseased crop (1970), several dock strikes at Gulf ports, occasional freezing of the Mississippi River, and a drought in 1974. Mr. Ōnuma did not believe Zen-Nō could safely continue relying on fewer than 800,000 U.S. farmers to satisfy its corn needs.[21]

Japanese perseverance in Thailand has paid off. Thai corn production rose rapidly in the 1960s (see Table Two) and has grown more modestly in the 1970s to an annual average of a bit under 3 million tons per annum.[22] Thailand now provides roughly 12 percent of Japan's annual corn imports.[23]

A number of problems have cropped up as a result of Japan's involvement in developing Thailand's corn belt. Ideally, a project developed with Japanese aid would export all its corn to Japan, but this has not exactly happened. Much of Thailand's corn is exported to third countries (see Table Three). While, as a perpetual heavy buyer, an increase in aggregate supply always benefits Japan, the Japanese are most satisfied when the corn ends up in Japan. The Thais have also found a number of domestic uses for corn. Feed, corn sugar, and starch industries have sprung up near the supply of cheap corn. Some of these products are competing with the Japanese in Southeast Asian markets and are even finding their way to Japan! The Thai boneless chicken exports mentioned much earlier in this article are also based on feed coming from the Thai corn belt.

Japan has tried to repeat the Thai experience in other parts of Southeast Asia with very unsatisfactory results. The Zen-Nō case examines the East Java corn project which began in late 1967 and found three reasons for failure: the small scale of the project (about 6000 hectares), generally poor management and communications, and the importance of corn as a local staple, which made corn exports to Japan a politically touchy issue and caused the Indonesian government to declare a corn export embargo after the bad harvest of 1973.[24]

Japan's second strategy for reducing its food vulnerability is to reduce risk by the means of long-term contracts. The Harvard Business School case *C. Itoh & Co., Ltd.*[25] discusses at length the mechanics of the Japan-Thailand Maize Agreement. Shipping schedules, quantities, buyers, sellers, and prices are all covered in the long-term agreement, the provisions of which are revised every year just after planting time. The result of the long-term agreement is to provide the Japanese with a steady supply of corn, while giving Thai farmers and middlemen steady demand at a reasonable price. This encourages them to invest more in corn production which makes both the Thais and the Japanese happy.

---

21. Ibid., 8.
22. Ibid., 24.
23. Ibid., 22.
24. Ibid., 30.
25. *C. Itoh & Co., Ltd.*, Harvard Business School Case (4-576-041), May 1976.

Table 3

Volume of Thai Corn Exports by Destination 1957-1974

(Metric tons)

Year	Hong Kong	Singapore	Malaysia	Japan	Taiwan	Others	Total
1957	2,925	9,586	15,432	36,393	–	1	64,337
1958	3,879	14,880	14,471	129,683	–	1	162,914
1959	10,170	18,384	20,587	189,185	–	103	238,429
1960	11,327	35,601	24,865	441,046	2,052	50	514,941
1961	57,245	82,495	31,560	338,346	719	54,697	569,131
1962	104,300	97,551	50,596	229,686	–	1,995	484,123
1963	113,253	88,702	61,629	453,414	9,911	40,576	767,485
1964	111,325	88,063	64,883	844,936	9,573	28,152	1,146,932
1965	85,099	96,518	62,701	559,749	8,990	18,296	831,353
1966	80,597	165,676	82,515	826,289	57,116	49,363	1,261,556
1967	85,614	131,639	87,642	670,797	143,993	26,296	1,145,981
1968	140,378	186,826	135,903	666,272	395,475	33,344	1,558,198
1969	144,841	188,456	132,553	486,686	450,498	151,781	1,554,815
1970	112,078	109,706	92,798	649,903	447,229	36,171	1,447,955
1971	143,780	167,513	92,806	925,277	322,098	219,987	1,873,401
1972	119,978	225,959	107,962	842,204	502,775	44,741	1,843,619
1973	142,264	172,759	121,781	490,380	311,247	156,209	1,394,643
1974	127,292	283,071	100,704	781,443	251,571	227,666	1,871,840

Note: Including cornmeal.
Source: Harvard Business School Case *C. Itoh & Co., Ltd.*, 16.

Andrew Wellington Cordier Essay

The Japanese have also considered projects in the People's Republic of China, Brazil, and Vietnam, but each of these countries has serious drawbacks. This inability to produce another Thailand has led Japanese trading companies to begin buying heavily into grain infrastructure in the United States.

> In 1978, Mitsui Bussan purchased from Cook Corporation, a grain major, a pierside elevator in the suburbs of New Orleans, seven inland elevators on the banks of the Mississippi, and a number of freight cars. Marubini also secured a 4-million-ton-class pierside elevator from Cook, on a lease contract in Portland in 1978, and is heading in the direction of purchasing it in 1985. Mitsubishi has set up a joint venture company with Coppel in Los Angeles and has launched into the owning of grain elevators.[26]

Buying part of the American grain transportation infrastructure is one way for the Japanese to gain better control over the supply lines which move Iowa's products to Tokyo's dinner tables. But owning American grain elevators and barges is only useful if there is a grain surplus, if the U.S. government will let grain be shipped to Japan, and if the trans-Pacific shipping lanes are open. Since no amount of Japanese ownership of American agribusiness can overcome these obstacles, the Japanese are likely to find themselves promoting corn-for-export projects in Southeast Asia again in the future. They will have trouble making such projects work because they are unlikely to again encounter the lucky combination of land, climate, and infrastructure that made the investment in Thailand pay off so handsomely. The circle remains intact.

Although Japan cannot solve its dilemma of dependence on the United States, barring a major change in agricultural technology, there are a number of measures which the Japanese should take in order to further reduce their vulnerability to short-term food import interruption:

- The Japanese should subsidize private stockpiles of crucial imports such as corn or soybeans. They can use the fiscal gimmick of their choice: tax relief for those who hold larger inventories or subsidized loans might be the answer. Privately held reserves will assure dispersal, and dispersed reserves will insure a greater chance of survival in the unlikely event of a Soviet air raid or the all-too-likely event of a major earthquake.

- More agricultural aid should be provided under the rubric of comprehensive security. As a long-term heavy buyer of corn and soybeans, it is always in Japan's interest to increase both the number of potential sellers and the aggregate quantity supplied. Japan must persevere in trying to develop promising Third World corn projects.

- Improvements in the Maritime Self Defense Force's convoy and anti-submarine capabilities would increase both food and oil security in the event of a Pacific naval war.

- Agricultural protectionism should be reviewed. Japan's case for strategically necessary protection will be much stronger it its agricultural trade policy is not filled with goodies for important LDP constituencies.

- Japan should push for a long-term minimum annual purchase agreement similar to those the

---

26. "*Nihon Nōgyō Shimbun* Says Trading Firms Up U.S. Feedgrain Sources," *Foreign Agriculture* (January, 1981): 15 (translated from the front page of the August 6 *Nihon Nōgyō Shimbun*).

189

Americans have negotiated with the Soviet Union. Such an agreement would formally recognize Japan's unique dependency on North American farm products and commit the Americans to selling the Japanese at least enough grain and oilseeds to avoid a food panic in the event of a failure of the North American crop.

Each of the above points could help ensure Japan's food security in the event of a brief crisis, but none of them could help the Japanese indefinitely in the wake of a major climate change or a long war in the Pacific. Fortunately, the Japanese do have a strong defense against a long-term interruption of imported grain and oilseed supplies: the traditional Japanese diet. Readoption of the traditional rice-intensive diet—however undesirable that return may be—always stands as a plausible option in the event of a catastrophic change in the international grain and oilseed markets. The Japanese are fortunate in that the simpler traditional diet remains part of their national memory. The past is the ultimate source of food security for Japan's future.

Tim Sears graduated from Columbia University with the M.I.A. degree in January 1983. He entered the U.S. Foreign Service in April.